THE ALAMO

This Large Print Book carries the Seal of Approval of N.A.V.H.

THE ALAMO

A novel by
FRANK THOMPSON based on the
screenplay by
LESLIE BOHEM and STEPHEN GAGHAN
and JOHN LEE HANCOCK

Thorndike Press • Waterville, Maine

Published in 2004 by arrangement with Hyperion, an imprint of Buena Vista Books, Inc.

Thorndike Press® Large Print Americana.

The tree indicium is a trademark of Thorndike Press.

The text of this Large Print edition is unabridged.
Other aspects of the book may vary from the original edition.

Set in 16 pt. Plantin by Liana M. Walker.

Printed in the United States on permanent paper.

Library of Congress Control Number: 2004047911
ISBN 0-7862-6592-2 (lg. print : hc : alk. paper)

TO THE NEWTON FAMILY:

Annie, Callan, Jill and Nick
In whose happy home much of this book
was written

Acknowledgments

My deepest thanks go to the many people who have helped me along the way on the road to *The Alamo*. First, thanks to the screenwriters for giving me so much wonderful material to work with: Les Bohem, Stephen Gaghan, and John Lee Hancock. Everything good about this book came from them. Then to the wonderful folks on the set of the film who always made me feel so welcome and who were helpful and generous in so many ways: Philip Steuer, Mark Johnson, Katie R. Kelly, Ernie Malik, Michael Corenblith and again, and most especially, John Lee Hancock.

My gratitude also goes to the good people at Hyperion, particularly Natalie Kaire and Robert S. Miller.

Special thanks to Stephen L. Hardin and Alan C. Huffines, who are good friends and better historians.

And finally, my most heartfelt thanks go to my beautiful wife, Claire McCulloch Thompson.

The superiority of the Mexican soldier over the mountaineers of Kentucky and the hunters of Missouri is well known. Veterans seasoned by twenty years of wars cannot be intimidated by the presence of an army ignorant of the art of war, incapable of discipline, and renowned for insubordination.

— MEXICAN MINISTER OF WAR
JOSÉ MARÍA TORNEL Y MENDIVIL

☆

In 1821 Mexico won independence from Spain and with it the vast land holdings that included the northernmost states of Coahuila y Tejas.

In an attempt to further colonize this territory and help stave off marauding Indians, settlers were granted land and tax advantages to move to the state, which the Anglos called Texas. And they came — from every state in the union and from many countries in Europe. So many settlers arrived in Mexico, in fact, that Antonio López de Santa Anna Pérez de Lebron, Mexico's elected president-turned-dictator, closed the borders and sent occupational troops into the state.

In an effort to enforce their rights as citizens of Mexico and to form their own republic, the citizens of Texas — Anglo and Tejano — began to organize a provisional government.

And to prepare for war.

Prologue

March 6, 1836

Smoke.

Stench.

Silence.

An eerie silence, stranger still in contrast to the nightmare of sounds that filled this place only a few hours earlier.

His fellow foot soldiers — *soldados* — go about their work silently, wordlessly, but fifteen-year-old Jesús Montoya wonders if this is really true or if he has lost the ability to hear, just as he apparently has lost the ability to move and to feel. He crouches in a corner, near the large wooden fence that connects the compound's main gate to the ruins of the old church building, and watches numbly as the soldiers of General Antonio López de Santa Anna drag the bodies of the Texians toward the place where they are being stacked, where they will be burned like cordwood.

Jesús has heard this place referred to as Mission San Antonio de Valero, but most people call it by its curious nickname, the "Alamo." Jesús doesn't know why, but it makes sense to him that the name no longer carries any religious significance. If this ghastly site ever was a place of peace and of worship, no trace of those days remains. Now, in the bright sunlight of this Sunday morning, it looks more like a slaughterhouse than a church. Hundreds of stiffening corpses litter the ground, their eyes staring unblinkingly at the sky, their gnarled hands gripping now useless weapons, or still locked like vises around the necks of their enemies. The ground is so drenched with blood that each footstep brings bubbles to the surface, like a newly plowed field soaked by a horrible rain.

Jesús has seen some bad things in his life, but nothing like this. Only a few feet away, in a ditch by the fence, a skinny, scruffy dog sits on the chest of a dead Texian, whimpering and licking his face, urging his master to come back to life. Through the door of the church, on the ramp that leads up to the cannon platform in the rear, a Mexican soldier clutches the body of a

Texian and weeps. "Gregorio!" he cries. "My God, Gregorio, it cannot be . . . Do not die. . . ." The two men look very much alike. Jesús knows instinctively that they are brothers, men who somehow found themselves on opposite sides of this terrible fight.

Gradually, his shock begins to fade; feeling creeps back into his limbs. It is as if he is awakening from a trance, the scene before him gradually changing from silent nightmare to awful reality. Sounds and smells become more vivid, and Jesús wishes that he could go back to his numb state, to escape the horror spread before him.

Jesús hears the sound of plaintive weeping. Across the gory courtyard, two Tejano women from town cover their noses with cloths and cross themselves. They seem to be looking for someone in particular, and when one of them gasps and drops to her knees, Jesús knows that they have found him. The other woman's voice rises to a terrible wail, like that of a wild animal. All around her, Mexican soldiers continue working, dragging bodies, gathering weapons, seeing to the wounded. They do not react to the women's grief. It seems to Jesús that the soldados have reached a point where emotion — neither terror, nor grief, nor happiness — is no longer an option.

13

Their bodies remain animated but their hearts and souls have ceased to function. It is as if they have been completely emptied. It is, perhaps, the only thing that keeps them all from going mad.

Leaning against the low stone wall of the Alamo's well, a Mexican soldier mumbles a prayer. His hands clasp tightly at his stomach, cradling his intestines, trying to keep them from dropping onto the ground. Another stumbles about aimlessly, his nose nearly severed from his face by a bayonet or bowie knife. He is calling in a hoarse whisper for a doctor or a priest. But there are no doctors, no priests. There is no comfort for the wounded, no last rites for the dying. The passage from this life to the next will have to be accomplished alone, just as the pain of living must be endured alone. Ailments, both physical and spiritual, will either heal themselves or they will destroy. Jesús knows that a wound in a battle such as this — even a fairly minor injury — is a death sentence. He has not been hurt himself — his body, at least, is unscathed. But he wonders if the things he is seeing, the things he has seen since before dawn, will slash an unhealable wound through his very soul, if his spirit will bleed and wither and die from the agony of it.

Jesús slowly stands up and walks toward the compound's north wall, the point at which he first entered the fort three or four hours — or what seems like three or four lifetimes — ago. To his left, he sees a lone hand clutching a pair of broken glasses. Glancing up to the second floor of the barrack building beside the church, he recognizes the body of Colonel José Torres lying beside a flagpole. The Texians' flag is draped over him like a sheet. Torres would look like a man sleeping peacefully, except for the ragged musket-ball wounds in his cheek and forehead.

Just before Jesús, in a space directly in front of the old church, the mutilated corpse of a distinctive-looking man is being hoisted by four soldiers and carried toward the funeral pyre. Jesús watched this man die and heard what the president called him: Crockett. Davy Crockett. It was a name they all knew. When they heard the soft, raucous sounds of fiddle playing wafting toward them from the Alamo's walls over the long days and nights of the thirteen-day siege, the soldados would smile at each other and say "Croque." But today he learned what the Americano's true name was. His music somehow conveyed hope and defiance throughout the siege of the Alamo — it brought an odd note of beauty and fun into a place otherwise devoid of either. This Crockett was a famous man — a bear hunter, a great fighter. Jesús was told that he could charm a wild animal out of a tree simply by smiling at it and that he could shoot the wings off a firefly at one hundred paces. Before he saw him in person, Jesús had assumed he was a giant, as big as the stories told about him. But in death Crockett looked like any man here; an empty husk, drained of blood and life and whatever magic he had wielded in his many picturesque adventures.

Jesús hears a cry and turns around. "It is Bowie," cries a soldado in a tone that mixes contempt with awe. Another man is dragging Bowie's corpse from a room on the south wall, near where Jesús has just been crouching. Another soldado calls out, "He died in bed, hiding under blankets like a woman!" Jesús has heard of Bowie, too. He was rich, richer even than the president. Some said that he was actually a member of the Mexican aristocracy, even though he was clearly a gringo. Others told of the knife he had invented, a knife of fearsome size and power, which he named after himself. Jesús thinks about going into Bowie's room, to see if the famous knife is still there. He would like to see it, hold it for just a moment. That would be a moment to remember. But he doubts that such a weapon is real. Probably it is just another tall tale. Jesús knows that if it indeed exists, and if it really had lain in that room, another enterprising soldado has already made off with it. This Bowie was well known for his adventures, like Crockett. But, like Crockett's, all of his adventures have come to nothing, leading only to a terrible death in this awful mission ruin.

Most of the soldados are taking whatever they can find; the spoils of war. They are going through the pockets of the dead Texians, removing boots and shoes, taking top hats and watches, pistols and knives. Fancy handkerchiefs, pipes, silver whiskey flasks are laconically shoved into Mexican backpacks. It would, after all, be a shame to relegate all of these valuable items to the flames that will shortly consume the bodies of these pirates and rebels. Jesús considers taking a souvenir. But why would he want something to remind him of this day? The sooner he forgets the Alamo, Jesús thinks, the happier his life will be.

Jesús sees two officers nearby and immediately wraps his hands around the collar of a Texian and begins dragging him toward the pyre. He doesn't want to be reprimanded for being lazy — especially since he knows so well how harshly Santa Anna and his officers can reprimand when they put their minds to it. Although Jesús has had little contact with the two officers, he recognizes them both. General Almonte is rather short and intense; his lips curled in a perpetual sneer. General Castrillón is tall and straight, with the dignified bearing of an aristocrat and the deep, sad eyes of a man who has seen too much horror and death in his life. As Jesús passes them, he hears Almonte say with a note of pride, "A great victory, no?"

Castrillón looks around the hellish compound with revulsion. "Another such victory," he says quietly, "and we will all go to the devil."

Jesús continues to drag the body, taking care to look anywhere but into the dead man's face. But his gaze is drawn to the hooded eyes of the corpse; it is almost as if the Texian is trying to communicate a message from the other side of death. But Jesús knows that there is no message, no supernatural wisdom to be gleaned from any of this — only emptiness.

The words of Almonte have made him wonder. How can an event like this be considered a victory of any kind? The blood, the stink, the horror — none of it seems like winning. Even those who are still standing have lost something that can never be reclaimed. Jesús cannot imagine how anything good could come of such a "victory."

Suddenly wracked with nausea, Jesús braces himself against a cool adobe wall and vomits. He retches again and again as if, in emptying his stomach, he can also expel every horrible image and thought that has entered his consciousness this morning. When his retching becomes empty, dry heaves, he crouches once again in a corner and weeps. He has survived. But at the moment, that does not seem like much of an accomplishment. It does not even seem desirable.

Hours later, as the sun begins to set, casting a golden glow upon the sad face of the Alamo church, the funeral pyres are lit. There are two in the compound itself and another outside, toward the Alameda. That pyre is some distance from the Alamo — too far to drag bodies from the fort. Jesús thinks there must have been many Texian bodies out there in the field for a pyre to be necessary so far away.

The corpses of the Texians are stacked in alternate layers with wood gathered from a nearby forest. Most of the bodies are naked. Almost every usable piece of clothing, hats and shoes have been removed by victorious soldiers, who now feel themselves a bit richer with their gringo possessions. One at a time, the gruesome constructions are doused with lantern oil. Then, at the signal from a sergeant, torches are lighted and tossed onto the pyres.

The fire, dark orange and oily, shoots upward in the first explosion of flame. Moments later, they settle down and produce thick, black billows of smoke. The smell is nauseating. Jesús, like many others, ties a cloth around his face like a mask, leaving only his eyes visible. He watches sadly as the bodies of the Texians are consumed by the fire. Their ashes, borne by the noxious smoke, float languidly into the sky of the March evening. Eventually they come to rest, falling like a gentle black snow on the fertile Texas ground.

Chapter One

Washington City

"I'm a screamer."

James Hackett squinted into the dingy backstage mirror. A disgusted — and elaborately made-up — face peered back at him. Even here, in one of the top theaters in Washington City, the dressing rooms were small, filthy and dimly lit. How in God's name could anyone expect an actor to step directly from this squalor onto a stage before a discriminating audience of senators, congressmen and masters of industry — and to give a good performance as well? Paris — now there's a city that knows how to treat an *artiste*. Or London — ah, London. What marvelous sophistication. But even though this smelly marsh town was the capital of the United States, it still seemed to be populated primarily by yahoos and buf-

21

foons who barely knew how to attend a theater, much less maintain one for the comfort of its performers.

Hackett sighed as he daubed makeup onto his nose and cheeks, being careful not to smear any of the paste into his long wig or onto his buckskin hunting frock. *'Twas ever thus,* he thought, then murmured, ". . . a poor player that struts and frets his hour upon the stage and then is heard no more: It is a tale told by an idiot, full of sound and fury, signifying nothing."

Shakespeare.

Well, the play he was performing tonight surely was not Shakespeare. Far from it. *Lion of the West* was a raucous comedy about a rough-hewn, ill-mannered frontiersman named Nimrod Wildfire. It was crude, loud, obvious and totally lacking in poetry or greater meaning . . . and audiences loved it.

Hackett carefully placed the fur cap onto his head and felt Nimrod Wildfire stir to life within him. It was more than a cap made of fox fur — it was made of a fox . . . in its entirety. The angry face of the creature growled at the front, its jaws open as though ready to pounce upon its unlucky prey. At the back, the long tail hung over Hackett's neck. It was truly eye-catching. And Hackett had to admit that it was true — the headpiece was the most important part of the getup. Without it, he was just an ordinary man, not very tall, with a weak chin and tiny eyes set too closely together. But with it, he was colorful, bigger than life, outrageous — a genuine rip-roaring frontier hero.

He tried the line again.

"I'm a screamer."

James Hackett smiled a little to himself. This speech always brought down the house. He spoke louder, relentlessly rehearsing the lines that he had performed hundreds of times before.

"I got the roughest racin' horse, the prettiest sister, the surest rifle and the ugliest dog in the district. I am about the savagest critter you ever did see. My old man can lick anybody in Tennessee and I can lick my old man."

Carefully checking both sides of his profile, Hackett raised his voice to full stage-level volume.

"I can run faster, dive deeper, stay longer under and come out drier than any chap this side of the big swamp. I can outgrin a panther and ride a lightnin' bolt, tote a steamboat on my back and whip my weight in wildcats. I am half horse and half alligator, with a whiff of harricane throwed into the bargain!"

Even alone at his dressing table, it seemed to Hackett that he could hear the screams of laughter and the deafening applause that always greeted this scene. But he knew that it was not entirely the writing — or his own performance — that made *Lion of the West* spring to life night after night, month after month. It was because of *him* — the bumpkin congressman, the dim-witted bear hunter who had somehow parlayed his laughable character, his ignorance, his outsized eccentricities into national fame.

Hackett continued, gesturing to himself melodramatically, "I will kill a black b'ar for breakfast every mornin', pick my teeth with a tent spike and go through hostile redskins like a dose of salts. I could tell you folks more, but then I'd be braggin'!"

Hackett paused, smiling, holding for imaginary applause. He always had to stop at this point to take a modest bow.

The character in the play was named Nimrod Wildfire. But audiences everywhere knew who it really was: Davy Crockett.

Of course, Hackett and the play's author, James Kirke Paulding, had always denied it — in public, at least. But they both knew that the public's association of the congressman with the theatrical figure was no mistake. Indeed, it was the original intention of the piece.

A few years earlier, in 1830, Hackett had offered a prize to the playwright who could come up with a special kind of character. He wanted someone who represented the raw new American spirit, a high-spirited pioneer figure whose fractured English was hilarious and absurd but whose spirit was large. Paulding won the prize by suggesting that he base a play on the wildwood exploits of David Crockett from Tennessee.

The idea struck Hackett as a splendid one. The very backwoods characteristics that had already begun turning Crockett into a legend also made him something of a joke among the movers and shakers of Washington City. Placing this illiterate brute in the midst of high society, like the proverbial bull in the china shop, seemed to offer the perfect formula for crude comedy. Paulding even wrote to a friend to get some specific examples of "Kentucky or Tennessee manners, and especially some of their peculiar phrases and comparisons. If you can add, or invent, a few ludicrous scenes of Col. Crockett at Washington, you will have my everlasting gratitude."

His friend replied that Paulding would

merely have to check the Washington papers to find more than enough fodder for ridiculing Crockett. The man was unschooled, socially awkward and politically inept. Simply transfer the real man to the pages of a theatrical script and hilarity would undoubtedly ensue.

It had turned out just that way. *Lion of the West* was an immediate hit — in urban centers, anyway. James Hackett found to his consternation that whenever he portrayed Nimrod Wildfire before rural or pioneer audiences, the response could be cold, sometimes downright negative and — at least on a couple of occasions — dangerous. The one time in his life Hackett had literally been driven out of town on a rail was by outraged mine workers in Kentucky, who seemed to consider his absurd theatrical character a direct slap in their collective face.

But in New York, London, Paris, Boston and now Washington City, things were different. There were sophisticated audiences in those cities, people who were willing — indeed, eager — to, for the purposes of entertainment, look down their noses at the lower classes of people who lived in the mountains or on the frontier or in other savage conditions.

A sharp rap sounded on the dressing-room door and the stage manager stuck his head into the room.

"What?" Hackett said, annoyed. "What is it?"

The stage manager smiled slightly. He did not care much for Hackett and his pompous ways, and he had news that he knew would unnerve the actor.

"He's here," the stage manager said.

Impatiently, Hackett turned and demanded, "Who is here?"

The stage manager's smile widened. "*He's* here."

Hackett's face drained of blood. He had dreaded this day for almost three years. There was no doubt about whom the stage manager was speaking. David Crockett was in the theater. Crockett himself! And who knew how an uncouth barbarian like that would react to being mocked on the stage? Hackett already knew that Crockett was not a bit pleased by being publicly mocked by Nimrod Wildfire, knew that Crockett had even gone out of his way to make sure that people did not confuse him with that ill-mannered, rough-speaking lout. But for the congressman to actually show up at the theater — Hackett knew that this meant trouble. Nervous now, he daubed a little more makeup around his frightened eyes and whispered meekly to himself, "I'm a screamer. . . ."

The theater was packed with Washington's most prominent citizens: politicians and businessmen in impeccably tailored tailcoats, intricately embroidered vests and cravats of fine silk. Their ladies were resplendent in lavish gowns fresh off the boat from Paris, with full, ankle-length skirts and scandalously low necks, offering for their delighted gentlemen's enjoyment generous and tantalizing glimpses of décolletage. Their hair was arranged in elaborate cascades of curls and ringlets. There were rich and powerful men in that audience, and women who were the belles of Washington high society. But the murmurs that ran through the crowd all focused on one man. They had heard he was coming, and like Hackett, they anticipated trouble. Unlike Hackett, they were nearly giddy with anticipation; they simply could not wait to see what sort of ruckus their celebrated bumpkin congressman would cause. It was almost bound to be funnier than the play itself.

No one had to announce when David Crockett stepped into his private box, just above the wing at stage left. Everyone in the theater, as if by some mass instinct, turned their heads upward at the same moment. Some, inexplicably, felt like standing. He was a figure of fun, but somehow, at the same time, he possessed a powerful presence. Crockett commanded every room that he entered. Even his worst enemies had to admit that hc exhibited enormous charisma and personality.

Crockett was fully aware of the stir he was causing in the theater, but did not pretend to be humbled or surprised by it. Instead, he smiled warmly at the crowd and gave the house a friendly wave. He was greeted by applause, polite at first and thcn, like a wave of sound washing over the room, a thunderous ovation, mixed with cheers and *huzzahs.* Crockett's smile grew wider and, waving once more, he took his seat.

In the wings, only feet away, Hackett peered through the curtain at Crockett, sweating bullets. He was surprised that Crockett was not a bigger man. After all the stories he had heard — indeed, after all the stories he had himself made up — he was convinced that Crockett would be a giant of a man, like a true folk hero. Instead, Crockett stood at about five feet, ten inches tall, and his body could better be characterized as stocky rather than muscular and mighty. He wore his dark brown hair long, curling past his collar, and his amiable face was framed by a substantial pair of mutton-chops. There was a slight, almost effeminate, curl to his lip, and his eyes were dark and intelligent. He wore a long, black, expensively tailored frock coat and a cream-colored vest. His silk cravat, the color of gold, was elaborately tied, forcing his collar up high around his neck. *He does not look a thing like Nimrod Wildfire,* Hackett thought. *He looks like a . . . a . . . congressman!*

The orchestra gave a flourish, the lights dimmed and the crowd quieted in anticipation. Hackett muttered to himself, "Just another performance, just another performance, just another . . ."

The curtain opened. The rustic wilderness set was illuminated by the golden glow of the calcium limelights that lined the lip of the stage. Backing the scene was a large illustrated curtain depicting various heroic and comic scenes featuring the play's frontier protagonist. In one cameo, his arm was raised high, brandishing a dagger at a leaping mountain lion; in another, he was firmly standing his ground against an approaching bear; and in another, he sat on horseback, surrounded by stampeding wild stallions. Across the top, over a logo depicting a rifle, fiddle and coonskin cap, arched the words "Colonel Nimrod Wildfire." Under the logo in large red letters was the title of the play: "THE LION OF THE WEST;" underneath, in smaller black letters, the subtitle: "OR, THE KENTUCKIAN."

The illustrations on the backdrop were clearly based on some of the Crockett legends that many in the audience had read about in his best-selling autobiography, *A Narrative of the Life of David Crockett of the State of Tennessee*. Of course, no one much believed that he had actually written the book himself, but it was so filled with delightful incidents and hair-raising adventures that bookstores could not keep it in stock. And even if the sophisticated big-city readers did not exactly believe what they read in the book, that fact did not stop them from repeating the stories and laughing uproariously at Crockett's antics and adventures, both real and imagined.

Hackett glanced at the backdrop from his place in the wings and thought that the illustrations made it harder than ever to plausibly deny a link between Crockett and Nimrod Wildfire. Peeking back through the curtain, he saw Crockett grinning broadly. *That means he was happy, does it not?* Hackett thought. Then he remembered all those stories about Crockett "grinning" animals and Indians into submission. One grin, the stories went, and raccoons would simply climb down from their trees saying, "Do not shoot, Davy, here I come!" And now, Crockett was going to unleash that grin on Hackett — and it was working. The frantic actor was ready to surrender already.

The conductor tapped the podium with his baton and the small pit orchestra began playing the lively "Crockett March" — another indication of the congressman's widespread fame. Hackett began to perspire even more profusely. The gigantic fur hat had never felt so heavy and oppressive. At the sound of the familiar music, the audience burst into applause. Hackett, no longer able to hide, somehow managed to cover his face with a wide smile and stepped forward. The applause grew louder. Hackett bowed slightly in the direction of the crowd but there was really only one audience member on his mind at the moment. To his relief, Crockett was also smiling and applauding but — was it Hackett's imagination? — he had a sardonic look in his eye. It was the kind of look that said, "All right, Mr. Actor, show me."

Hackett was not the only person in the

room gauging Crockett's reaction. Nearly everyone in the theater seemed to be keeping one eye on the stage and one eye on the congressman. When the applause died, Hackett sighed and took a baby step forward, into the limelight of the stage. Still sweating he said, "Ladies and gentlemen, I thank you for your kind reception." He glanced upward again. Crockett seemed to be hanging on his every word. Hackett sighed. He knew he had to get this out of the way in the beginning or he would never be able to continue the play.

"Before we, uh, begin tonight's . . . performance," Hackett stammered, "I should like to acknowledge the presence of the man whose . . . life . . . inspired this humble play." He smiled, losing himself in the moment — and hoping for the best. "May I introduce to you the real Lion of the West . . . the gentleman from the Cane . . ."

Hackett took the fur hat off his head, bowed deeply in the direction of the box and said, "Good evening, Mr. Crockett."

A hush fell over the theater. This was it. Everyone in the place watched and waited. Crockett, unsmiling, slowly stood and faced off with Hackett. He remained there for a moment, allowing suspense to build. Then he smiled and bowed himself.

"Good evening, Mr. Crockett," he said.

The audience erupted into cheers and applause. Hackett smiled widely but his eyes retained their look of shock, like a man who has been pardoned from the gallows after the rope was already tied around his neck.

Standing outside the theater, listening to the faint sounds of cheers and applause, Sam Houston was not inclined to go in himself. It was not that he did not enjoy the theater, but right now he had a lot on his mind. Theatergoers, arriving late, walked quickly past the rough-looking man pacing the sidewalk. He stood over six foot, three inches, and was barrel chested. His stern face made him look like he was perpetually in the mood for trouble. Periodically he took a swig from a silver flask that he kept in the pocket of his tailcoat and mumbled to himself. It was the mumbling that really served as a repellant to others on the street. A man who talked to himself was very likely to be a man who simply was not right in the head. And when a big, muscular, mean-looking man was talking to himself, it was best to steer clear.

Houston's mumbling was a rehearsal of sorts. He had some convincing to do tonight, and he wanted to make sure that he used precisely the right words. And one of the people he had to convince was in that theater. Sam Houston had no interest in the fictional Nimrod Wildfire, but Congressman David Crockett was much on his mind. Houston knew that there was going to be a soirée at a nearby hotel after the performance and had been told that he could count on seeing Crockett there. If the audience was as filled with movers and shakers as Houston suspected, that soirée would be an excellent chance to talk with a few of them, too.

If anything, Houston had lived a more colorful life than either the real or fictional versions of Crockett. As a boy he had run off to live with the Cherokee, learning their language and adopting their ways. They accepted him, and he was named *Kalanu* — "the Raven" — by the chief of the tribe. He fought and was wounded in the War of 1812. In fact, the leg wound he received at the Battle of Horseshoe Bend had never healed, after more than twenty years. He was a politician and a Freemason. And he could even call himself an actor; he was a past member of the Dramatic Club of Nashville. And finally, after all those lives, he had become the governor of Tennessee.

It was not long after his election that

Houston had married twenty-year-old Eliza Allen. She was beautiful and her father was very rich, and Houston felt that he had made the best decision of his life. It turned out to be the worst. Only three months after the wedding, she abruptly left him and returned to her family home. Neither Houston nor Eliza ever commented publicly on the reasons their marriage failed; indeed, Houston never even talked about it with his closest friends. Nevertheless, the scandal was immense, and ruined his political future. He resigned as governor and went back to the Cherokee, to heal. Although he had not divorced Eliza, Houston married a Cherokee woman named Talihina Rogers.

But now he was back in Washington City with big plans. He often thought of himself in terms of a line from one of Shakespeare's plays, *As You Like It*: "And one man in his time plays many parts. . . ." Houston had indeed played many parts in his time — and tonight he had a new role. He was a salesman with a gigantic product and a very important pitch to make. In fact, it was life or death.

Houston stood outside the theater for a while, listening to the laughter from within, continuing to mutter under his breath and

36

fortify his nerve with the help of the flask. Then he headed for the bar in the hotel. That would be a far more congenial place to wait, he thought. When this damned comedy had played out in the theater, his prey would be coming to him.

Chapter Two

Sam Houston stepped up to the hotel bar and ordered a shot of whiskey. The bartender cracked off a chunk of ice with his ice pick and started to put it in his glass.

"Keep your ice," Houston said disdainfully. He dropped a coin on the bar, picked up the glass and walked back across the room to the two well-dressed businessmen he had lured into his net. They were named, rather unimaginatively, Smith and Jones.

Taking his place by their side, Houston downed his drink in one slow, steady pull. He swallowed the fiery liquid with a grimace and smiled. "If it doesn't burn going down," he said in a rather hoarse voice, "how can you be sure it is bad for you?"

Smith and Jones chuckled politely. And

they checked around the room for a convenient escape route.

But Houston was not letting them go quite yet. He was right in the middle of his spiel. Nodding at his whiskey glass he said, "I will be interested to see you gentlemen when you arrive in Texas and have your first taste of mescal."

Mr. Smith, the shorter and balder of the two, asked, "I have been told that in this Texas — this Mexico — men and women bathe together, in the open — in the altogether! Could this possibly be true?"

Houston smiled and said, "Cleanliness is next to godliness."

Mr. Jones, taller and broader, with a prominent nose and eyes set a little too closely together, frowned. "How godly can a place be if Jim Bowie calls it home?" he said.

"Now Mr. . . . um, Jones," Houston said, momentarily forgetting which was which, "Jim married into a fine Tejano family. Yes, sir, he found out you do not have to skirt the law to get rich in Texas."

Smith and Jones looked at each other skeptically. They both knew Bowie at least slightly. More to the point, they had both heard the stories about him. Knife fighter, killer, smuggler, slave trader, adventurer, drunkard. There was nothing about this reprobate that inspired anything in them but feelings of disgust and trepidation.

Across the room Crockett was holding court to a group of men while Hackett, grinning — and no longer sweating — stood alongside. Crockett's arm was around Hackett's shoulders, as if they were, and always had been, bosom friends.

Cocking his head toward Hackett, Crockett told the men, "More me than I am myself. I have half a mind to hire Mr. Hackett here to play me seven days a week — I would dearly love some time away. Of course, the citizens of Tennessee may grant me that wish come next election."

The men laughed uproariously. Perhaps a bit too uproariously for the mild joke, but Crockett was getting used to that. It seemed to him that as his reputation as a humorist — or, at least, as a source of humor — spread, people were so determined to find him funny that they busted a gut at just about every word he said. That was all well and good when he was trying to be funny. . . . Crockett noticed Houston across the room. "Excuse me, Mr. Nimrod Wildfire, gentlemen. I need to see a man about a dog." As he crossed the room to Houston, he shook a few more hands, locked smiles with many a gentleman, and made polite bows to several ladies. Had there been a baby present, he would have kissed it, too. If working the room were a paying job, Crockett thought, he would be a wealthy, wealthy man. When he reached Houston, Mr. Smith was speaking.

"What say the Mexicans of all this? I mean, is the Mexican army not occupying San Antonio de Béxar as we speak?"

"For now," Houston said.

That was apparently not the answer Messrs. Smith and Jones wanted to hear. Jones pretended to see someone across the room with whom he desperately had to speak, and the two men politely made their excuses and wandered off.

Houston called after them, "Invest now, gentlemen. Or lament later."

Crockett clapped Houston on the shoulder. "Making friends wherever you go."

Houston gave Crockett a sour look and downed another drink.

"Enjoy the performance?" Crockett said.

Houston looked Crockett in the eye and said, with a little smile, "From the day I met you."

Houston walked back over to the bar and accepted a refill. When he returned to Crockett's side, Crockett raised his glass.

"To Tennessee," he said.

"To hell with Tennessee, David," Houston said. He raised his glass. "To Texas."

"You will turn on an old girl quick, will you not, Sam?" Crockett said.

Houston laughed sharply; there was not much humor in it. "Wait until she turns on you. That is what you deserve for defending Indians."

Crockett said, "Least I will earn the honor of being diselected." Houston's look reminded Crockett that this was still something of a sore spot. "Beg your pardon, Governor," he said.

Smith and Jones, off to the side, watched Houston and Crockett drink and laugh together. Smith shook his head and said, "Sad, is it not? A year ago we'd have been looking upon two men with their caps set for the White House. Now . . . ?"

Jones shrugged. He knew, as everyone in the room knew, that the political future of both Crockett and Houston was absolutely nonexistent.

Crockett knew it, too. But Houston did not seem to — at least, not to Crockett. "What are you peddling, Sam?" he asked.

Houston leaned in conspiratorially, tipped his glass in Crockett's direction and said, "Something a certain congressman might need before long."

Crockett laughed. "You selling rocking chairs?"

Houston drained his glass and wiped his lips. "I am selling Texas," he said.

Crockett shook his head, thinking, *Here's another one of Sam's high-flown schemes.* "What would I want with Norte Mexico?" Crockett said.

"Texas," Houston corrected him. "No man will invest in a war to remain a province of Mexico."

Crockett's brow furrowed. "You figger on becoming part of the U.S.?"

Houston smiled and raised his glass: "To the Republic of Texas."

Crockett reluctantly raised his glass to Houston's toast. They both drank.

Houston said, "Remember how Tennessee was, David?"

Crockett nodded warily.

"Texas is better," Houston said. "Timber, water, game, cattle and more land than you have ever seen in your life. It is a virtual paradise, and you can go to dwell there without the formality of dying first."

Crockett looked impressed.

Houston continued, "Take the oath for militia duty and you will receive six hundred and forty acres of your choosing."

As Crockett considered this enticing incentive, Houston spotted a wealthy-looking man in the middle of the room. "Now that man looks to have capital," he said. He patted Crockett's shoulder and walked away.

Crockett called after him. "Sam?"

Houston stopped and turned.

"You figger this new republic is going to need a president?"

The two men shared a look and a smile. Then Sam Houston continued across the room, looking to plant one more seed for the future.

Chapter Three

George Kimball opened the door with a flourish.

"Here it is, Almeron," he said, smiling proudly. "Our own hat shop — Kimball and Dickinson."

Almeron ushered in his wife, Susanna, before him, and then stepped into the small shop. The shelves were lined with hats of every description, from expensive tall beaver hats to cheap cloth caps with narrow brims. As a hatter, Kimball was proudest of his fine hats, produced especially for the upper crust. But he was pragmatic enough to know that Gonzales was not exactly New Orleans, and that the bulk of his business would come from farmers and storekeepers, mostly Anglo newcomers to Texas with little money to spend.

"Oh, Almeron," Susanna said, clutching his arm. "It is beautiful. But are you sure this is a wise decision?"

Almeron laughed. They had talked over the subject a dozen times. "Did I not tell you, George?" he said. "Women these days just do not appreciate the finer points of big business." He affectionately gripped Susanna's shoulders. "I am just a co-owner of the shop, Sue," he said. "George does not expect me to help run the place." He turned to Kimball with a teasing look on his face. "Or do you, George?"

Kimball smiled. "Oh well," he said, "perhaps you can sweep up in the evenings."

They all laughed.

"I know," Susanna said. "But you remain so busy with the blacksmith shop. And now this . . . I just worry that you are taking too much on." She patted her rounded stomach. "Besides, you are going to have yet another job before too long . . . Papa."

Almeron embraced her. "That is exactly why I want to do this. As Gonzales grows larger, my blacksmith business will grow more prosperous, and so will our hat shop. Why, by the time my son is born . . ."

". . . or daughter," Susanna corrected him, smiling.

Almeron returned the smile. "Or

daughter. By that time we will be well on the way to making our fortune. It is why we came here, all this way from Tennessee."

Susanna placed her head on her husband's chest. What he said was true. Their lives had been one of constant struggle on their old farm back East. Like so many of their neighbors, they came to Texas firmly convinced that it was a paradise of promise, that it was big enough to fulfill all of their wildest dreams.

Susanna looked at Kimball. "Do you see what you have done to my husband, George?" she said. "You have turned him into a business tycoon, more concerned with making a fortune than spending time with his poor wifey and baby daughter."

"Or son," Almeron corrected, grinning.

"Do not worry, Susanna," Kimball said. "It may turn out that Almeron might not be a millionaire for weeks and weeks yet. You will have plenty of time to adjust to your incredible fortune."

"Oh well," Susanna said brightly. "If it will be weeks and weeks . . ."

In due course, those weeks and weeks passed. Almeron was not quite a millionaire yet, but he divided his time between his two businesses while caring for his pregnant

47

wife. And when their baby daughter was born, Almeron took on a new job; not a high-paying one, but the most rewarding of all.

Almeron never actually worked in the hat shop; that was Kimball's territory and Almeron was content to remain a silent partner. But Susanna enjoyed helping out there from time to time. Angelina was a quiet child who slept easily and was almost always in a good mood. She had a comfortable crib in the back room of Kimball and Dickinson's for when Susanna took her turn behind the counter.

On a day late in September, Susanna and Kimball were taking inventory. There had been few customers that day but business had generally been so good that neither of them was worried. They looked upon the slow day as a good thing — a little breathing room. Almeron walked in with a large tin pail. "I have brought the midday meal," he announced.

Kimball smiled. "You will make a wonderful wife for someone someday," he said.

Almeron laughed. "Well, it is certain that I am that rarest of husbands. Who else would allow his wife to work in a store while he has to cook his own meals and wash his own dishes? It is not natural!"

Susanna kissed him on the cheek and took the pail from his hand. She had already set the table in the back room so they could eat while gazing upon their beloved daughter. "I did not marry you because you were natural," she said teasingly, "but because you are the best of all possible husbands."

Almeron bowed. "I must humbly agree with your sentiment."

The door of the shop slammed open. Sixteen-year-old Galba Fuqua burst into the room, panic on his face. "You are here," he said breathlessly. "The mayor wants every man to meet up by the crossing on the Guadalupe. As soon as you can!"

Susanna felt a jolt of fear travel up her spine.

"Galba," she said, "what is it? What is the matter?"

"Mexicans!" he said, his eyes bright with excitement. "The mayor said bring your guns." The boy turned without another word and raced out of the store.

Almeron looked at Susanna and smiled a little in a vain attempt to calm her. He turned to Kimball and said, "Fetch your rifle, George. I highly doubt if we will need it."

To Susanna he said, "Stay here, Sue. Everything will be fine. You know Galba —

he is a very excitable boy."

Susanna kissed her husband and glanced at Kimball. "George," she said in a tight voice, "take care of . . . take care of both of you."

The crossing was about four miles north of town. By the time Almeron Dickinson and George Kimball arrived there looked to be over a hundred men present, milling around, waiting for instructions. Andrew Ponton, the mayor of Gonzales, walked through the crowd, responding to questions with terse answers. His soft belly and pallid complexion indicated a life lived indoors and in relative inactivity. He did not seem to be exactly in his element, in command of what looked to be a war party. Ponton spotted Almeron and walked toward him.

"This could be bad, Almeron," he said.

"What is it, Andrew?" Almeron said.

"You know that old cannon we have had around here for years?" Ponton asked.

Almeron nodded. "It was here when I got to Gonzales four years ago. Not much of a gun."

Ponton said, "No, not much of a gun. But now the Mexicans want it back."

"Whatever for?" Kimball said.

Ponton shook his head. "I do not know. I can only assume that they believe we will

50

use it against them. As if we could even cause any harm with that pathetic instrument. Anyway, they sent a Colonel Ugartechea to retrieve it."

"What did you do?" Almeron said.

Ponton smiled a little. "I had a very polite parley with him. I told the man I had no authority to turn the cannon over to him. Told him if I made a decision like that, I would be kicked out of the mayor's office and would never be elected again. I said I would have to consult with my constituents to decide what to do."

Kimball said, "And he just left?"

Ponton nodded nervously. "He said he would be back today and that I had better have the cannon ready to turn over to them or there would be . . . reprisals."

Almeron said, "Where is the cannon now?"

Ponton's smile widened. "I buried it. In the peach orchard."

Almeron looked to Kimball and then to Ponton. "Well sir, I think you had better dig it up."

"Dig it up?" Ponton said.

Almeron nodded. "If the Mexicans want our cannon, I believe we ought to give it to them."

By sundown, the crowd at the riverbank

had swollen to over 150 men — nearly all the adult males in Gonzales. Some of them laughed when the cannon was wheeled into their midst. It was a small, slightly ridiculous gun, capable only of firing six-pound shells. It may have once been mounted on real wheels, but they were gone now. Someone had cobbled together rough wheels from tree trunks and the little gun swiveled and wobbled on them like a silly child's toy.

The men examined it. Young, a recent immigrant from Illinois, said, "Will it even fire?"

Almeron said, "I do not have much confidence that it will shoot a shell, but it may just make enough noise to send a message to the Mexicans."

Kimball shook his head ruefully. "If it makes even a small farting noise, it is a better gun than I currently give it credit for being!"

The men laughed. Under Almeron's direction, they cleaned the dirt off it and began preparing it to fire. There were no shells handy, so they loaded it with scrap iron, horseshoes and nails. And then, they waited for sunrise.

The mist was heavy over the Guadalupe, and light was just beginning to peek over the horizon, when a voice called out, "There they are!"

The Texians could see that, across the river, the Mexicans had quietly set up camp overnight. It looked to Almeron like there were about a hundred of them. An officer stood on the opposite bank, smiling a conciliatory smile.

The officer called out, "I am Lieutenant Francisco Castañeda. I have been ordered by Colonel Domingo de Ugartechea to take back a cannon that is known to be in your possession."

Almeron called back, "I am pleased to meet you." The other men of Gonzales gathered behind him. "Please give the colonel our regards and deliver this message. . . ." Almeron raised his voice. "If you want our cannon," he shouted, "come and take it!"

The other men cheered. Someone had already prepared a banner with a crudely drawn picture of the cannon and the words COME AND TAKE IT! printed above it. They waved their banner and shouted at the puzzled lieutenant.

Without a word, he turned and stormed back to his camp, deeper in the woods. "Get ready, fellows," Almeron said. "They might just come and take it after all."

But the Mexicans did not make a move. All day long the Gonzales men stood at the ready, but the enemy took no action.

Just after sundown, the Texians had a meeting to decide what their next move should be. Kimball said, "I believe we had better take the bull by the horns." The others looked at him, concerned and questioning. "Here's the way I see it," he said. "We outnumber them. This cannon is little more than a pop gun, but it is one more cannon than they have. I figure if we hit them hard and unexpectedly, we can have them skedaddling back to Mexico with their tails between their legs."

Almeron nodded. "I think George is right. If they are not going to attack us, I say we attack them. Something tells me our brave Lieutenant Castañeda will not be able to mount much of a defense. He looks like he just started wearing long pants."

Mayor Ponton nodded. "Then it is decided. What is your plan of attack?"

In the hour before dawn, thick fog blanketed the ground. During the night, the men of Gonzales had quietly moved about half a mile down the river, to a shallow crossing point. They placed the cannon on a rudely constructed raft and floated it across. The men waded or swam to the other side. Once on shore, as silently as possible, they felt their way through the dark woods in the direction of the Mexican camp. When they were about three hundred yards away, Almeron pointed to the dim glow of two campfires in the distance. "Aim there," he whispered.

The men raised their rifles to their shoulders and aimed, waiting for Almeron's order. Kimball handed him a lighted torch, and Almeron nodded for the men to prepare themselves. He touched the torch to the cannon.

The blast was deep and loud. There was no way of knowing if any of its ersatz ammunition even reached the camp, but it did not matter much. The men of Gonzales fired a volley in the direction of the Mexican troops, and the sleeping soldiers awoke in panic and confusion.

Lieutenant Castañeda, shirtless and hatless, was rudely rousted from a deep sleep and leaped from his tent. Holding a saber in his left hand, the young officer looked as though he had stepped from one nightmare to another. Almeron almost laughed at his skittish terror. Castañeda waved his arms at the Gonzales force and shouted as loudly as he could. "Parley!" he called. "I request a parley!"

Almeron had already reloaded the cannon. It lobbed more scrap metal in the direction of the camp, followed by another volley of musket fire. The young lieutenant stopped calling for a parley and began running, along with most of his men, toward the main road. "Come and take it!" the conquering army taunted the retreating soldiers. "Come and take it!"

Kimball slapped Almeron on the back. "Think we got any of them?"

"Hard to tell," Almeron said. "But they no longer seem to desire our cannon."

The men laughed and cheered. Pathetic cannon or not, at that moment the Texians thought there was no army on earth that was the equal of them.

Susanna wept.

"Oh, darlin'," Almeron said, lightly massaging her shoulders. "We will be back in no time at all."

She said nothing.

Almeron said soothingly, "You saw how quickly we ran off the Mexicans from here in Gonzales. We will run them off from Béxar, too, just as easy. Then the war will be over and we can get back to more important things."

He smiled toward the crib that he had

crafted himself from the wood of a walnut tree. In it, their baby daughter, Angelina, gnawed on a piece of pork rind. She was over a year old, beautiful and bright. She would be walking and talking soon, making her next efforts toward becoming a full-fledged human being.

"You cannot blame me for worrying about you," Susanna said. "Any kind of battle can turn deadly for someone. Even if you win, there are bound to be casualties."

"I will not be hurt," Almeron said. "I cannot. I have forged a special suit of armor in my shop. I will clink and clank at the Mexicans and they will flee in fear."

Susanna laughed a little despite herself. What she did not want to say was that she was also worried about herself, and about Angelina. Even as more trouble was brewing with the Mexican army, there were unexpected threats at home, too. Roaming bands of white mercenaries were taking advantage of the confusion of war. Susanna had heard terrible stories. It was said that these terrible men were looting businesses, raping women and taking over private homes for themselves. Almeron and many of the town's good and honest men were leaving to fight the Mexicans in Béxar. But there were new men in Gonzales now, and they did not seem to be good or honest. Susanna feared that among them were some of these terrible brigands. These men looked at her in the most disconcerting way as she passed on the street. Sometimes they muttered things under their breath. Susanna could not understand what they were saying, but the tone was clear enough. She felt vulnerable enough while Almeron was there. With him gone with the army to San Antonio de Béxar, she would be alone and helpless.

Almeron knew about the marauders, too. He did not mention his own fears to Susanna but had been quietly making arrangements of his own.

"I will only be gone for a few days," he said. "In the meantime, I have asked Smither to check in on you from time to time."

Launcelot Smither was a farmer who lived just on the outskirts of Gonzales. Some said that he had once been a doctor but Almeron knew little about him; Smither was not the kind of man to answer questions about himself, and he certainly never volunteered any personal information. But Almeron knew that he was both honest and trustworthy. Smither was an accomplished shooter and could be relied upon to protect Almeron's family just as well as Almeron himself could.

Susanna crinkled her nose. "I do not like that Mr. Smither very much. That smell . . ."

"He raises pigs," Almeron agreed, "and perhaps he does not keep himself as tidy as you might prefer. But he's a good man. You can count on him completely. If you ever . . . need anything, just get word to him and he will be by your side. He will also stop by every day, just to make sure you are doing all right. And do not forget, George Kimball will remain here. Everything will be fine."

Susanna looked at her husband suspiciously. "You have never sought protection for me before," she said. "Why now?"

Almeron did not meet her gaze. "These are troubled times. The Mexicans . . . and everything. I just want to keep you safe."

The next morning, Susanna, holding Angelina in her arms, watched as Almeron and a few other Gonzales volunteers headed down the road to Béxar. He turned to give her a final wave and a reassuring smile. Susanna smiled in return, forcing herself to remain in a good mood about the temporary separation. Once the small group of riders disappeared over the last rise, she walked back home. She was already lonely, only moments after Almeron's departure, and was too preoccupied with her own sense of loss to notice that three men sat on the porch of the hotel, watching her intently as she entered her house.

For the next weeks, Susanna's life was too busy for her to dwell much on her unwelcome solitude. Angelina was getting livelier all the time, and it required an enormous amount of work just to keep up with her. As often as possible, Susanna helped out in the hat shop and kept an eye on Almeron's blacksmith shop, being run in his absence by young Galba Fuqua. She had to step gingerly around the boy. It was quite obvious to her that he had developed a schoolboy crush on her. She thought it silly, and allowed herself to feel slightly flattered by his overt affection. But she made it a point never to give him any inkling that his emotions could be shared. That would just be cruel.

Susanna had only received one letter from Almeron. In it, he insisted that he was well and in no danger. Trouble was brewing in Béxar, but so far there had not been much action. He repeated more than once in the letter that he was safe and promised that soon they would be together again. She wrote to him almost every day, telling him about the cunning things that Angelina did, or about the good day of business George Kimball had just enjoyed, or about an unusual task of smithing that Galba had been asked to do. She did not tell him how lonely she was, or how afraid she was growing, day by day. More than ever, the streets of Gonzales seemed to be alive with danger and Susanna tried never to go anywhere without the company of Kimball or Smither.

One morning, after cleaning up after breakfast, bathing and dressing the baby and writing to Almeron, Susanna walked over to the hat shop to go through some of the recent receipts. She had never been to school but had been well taught by her educated grandmother. She could not read very well, but Susanna had learned her sums better than Kimball ever did, and he was always grateful for a helping hand.

When Susanna arrived at the shop, she saw three men pawing roughly through the hats on the shelves. Their clothes were filthy and mismatched, as though they had been gathered haphazardly, at different times. The men laughed uproariously as they tried on tall beaver hats and then flung them to the floor. When Susanna stepped into the shop, Kimball looked at her with alarm. "I am sorry, ma'am, you must be in the wrong establishment," he said. "This is a men's hat shop."

Susanna saw at once that he wanted her to turn and leave. She nodded politely and said, "I must have been mistaken, sir. I thought this was a mercantile."

As she reached for the door a calloused hand grabbed her by the wrist. The tallest of the men, a red-haired bully named Mahoney, held her firmly and leaned in close. His cronies, Edmondson and Bearden, looked on leeringly. Whenever they attacked women, Mahoney always went first because he was the boss. The other two did not mind very much. They were just delighted to be included in all the fun.

Mahoney's breath was sour and his face was prickly with several days' growth of beard. "I do not believe you were mistaken at all, madam," he said in a low, insinuating tone. "I believe it was fate that brought you to me."

Angelina began to cry, and Susanna, holding her with only one arm, drew the baby closer to her chest. Trying to remain calm, she said, "Sir, I am a married woman."

Mahoney laughed. "Married? That may

be so. But did not I see your husband go ridin' out of town? Oh, must-a been about three weeks ago? A month, maybe?"

Susanna looked at him with shock. She glanced over at Kimball with a pleading look in her eyes.

"Now," the red-haired man said, "if I was married to a lovely thing like you, I would not go ridin' out of town, no sir. I would stick close to you, madam. Day and . . . night."

Kimball stepped out from around the counter. "Take your hands off that woman, sir," he said as brusquely as he could manage. Some merchants kept firearms handy, but Kimball believed that his shop would attract only the gentlemen of Gonzales, so what would be the need? Lacking a weapon, Kimball balled up his fists in what he hoped was a menacing manner.

The effect was not quite as terrifying as he had hoped. All three of the men looked at him and howled with laughter. "Sir Galahad," one said. While the tall man gripped Susanna's wrist even tighter, bringing his face close to her neck, Bearden punched Kimball hard in the stomach. Breathless, eyes bulging, Kimball fell to his knees. Edmondson hit him in the jaw, knocking him to the floor. Both men began

63

kicking him in the ribs, laughing all the while.

Now both Susanna and Angelina were screaming. The tall man started to pull Susanna toward the back room while the others went to empty out the cash drawer.

The sound of a shotgun blast brought everything in the room to a sudden halt. Launcelot Smither stood at the doorway. He had fired the first shell into the air but now he aimed the shotgun directly at Mahoney's head. He stepped inside the shop. "Unless you want to begin your sojourn in hell in the next half a minute," Smither said quietly, "you will remove your hands from the lady right now, and you will all three walk out that door."

From behind the counter, Bearden and Edmondson pulled knives from their sheaths and looked to Mahoney, waiting for orders. Smither cocked his head in the direction of the two men and said calmly, "If either of them takes a single step toward me, I will kill you first. And then I will kill each of them with my bare hands."

Mahoney glared at Smither for a long moment, sizing him up, calculating the odds. Smither was unkempt and slight of build. Even with the shotgun in his hands, he did not look all that threatening. A smile crept across Mahoney's face.

"He doesn't have the sand, boys," he said. "Get him!"

Edmondson and Bearden had not taken a single step in Smither's direction when another blast sounded. Where the tall man's face had been was now a mass of crimson. A swirling red mist hovered in the air for a moment. Susanna screeched in horror. Angelina seemed to have lost her breath and gasped in her mother's arms, her face turning a dark shade of purple.

Bearden and Edmondson charged Smither. He held the shotgun by the barrel and swung it, cracking open Edmondson's skull. Bearden lunged at him with the knife, slicing through his shirt and drawing blood from his chest. Smither swung the shotgun again but missed. He lost his balance and fell to the floor and Bearden kicked him in the head. Smither nearly lost consciousness and was aware of little except Susanna's screaming. He wondered almost whimsically why no one else had come to their aid, especially after the noise of two shotgun blasts.

Bearden bent over Smither and grabbed his hair. He pulled Smither's head back and prepared to draw the blade across his throat. Suddenly he stopped. As through a bank of heavy fog, Smither saw a look of surprise come over the man's face. He fell forward and Smither saw the hilt of a bowie knife protruding from his back. Behind him stood Kimball. His nose and temple were bleeding and he could barely stand up straight from what he believed was a broken rib. He had pulled the knife from the tall man's belt and lunged at the last moment to save Smither's life.

Smither pulled himself to a sitting position, waiting for the fog to clear. Susanna ran to the back room to put the now-squalling Angelina into her crib and then came back out with a small bolt of muslin to use as bandages.

Kimball sat on the floor beside Smither and surveyed the carnage around the room. Outside, a small group of men had gathered, but still no one had the nerve to step inside.

Smither grimaced; it could be that he was attempting to smile. Since Susanna had never seen him smile, it was hard to tell. "Miss Susanna," he said. "We'd better get you out of this town." Smither nodded solemnly. "We'd better get you to Béxar, where it is safe."

Chapter Four

General Edward Burleson was in command
of the Texian troops in Béxar. Under other
circumstances, that might have been a position of power. To most of his men, however, it
seemed that Burleson's idea of commanding
was to wallow in indecision, waiting for
someone to make up his mind for him. While
General Martín Perfecto de Cós occupied
Béxar and the old Alamo mission with over a
thousand troops, the Texians under Burleson
sat on their hands on the outskirts of town.
Meeting after frustrating meeting only
seemed to polarize the issue. Burleson would
not budge — and nobody else could make a
move without his orders.

To gritty fighters like Sam Maverick and
Ben Milam, Burleson's unwillingness to attack the Mexicans and drive them out of

Béxar was incomprehensible and infuriating.

Maverick and Milam sat in the shade of a cottonwood tree and sipped coffee from tin cups. Occasionally, Milam took a meditative draw from his long clay pipe. Maverick was thirty-two and a South Carolinian by birth. He came from a fighting family. His grandfather on his mother's side was a general in the Revolutionary War. Another ancestor, also named Samuel Maverick, was killed during the Boston Massacre on March 5, 1770. Maverick had only recently moved to Béxar, but he liked it, and wanted to stay.

Milam was forty-seven years old, a veteran of the War of 1812. He was born in Wales but grew up in West Virginia. Milam had survived battle, yellow fever, shipwreck and Indian raids. Like Maverick, he was a born fighter. And like Maverick, Milam was not the kind of man who took things lying down.

"My friend," Maverick said, "I believe it is time to fish or cut bait."

Milam nodded, frowning. He cocked his head toward Burleson's tent. "This feller must think if we sit here long enough, we will just bore the Mexicans to death." His voice still bore a trace of his Welsh roots.

Maverick took another sip of coffee. He

said, "Some of the fellers, they are talking about clearing out. Came here to fight, didn't come here to sit by with their thumbs up their arses."

Milam said, "What if Burleson never will make up his mind?"

Maverick smiled. "Then I reckon it would be time for us to make it up for him."

"Officers' call!" Milam and Maverick looked up at the call. A young adjutant named Winders stood outside Burleson's tent. He yelled again, "Officers' call!"

Milam and Maverick stood up. Maverick tossed the rest of his coffee onto the grass. He said, "Maybe Burleson has finally decided to take charge of this thing."

"If he don't," Milam said, "I reckon somebody else will have to."

They gathered outside his command tent. The December evening was brittle with frost. Dr. James Grant, a fiery, bad-tempered Scotsman, was there. So was the more reasonable J. C. Neill, whose understated leadership qualities made the others wonder why he was not in charge.

Then there was James Fannin, who seemed to emulate all the worst aspects of Burleson's indecisive character. At thirty-two, Fannin seemed much younger than he was. He tried his best to carry himself with the dignified bearing of a soldier, but looked more like a puppy longing for approval.

Sam Maverick had decided to advocate an early attack, and Ben Milam was going to offer to lead it, if need be. Maverick had been captured by the Mexicans. They had nearly executed him, had, in fact, actually marched him to the firing squad. But they changed their mind and Maverick had later escaped. There was, some of the men thought, a sheen of personal vendetta that lent additional urgency to his furor for battle.

Major Robert Morris was the only one in the group who actually looked like a military man. He was dressed in the casual uniform of the New Orleans Greys.

The officers' call almost immediately degenerated into something like a brawl, all of the officers' voices competing for supremacy.

"We should attack now!" Maverick shouted. Several of the men cheered in agreement.

Burleson bellowed, "I believe we should put the issue to a vote."

Milam was outraged. "No more votes, dammit!" he shouted.

Burleson, undaunted, continued. "All in favor . . ."

Sam Maverick's voice overrode Burleson's: "We need action right now, or this whole deal is going to . . ."

Burleson would not give up. He brought the volume of his voice up. "All in favor of mounting an attack on the Mexican positions . . ."

Fannin raised his hand like a conscientious schoolboy and said, "If we weren't ready to attack two months ago, I do not see how . . ."

"When I escaped," Maverick butted in, "the Mexicans were starving in there."

Neill said, "But their artillery —"

"Their artillery," Grant said, impatiently, "is the same as it was in October."

"They've dug in," Neill said, "drilled their crews . . ."

Burleson tried again — "My good fellows, we are voting . . ."

Morris shouted, "Near a third of your men have gone back home or God knows where, and that was the best of them!"

Grant agreed. "If we do not attack now," he said, "the rest of the men will leave."

Fannin shook his head. He hoped that Burleson would have his way and that they would continue to wait and think about it. "We sure as hell cannot keep this siege up," he said. "The only thing we haven't run out of is corn liquor."

If obstinacy were a good leadership quality, Burleson would have been commander of all the armies. He wanted a vote and, by God, he would have a vote. "All in favor of the attack raise your hands."

Only five of the officers raised their hands. Burleson shook his head.

Burleson looked relieved. "That is it, then. I recommend we fall back to Goliad until the Consultation can sort this regular army deal out. . . ."

Ben Milam had been scowling through the entire proceedings. He stepped away from the group and faced them. "You can all just go do that, then," he said. "I come here to fight!" He turned on his heel and stormed away, toward where the volunteers were assembled. Maverick went with him. Burleson called after him, "Well, Ben, if you choose to call for volunteers on your own, there's nothing I can do to —"

Milam called, without turning, "You are goddamned right there's nothing you can do about it!"

As Milam and Maverick approached, the volunteers eyed them with keen interest. Some stood up, sensing that something was about to happen. They had not been able to hear the officers' meeting — even though it had been conducted at the tops of the officers' voices — but they, like Milam, were ready to make a move.

Milam stood before them. "Men, you know what the situation is," he said, "and I wager that you are as tired of it as I am."

The men murmured in agreement.

"The officers seem unwilling to attack," Milam said. "But I have the distinct feeling that you do not share their point of view."

The men were shouting now — "No!" "Let's get 'em!"

Milam turned to Maverick. "Can I borrow your sword, Sam?" he said. Maverick unsheathed his saber and handed it to Milam. Milam stepped to one edge of the crowd of men and placed the sword point in the dirt. He walked to the other edge, dragging the sword after him, drawing a long, ragged line.

"If you are with me, cross over the line to me," he said. He stepped back and held his arms out, Maverick's sword pointing to the sky. "Who will go with me?" he demanded. "Who will go with old Ben Milam into San Antonio?"

The men surged forward, shouting and cheering. "We are with you, Ben!" one called out. "You just say when!"

More volunteers rushed forward to hear

the news — "We are going to fight!" Burleson rushed over. "Men, men, please do not do anything rash," he cried. "I fear that it is highly imprudent to attack the Mexicans with so small and so unprepared a force."

Milam handed the sword back to Maverick. "Unprepared they may be, sir," he said to Burleson. "But they are fighting men. They came here to fight, and neither you nor all the demons in hell can stay them from their course!"

The men cheered. Burleson walked back to his command tent, staring dolefully at the officers who stood there, wondering what had happened to their democratic vote.

That night, Neill supervised the hurried construction of an earthworks emplacement behind which to place the Texians' twelve-pound cannon. The men, who usually complained loudly when ordered to do physical labor, pitched into the project happily. They shoveled trenches, cut down trees and built a rough but serviceable barricade.

Behind the emplacement lay the river. Beyond that stood San Antonio de Béxar, where most of the volunteers waited impatiently for the signal to attack. Before it, in a direct line of the cannon barrels lay the old mission, the Alamo. General Cós and his men had been fortifying it for weeks, but the Texians knew that it was in poor repair, with crumbling walls and major defensive deficiencies. Under the right circumstances, the Alamo could easily be taken, even by so "small and unprepared a force" as the Texian army.

As the sun rose, Neill's crew prepared the cannon for its first shot. He turned to them and said, "If they come out after us, get ready to swim." Neill checked his watch, and then nodded to the gunnery sergeant.

The sergeant touched the fuse with his torch. A cannonball arched through the air toward the Alamo. It landed with a thud, taking a large chunk off the top of the fort's north wall.

Immediately, a hundred Mexican soldiers double-timed across the narrow wooden bridge that crossed the San Antonio River heading east out of Béxar. They wheeled left to run toward the south wall gate of the Alamo.

From Béxar, Milam watched the retreat through a spyglass. "They bought it," he said with a satisfied smile. He was standing at the edge of the woods on the Béxar side of the river, just north of town. Red-haired Colorado Smith, one of the Texians' best riders and scouts, waited with him, along with several other volunteers.

"If we can get up on the roof of my workshop," Smith said, "we will have a clear shot at the plaza."

"Are there Mexicans in any of the houses?" Milam said.

"Most of 'em," said Smith.

Milam nodded. "Well, let us see how far we can get before they see us."

He waved forward and they ran toward the edge of town in a crouch, in groups of six or seven, fanning out onto either side of Acequia Street.

Coming parallel to Milam's party down Soledad Street, Frank Johnson led another sixty Texians toward the Veramendi House. The most lavish home in town, it was once occupied by James Bowie. Situated on the east bend of the river, its courtyard offered an unobstructed view of the Alamo.

A shot rang out and a Texian named Curilla grabbed his arm in pain, blood seeping through his fingers. Erastus "Deaf" Smith snapped his rifle up and shot the sniper off the roof of the Veramendi House. At forty-eight, Deaf Smith was one of the oldest men in the fight, and he had been drawn into the conflict only reluctantly. A cattle rancher, originally from New York, he

76

had a Mexican wife and four children. He only wanted to live in peace. But if the Mexican army was going to prevent that, so be it — he would fight for his home.

The rest of the men scurried down the street until a blast of canister shot cut through them from an emplacement at the corner of the plaza. Men cried out and scattered to the sides of the street. Hermann Ehrenberg, a young German volunteer, threw himself to the ground in the middle of the street. *"Gott in himmel!"* he said, his arm over his eyes.

Musket fire followed the cannon, balls pinging off the stone walls, kicking up dirt around Ehrenberg on the ground. "'Take cover!" Milam shouted. Ehrenberg scrambled up and ran back, joining the other men as they retreated to the Veramendi House, pausing along the way to help a wounded comrade. At the Veramendi House, the Texians smashed through doors and windows with boots and rifle butts. Another canister shot whistled through them. Four men fell to the ground wounded. One of them gaped dumbly at the gushing stump that, seconds earlier, had been his left leg.

Now the fighting was door to door, house to house, all around Béxar's main plaza. Men popped out from doorways and windows to take potshots at each other. The combatants were separated at times by only ten or twenty yards. Texians darted from one side of the street to the other. At every step they were fired on by riflemen on the rooftops, causing the Texians to scurry back to their original cover.

Deaf Smith and Lieutenant Hall of the New Orleans Greys clambered up a wooden ladder to the roof of the Veramendi House, crawling on their bellies to the lip of the south end. They looked down toward the plaza, where almost two hundred Mexican troops were dug in around San Fernando church. Smith took a bead on one of the cannon crew at the northeast corner of the plaza, but before he could fire, a small hail of bullets descended on his position from above. He scrambled for cover but found little. He looked up to see snipers firing down on them from the belltower of San Fernando. "God bless it!" Hall, a moral man, cried out as a bullet hit his left hand. Smith hammered at the roof with his rifle butt, trying to open a hole large enough to escape through.

Texians gathered under the ceiling of the Veramendi House's dining room looked up in alarm as plaster began to rain down upon them. Seconds later, Deaf Smith came crashing through the ceiling and landed on the dinner table with a loud thud. Lem Crawford, a recent arrival from South Carolina, cried out, "Jesus Mary, Deef. You 'bout skeered the livin' shit outen us!"

Smith was bleeding from a wound in his arm but immediately got up and grabbed a chair. He positioned it under the hole and said, "Help me get Hall off that roof!" Hall was still sitting where Smith had left him, holding his wounded hand in pain, bullets hitting all around him but, miraculously, always missing the mark. Smith said, "Time to come inside, Hall." Hall looked at him pleasantly, as if Smith had just asked him to join him for lunch. "Oh," Hall said, "all right, Deef." Smith put his arms around Hall's chest and dragged him to the hole in the roof. The other men, reaching upward for him, lowered Hall gently into the room. Smith, although wounded more seriously, climbed back inside under his own power. The experience had been so unnerving that he sat down in a straight-back chair and began to laugh uncontrollably.

A lone Texian, Henry Karnes, raced across a narrow street leading to the northwest corner of the main plaza, musket balls kicking up eddies of dust around his feet. He leaped through a doorway and rolled into a room where Ben Milam and a dozen other Texians were whaling away at a wall separating them from the next room, using a table leg and an axe to open the hole. Milam heard something. He raised his arm and said, "Hold off a minute!"

The men stopped chopping. They also heard the *chunk! chunk! chunk!* of hammering coming from the other side of the wall.

Colorado Smith grinned and said, "They are trying to get to us, too."

Milam nodded. "Let 'em. They can do all the work for us! Now charge your rifles, boys, and stand back . . ."

Within moments, the wall collapsed. A dozen surprised soldados stood on the other side, blinking through the adobe dust.

"Get 'em!" Milam shouted.

The Texians fired a volley, and then charged the room. The Mexicans who did not fall in the volley began hammering away at the attacking Texians using the same tools with which they had just broken through the wall. They fought each other with knives and bayonets, fists and teeth, rocks and broken bottles. The Mexicans were outnumbered and in seconds, they were all dead. Milam dispatched the last one with a quick thrust of his bayonet. The

Texians stood in the ruined room, breath-less, covered in dust and blood. They had been eager for action, and here it was.

In the later afternoon, Milam, Maverick, Fannin and Frank Johnson crouched in the courtyard of the Veramendi House. Johnson, kneeling, drew a crude map of Béxar in the dirt. "We have cut the last of them off in the Plaza de Armas down here," he said, making a mark.

"So we take the plaza tomorrow morning," Milam said, "then go after the Alamo."

Fannin shook his head. "I would not want to have to charge into all that artillery."

Milam turned his spyglass to the fort across the river.

"If we come at them from all sides," he said, "and spread out their fire . . ."

Johnson interrupted, "There are hun-dreds of men inside those walls. . . ."

"Starving men," Milam said. He turned to Maverick and said, "Hey, Sam . . ." The crack of a bullet sounded. Milam looked mildly surprised as blood began to trickle through a neat round hole in his shirt. "Oh Lord," he said, and slumped to the ground. Another ball hit him in the dead center of his forehead.

Johnson looked around wildly. He spotted a sniper in a cottonwood. "In the trees!" Johnson shouted. All the Texians raised their rifles and fired a ragged volley. The sniper, hit by three musket balls, dropped from the tree, hit the riverbank and rolled into the river.

They turned back to Milam. The pool of blood was spreading beneath his head and his sightless eyes stared into the Béxar sky, tinged with the first pink and orange streaks of sunset.

Ben Milam was buried that night in a hastily dug grave in the courtyard of the Veramendi House, just a few yards from where he had died. There was no time for a proper funeral, but Sam Maverick and Frank Johnson stood for a moment beside the grave.

Johnson said, "He was like no other."

"That, my friend, is an understatement," Maverick said. "So you are taking his place?"

Johnson nodded. "I have been elected to step in for Ben." He smiled. "But no one could really take his place."

They were silent for a moment. "Ben once told me a story about when he was a young man in New Orleans," Maverick said. "For some reason he had worked up some sort of business deal to sell flour to a company in South America. They chartered a ship and laid their hands on God knows how many tons of flour. The skipper of the boat — a man named Zunno — was an atheist, a fact that he very loudly proclaimed every chance he got. It made Ben nervous."

Johnson laughed softly.

Maverick said, "Now, Ben was not the most religious man in the world, but in his mind you simply did not start out on a long and dangerous voyage with a man who scoffs in the face of the almighty! That was just poor planning. Ben figured that a seafaring man needed all the help he could get, both natural and supernatural." Maverick crouched by the grave and patted the dirt. "Well, his other partners in this endeavor thought that Ben was turning a molehill into a mountain, and they reminded him that they all had a very considerable amount of money tied up in this thing — and where he got the money, I would love to learn. Ben never had a dime to his name the entire time that I knew him."

"What happened?" Johnson said.

"Well, sir," Maverick said, standing up again, "they left New Orleans with this God-hating captain and they began heading south. The voyage was to last several weeks, and before the second week was done, some of the crew began coming down with yellow fever. Next thing you know, more of the crew caught it. They started to drop like flies. Ben told me they were dropping bodies over the side four and five a day. Even the captain died, damning the good Lord from his deathbed. Ben felt that the good Lord had made his point pretty concisely. Well, even Ben got sick. So did all his partners. In fact, he landed in South America with fewer partners than he started off with. Ben was not a cold-hearted man, but he looked upon this as not altogether a bad thing. Fewer partners meant fewer splits in the profits."

Johnson said, "And were there any profits?"

Maverick laughed aloud. "Not a penny! The crew had been cut down by half, the captain was dead and most of the passengers were dying or already dead. That is when the squall hit. For four days and nights, every able-bodied man on the ship fought to keep it afloat. Some of the men who had survived the fever were washed overboard. The ship started taking on water at a prodigious rate. Ben and a few others even readied the lifeboats, expecting it to founder at any moment.

"But it didn't. No sir," Maverick said,

"that very unlucky ship managed to limp to shore at some vermin-infested little port. Ben felt very lucky to be alive. But his flour was not so lucky. It was submerged under ten feet of water in the hold of the ship."

Now the darkness was almost total around Milam's grave. Johnson said, "What did Ben do then?"

"Kept alive as best as he could," Maverick said, "until he got a job on a ship returning to New Orleans. And that ship ran aground and sank in full view of shore. Ben said he jumped off and walked almost the entire way to safety."

Johnson laughed loudly. "Do you think Ben might have exaggerated that story a little?" he said.

Maverick looked at him and then back down to the grave. "I think it is more likely that Ben understated the facts. He was downright reticent when it came to telling a story."

Johnson glanced toward the Alamo. "Look," he said.

A small group of men was walking out of the mission's main gate. One of them held a white flag over his head.

Maverick said, "Looks like they are ready to parley." He looked down. "Damn it, Ben, if you had just kept out of the way for another hour . . ."

Inside the Alamo, Cós stood grim-faced on the walls, watching as his young officer, Colonel José Juan Sanchez-Navarro, walked across the river to Béxar to beg for clemency for his sake. This would ruin him, Cós believed. His army had outnumbered the Texians. They had held the best strategic position. They were well-trained soldiers, while the Texians were nothing but rabble — farmers and slave traders, not fighting men at all. Yet he had lost the mission, lost the city and, it seemed to him, lost the war. General Santa Anna was not a forgiving man. The fact that Cós had married Santa Anna's sister gave him no preferential treatment at all. In fact, he was convinced that the president was even harder on him than on his other officers, just to avoid any hint of nepotism or favoritism. Or maybe it was simply that Santa Anna hated him, and always had.

Like any soldier, Cós dreaded defeat. But even more than that, he dreaded reporting the results of this engagement to his brother-in-law.

Sanchez-Navarro arrived in the camp and was greeted by Juan Seguin. Seguin was a Tejano, born right here in Béxar twenty-nine years earlier. Indeed, his family had been among the founding fathers of the city, and his father, Erasmo, was *alcalde* — mayor — when Stephen F. Austin made his first visit to San Antonio. The year before, he had been appointed the city's political chief. But, like many Mexican citizens, Seguin had become more and more concerned about the outrages of Santa Anna's dictatorship. He raised a company of other Tejanos who were loyal to Texas and bitterly opposed to Santa Anna. Now he, and they, found themselves in the distinctly uncomfortable position of taking a stand against the Centralist government of their homeland, fighting side by side with the rebels, who were mostly Anglos. Many of the Anglos did not trust him because he was Mexican. And many of his own people considered him a traitor. He was aware that some of the men wanted to make Texas a part of the United States. Others wanted the territory to remain a part of Mexico. But Seguin wanted neither. He wanted Texas to be an independent republic with no ties to either country.

But even though some of the Texians wondered about Seguin's loyalty, they all had to admit that he was indispensable at times like this: None of the others spoke Spanish as well as he did.

Sanchez-Navarro saluted Burleson, Johnson, Morris and Fannin at a table near Burleson's command tent. Burleson indicated that he should sit down. He did, but the others in his company stood behind him.

He spoke and Seguin turned to the Texians. "The general requests that his men be allowed to carry their arms, with ten rounds per soldier," he said.

"Absolutely not! They will lay down their arms!" demanded Johnson.

Sanchez-Navarro said something else and Seguin turned to the Texians. "It is only to protect themselves against the Comanches on their march."

Burleson nodded and said, "And his general promises not to return or engage in any other military action against Texas?"

Seguin translated, heard the colonel's reply, and said, "The general will make this promise."

Johnson said to Burleson, "You trust him?"

Burleson nodded toward the Alamo. "Do you want to charge those cannon?"

The Mexican army under General Martín

Perfecto de Cós rode out of San Antonio de Béxar with considerably less pomp than when they rode in. Column after column of forlorn, humiliated troops filed through the plaza past the jeering Texians who had just defeated them, as the bell in the tower of the San Fernando church rang out peals of victory.

Captain Juan Seguin sat astride his horse, watching the scene with decidedly mixed emotions.

A local merchant, Don José Palaez, drew up alongside Seguin in a horse-drawn cart. "Will they return?" Palaez asked.

"No," Seguin said. "General Cós gave his word."

The man in the cart gave a short, bitter laugh. "When I heard that the Mexicans surrendered," he said, "I did not believe it. How did the bastards accomplish this?"

Seguin did not look at him, but continued staring forward at the defeated troops. "With our hearts," he said.

At the edge of town, a number of Texians watched the Mexican troops file past. Though members of the victorious army, only a few of these observers were in uniforms, of sorts. The New Orleans Greys had been formed in Louisiana a few months ago with the express purpose of fighting for

Texas against Santa Anna. Their dress was not military, exactly, but their "uniforms" were at least close enough in design and color to make them appear to be a unit. They wore matching gray jackets and large caps with puffy, oversized bells and black visors. There were only a hundred Greys in all, but today, having turned back an army of over a thousand, they felt like great warriors indeed.

Some of them could not help chiding the Mexicans as they passed.

"Loosianna just whipped your arse!" jeered a rifleman named Boldt.

Another, a skinny private called Jaxon, laughed and shouted, "No, *Kentucky* just whipped your arse!"

A third, Logan, yelled, "Wrong, gentlemen! *Tennessee* just whipped your arse!" He turned to the group and called out gleefully, "Sant'anna sends 'em here, we send 'em back!"

"Yer lucky we let you keep your muskets," shouted another Grey, a recent immigrant named Dubravsky. "Should just let the savages swallow you whole!"

Gagliasso, a former member of the Italian navy, tossed a pebble after the Mexicans, catcalling, "Now scat, and don't come back!"

Several of the men spat in the direction of the army. General Cós saw this and hesitated for a moment, staring at the men and trying to retain some shred of pride. Then, with a sigh, he rode on.

Chapter Five

To Jesús Montoya, his grandfather's farm was both heaven and hell. Rugged and remote, the little jacal they shared was far from the luxuries and enticements of San Antonio de Béxar. They had gone there once, to sell a flock of goats, and Jesús had been mesmerized by the sights, the smells, the colors, the splendor of the huge city. At least, it seemed splendid and huge to Jesús; the largest town he had ever seen before then was a haphazard collection of one store, one saloon and five small houses. In contrast Béxar seemed, to his eyes, like a metropolis. It was dazzling.

As were the señoritas. What few women and girls Jesús ever encountered in their tiny village were sturdy, coarse and plain, made older than their years by ceaseless back-breaking, spirit-annihilating labor. But in

Béxar, Jesús had seen women who were fresh and smooth, dressed in beautiful skirts and wrapped in shawls into which were woven all the colors of the rainbow. They did not smell of earth and sweat but of flowers and fruits, and strange, alluring perfumes.

Jesús longed for those women, as fragile and lovely as the painted figurines of the Virgin at the little adobe church in his village. Even more, he longed for travel, for adventure. He wanted to see beyond even Béxar, to drink a long, soothing draught of freedom.

But even though his grandfather's tiny farm was something of a trap, it was also a warm and welcoming home to Jesús. It sat on a gentle slope, framed by tall, green mountains and bordered by two wide streams, one white and furious with eddies and little waterfalls, the other placid as a pond. The nearby forest was rich with game and the fertile soil easily offered up corn and tomatoes, beans and jalapeños. Jesús's mother had died when he was just a child, so long ago that only with effort could he even conjure up a few hazy images of her. His father had died much more recently. Of that event, he still had vivid and terrifying memories. His father's death lived on in Jesús's frequent nightmares, which played and replayed the anguish of the event night after night.

From that time, Jesús had lived with his grandfather. It had not been an easy period in either of their lives. One had lost a father, the other a son. But Jesús's grandfather was a kindly man who listened patiently to his grandson's plaintive chatter about the glorious life he would someday live. He was also a man whose own colorful way of telling tales made his life seem far more interesting than it actually had been.

All in all, as he sat on the bank of the placid stream watching his fishing line drift lazily in the water, Jesús felt at peace. He knew he was probably happier here than he would be anywhere else. That did not stop the yearning, but it filled the moment with contentment. Besides, he knew that he had a long life ahead of him. There would be plenty of time for traveling the world, seeing unforgettable sights and romancing exotic women.

A sharp tug suddenly dipped the fishing line under the surface, and Jesús sat up with a start. He let the fish play the line for a moment and then, with a jerk, he lifted the rod and brought it home. It was a trout — easily large enough for supper for both Jesús and his grandfather. He held it up proudly and was about to run over to the cornfield to show it to his grandfather when he saw something else in the distance — something ominous.

On the horizon, two Mexican cavalrymen — dragoons — on horseback were approaching the field where Jesús's grandfather was plowing with a team of oxen. The dragoons carried long lances and wore bright red tunics and shiny silver helmets that glinted blindingly in the sunlight; it made them look to Jesús like creatures out of mythology, with heads of flame.

The two dragoons casually rode up to the old man and stopped.

"Hello, patriot," said one of the men. "We were told you have a son."

Grandfather looked up at both of them gravely, trying not to show fear. "My son was hanged," he said. "I am alone." He gestured toward his *jacal* as if its emptiness were a testament to the truth of his statement.

One dragoon nodded to the other, who immediately rode toward the creek to have a look around. As he rode away, the first dragoon began walking his horse slowly around the old man, forcing the old man to turn around and around in a circle in order to keep the horseman in sight. The dragoon said nothing for a long time, merely staring at the grandfather, smiling slightly, knowingly.

Nervously, the grandfather said, "I live in Tejas, but I am a loyal Mexican."

Jesús watched the disturbing scene for a moment, but when he saw the searching dragoon riding his way, he flung the trout to the ground and ran for the cover of a ditch. The dragoon did not see Jesús, but he did see a fish go flying through the air. He whistled for the other, then rode directly toward the ditch. In it, Jesús cowered low, but in plain sight.

Jesús looked up at the dragoon. The horse stood over him, menacingly. One step forward and Jesús would be crushed. The dragoon was even more menacing. Was he about to skewer Jesús with his lance? Or were Jesús and his grandfather about to be dragged away and hanged from a tree, as his father had been?

As fearsome as he seemed to Jesús, the dragoon actually had a benign, even friendly, look on his face. Gazing down on Jesús from his horse, the dragoon smiled warmly and said, "Welcome to the army of General Antonio López de Santa Anna."

Jesús instinctively put his arms over his

head, bracing himself for the attack.

"Come, come, boy," the dragoon said. "We are not going to hurt you. Stand up now."

Very reluctantly, Jesús stood up. He glanced around, looking desperately for another escape route, knowing that he had absolutely no chance of outrunning the horse, or of escaping the point of that lance.

"What is your name, boy?" the dragoon said.

"Jesús Montoya."

The dragoon said, "Are you married?"

Jesús shook his head no.

The abandoned fish, not yet dead, desperately worked its gills as it lay on the banks.

The dragoon smiled and said, "Plenty of time for marriage, when you are older — and a war hero. You are to come with us."

Jesús stammered, "Where . . . what . . . ?"

The dragoon gestured for Jesús to start walking. "Everything will be explained to you in due time, boy," he said. He began herding Jesús back to where his grandfather waited with the other horseman. As Jesús stumbled along, he turned to the rider and, with a pleading look in his eyes, said, "My family . . ."

The dragoon smiled. "They will be very proud of you," he said. "It is an honor to fight for your country."

Jesús walked toward his grandfather, but the dragoon would not let him stop to say good-bye. Jesús waved and murmured, "Grandfather . . ."

The old man only shook his head sadly. They both knew there was nothing he could do. The other dragoon fell into step beside the one who had captured Jesús. The boy turned a little. He could barely see their faces for the bright silver glow that emanated from their helmets.

"Where are we going?" Jesús said.

The first dragoon snapped, "Quiet! Just walk!"

Jesús's dragoon was still smiling. He said to his partner, "Do not be so hard on the boy. He is only curious." He looked down at Jesús and said, "Where are we going? We are going to punish the gringos."

Chapter Six

"You marked the coat as swallowtail?"

Mr. Ingram, the owner of Ingram's General Store and Barroom, was beginning to tire of this, but maintained a steady smile on his face. A customer is a customer. Even an exacting, nitpicking, condescending — basically insufferable — customer.

"As you desired, Mr. Travis," Ingram said with bland pleasantness.

"Lieutenant Colonel Travis," the young man corrected him. Ingram simply raised his eyebrows a bit and nodded.

Ingram's was the best-appointed store in San Felipe. In fact, it was just about the only store in San Felipe. Its owner prided himself on stocking almost anything that a person could need to get through life. In the front he kept food, tobacco, Mexican blankets, gourds, guns, saddles, cooking utensils, candles, knives — even pieces of sugar cane and cactus candy for the delight of the children. In the back, there was a barroom with rickety tables; it also served as a storeroom. Crates lined the walls, and goods of all kinds were piled anywhere there was an empty space. That did not seem to matter much to the patrons. When they came there to drink, they did not care much about ambience.

William Barret Travis would never have had the occasion to see the back room. He was a teetotaler; more than that, he was the kind of teetotaler who made sure that everyone he met heard his views on the subject. As Mr. Ingram was finding out, twenty-six-year-old Travis liked to make himself perfectly clear, no matter what the subject.

Travis was a handsome man, tall and erect with a natural aristocratic bearing. His eyes were dark and penetrating and his face smooth and unlined. It gave the distinct impression of a face that had almost never experienced the disturbance of a smile. At the same time, it looked far younger than it was — and, undoubtedly, more innocent than it was.

Travis had not been in San Felipe very long, but Mr. Ingram had already learned to dread his appearance. Whenever the young lieutenant colonel walked into the store, the proprietor knew that he was in for a session of extremely precise orders, spelled out in numbing detail and repeated ad nauseam.

Today was even worse than usual. Travis leaned over the counter, intense and humorless, spelling out the minute particulars of the handwritten sales order that was spread on the counter between the two men.

"And the piping is onyx?" Travis said, not for the first time. He pointed to a sketch of a man in the exact uniform he was ordering. The man in the drawing looked a lot like Travis.

Mr. Ingram nodded again. "Yes, sir, exactly as you have specified." He indicated the drawing. "Should be quite a sight. Where would you like the uniform sent?"

Travis drew himself up a bit.

"San Antonio de Béxar," he said. "I will be posted there. To defend the town."

"Defend against what?" Mr. Ingram said. "Mexican army left Béxar with their tails between their legs."

The response deflated Travis a bit — but only a bit. He could not expect a rank civilian such as Mr. Ingram to understand the sober responsibilities of the military life.

"Mister William?" Travis's manservant, Joe, was standing in the doorway. He was about Travis's height and was dressed in obvious hand-me-downs that nevertheless were clean and well-maintained. Actually, Travis and Joe himself were the only people who referred to Joe as a "manservant." Everyone else knew that the twenty-three-year-old Negro was a slave.

"She here," Joe said. "In yer office. Waitin'."

The statement had so little to do with the uniform currently under consideration that Travis did not quite follow what Joe meant. He looked at the young man with eyebrows raised, as if asking, "Who?"

Joe lowered his head a bit. "Yer wife," he said.

Across the street, James Bowie staggered into the narrow space between two buildings. His slave Sam — and Bowie never thought of him as his "manservant" — stood behind him, thinking that his master looked like death warmed over. Bowie was coughing, something that seemed to afflict him more and more these days. Sam had no idea if Bowie was sick or dying — and he did not much care. Sam thought of himself as a slave as well, and thought of little else than how he might someday escape and be a free man, somewhere. Until that day, Sam would take orders and abuse with as much stoic grace as he could muster. There was no alternative.

"Mister James?" he said, softly.

Bowie's coughing began to turn to gagging. With a convulsive fit, he spewed vomit all over the wall. *Well,* Sam thought, *that answers that.* His master was neither sick nor dying — just drunk. As usual.

A group of riders raced down the street behind Sam. He had been placed there by Bowie to keep watch, to make sure no one saw him in his weakened condition. The sound of the riders seemed to snap Bowie out of his misery and he quickly straightened himself up and hurried toward the street. Sam stepped aside to let him pass. With a heavy sigh, he followed him.

Bowie saw with an inward groan that Travis was walking down the street toward him, with Joe in tow. Bowie straightened further and walked in Travis's direction, as though headed somewhere with great purpose. Nearly every man in the street who saw Bowie gladhanded him, patted him on the back. He was clearly a favorite among the Texians in this town. Travis was greeted by no one.

As Bowie and Travis passed each other on the street, each touched the brim of his hat in polite greeting.

103

"Colonel," Travis said.

Bowie replied, "Buck," knowing that Travis found the nickname annoying in the extreme.

Their slaves also greeted each other in a way, sharing a look that hinted at the relationship, or lack thereof, between their owners. Sam clearly felt himself to be more than a little superior to Joe. Joe had heard the scandalous stories about Bowie's raucous and reckless behavior, his drunkenness and wildness. The moral young man took some modicum of comfort in being owned by such a high-class gentleman as Mr. William.

As soon as Travis and Bowie were out of earshot of each another, they spoke again.

"Drunken Hottentot," Travis said, under his breath.

Bowie muttered, "Two-bit swell."

The group of riders that Bowie had heard were dismounting in front of Ingram's, rushing in to cut the dust from their throats in the back room. Bowie recognized one of them as Deaf Smith, a great scout and an old friend.

Bowie strode toward him, calling loudly. "Deaf" was not just his nickname.

"Deef!" No response.

Bowie tried again, louder, "Deef!"

Deaf Smith happened to turn around at that moment and saw with surprise that Bowie was behind him. They shook hands. "Deef, you come from Béxar?" Bowie said.

"Ain't it so?" Smith said, nodding.

Bowie said, "How's my home?"

Smith looked Bowie in the eye, wondering how much to tell him. "Free of the Mexican army," he said. "Fought 'em straight into the old mission, then right out again."

"Is it wrecked bad?" Bowie said. "The house?"

Deaf hesitated, choosing his words carefully.

"There was quite a bit of cannon shot, Jim."

Bowie's mind immediately conjured up images of his beautiful home in ruins. The Veramendi House was owned by the family of Bowie's wife. Even today, when it was no longer occupied by members of the family, people all over Béxar referred to it as the "Veramendi Palace." But Bowie's mind did not linger long on thoughts of the house, for to him, the house only meant one thing — the place where he had lived with his beloved Ursula. The house, whatever the damage, could be rebuilt or written off. But Ursula . . . Travis approached his law office and stopped at the doorway. A towheaded, somber-faced little boy of seven stared back at him. Behind the child, a woman with sad eyes stroked the golden hair of a three-year-old girl, who clung to her mother's leg and shyly avoided looking at Travis. The woman gave the boy a little nudge. "Go on, Charlie," she said. "You remember him. Do you not remember your father?"

Travis forced a smile that he did not feel and held his hand a couple of feet above the floor. "When I last saw you," he said in an unconvincingly hearty voice, "you were *this* tall."

There was no reply. The boy just looked at Travis, without anger, without fear, without . . . anything. Still smiling his frozen smile, Travis turned his gaze toward the little girl.

"What are you calling her?" he asked. "Lizzy? Betsy?"

"Elisabeth," the woman said firmly.

The little girl buried her face in her mother's skirts. Travis, still avoiding the woman's eyes, turned his attention toward some papers on the desk.

"Well, Rosanna," Travis said in a businesslike tone, "the choices are abandonment, adultery, or cruel and barbarous treatment. I think abandonment's the most accurate."

Rosanna Travis was twenty-four years old, but life had caused her to age prematurely. Although she was still a pretty woman, her eyes were hard and her mouth grim. It was difficult for Travis to reconcile this wounded face with the lovely vision he had first encountered at that dance in Claiborne, Alabama, seven years ago. It did not occur to him that perhaps her stern countenance was worn only for such occasions, when her heart felt as if it were being ripped from her body.

In a low voice, almost a whisper, Rosanna said, "Last time I saw you, you were lying in bed next to me. Then I closed my eyes. That was four years ago." She nodded toward the papers on the desk. "Any of the choices would be appropriate."

Travis said softly, "That is true, Rosanna. That is certainly true."

Rosanna sat in a leather-bound chair beside the desk and pulled little Elisabeth into her lap. "They talk about you a lot back in Claiborne," she said.

Travis looked at her, interested, as he always was, when the topic was himself. "What do they say?"

Rosanna smiled bitterly. "Rumors. You . . . we . . . are the subject of many and various rumors."

Travis sat on the edge of his desk. "For instance?"

"Some people hold that it is I who was unfaithful to you," Rosanna said.

Travis grimaced a little. "Perhaps we should not speak of such things in front of the children. . . ."

Rosanna snapped, "Charlie has heard these things almost every day. Well-meaning people in church, other children taunting him. There is nothing we can say now that he does not already know. Elisabeth, thank God, is too young to understand any of it."

Travis nodded solemnly. Charlie continued to stare at him, but Travis avoided his gaze. He said to Rosanna, "What are the other rumors?"

"They say you killed a man," she said.

"What?"

She nodded. "Those who believe that I was unfaithful to you say that you discovered the man in question and murdered him. I have heard that you stabbed him and that you shot him. I even heard that you tied him to his bed and set his house on fire," Rosanna said.

"What unutterable nonsense!" Travis said, standing up abruptly and pacing the floor. "Who would say such things about me?"

Rosanna shrugged a little. "Almost everyone," she said. "When you departed in the dead of night, leaving unpaid debts, abandoned law clients . . . After that, no one regarded you with very much admiration. Oddly, I find myself having to defend you from time to time." She laughed, quickly and bitterly. "Yes, I have to stand up for your character. Is that not a priceless irony?"

Travis said nothing. Shame burned at his face.

Rosanna's face was still impassive, but her voice was choked with emotion. "Are you going to marry her?"

Travis was startled. "Who?" he said.

Rosanna looked at him, smiling bitterly. "Who? That kind of response is unworthy even of you, Will."

Travis lowered his eyes. "I had no idea that you knew anything about her."

"I do not," Rosanna said. "Except that I have been told you are engaged to her."

"That is not precisely true," Travis said. "We have been . . . keeping company for some time now. But the subject of marriage . . ."

"What is her name?" Rosanna asked.

Travis hesitated. "Rebecca," he said finally. "Rebecca Cummings."

Rosanna nodded. "Rebecca. Not very different from Rosanna, is it?"

Travis smiled, trying for a note of levity. "Different enough," he said.

Rosanna's eyes filled with tears and Travis immediately regretted saying it. He pulled a handkerchief from his coat and stepped toward her. She raised her hand, stopping him in his tracks. Rosanna reached into her purse and pulled out a handkerchief of her own. She dabbed her eyes with it and sat silently, composing herself, her face once again freezing into an emotionless mask.

Charlie stayed close by, never taking his eyes from Travis's face, still showing no emotion of any kind. Rosanna glanced over the document. There was nothing there that she had not read a dozen times before. "Are you sure you want to do this?" she said.

Travis, looking uncomfortable, spoke with some effort. When he did, his voice was raspy. "We have signed the papers."

"I meant Charlie," Rosanna said.

"My dear," Travis said, "I do not intend this harshly, but he should have a manly example in his life."

She said nothing, but the look she gave him spoke volumes about the kind of "manly example" she expected Travis to be to her son. Travis ignored the look and plowed on. "I have already made arrangements for him to stay with a fine family while I am away: the Ayerses. Wonderful people. The wife is quite a bit younger than the husband but . . ."

Travis stopped. Rosanna was nodding, her eyes brimming with tears.

In a brighter voice, Travis said, "They promoted me to lieutenant colonel. Did I tell you that in the letter?"

"I cannot say I am happy for you, Billy," his wife replied. Abruptly, she stood up. "Well," she said a little too loudly, "we have a long way to travel."

Rosanna knelt and wrapped the boy in her arms, holding him as tightly as she could. Charlie was a little bewildered by the fierce hug and struggled a little to free himself. She finally released him and held both shoulders, looking at him intensely, as if trying to memorize his face. Rosanna then kissed his forehead and took another long look at his face, smoothing the hair back out of his eyes.

Travis could not stand watching their farewell and stood at the window, staring out onto the busy San Felipe street.

"Your father is becoming a rich man," Rosanna said, "and he will be able to see to your education." Charlie did not say a word, did not cry, did not exhibit any emotion at all.

Rosanna stood and gazed sadly at her son one more time. Then she took Elisabeth's hand and, without a word to her former husband, walked out of Travis's law office. Elisabeth stole one look back at her father as the door closed. Travis stared after them for a moment, then turned to Charlie. He knelt before the boy and stretched his face into a smile. Once again, his voice tried for hearty and enthusiastic.

"We have a tutor," he said, "to teach you Spanish." Travis smiled widely, "Hola, Carlos. That means 'Hello, Charlie.' "

Charlie, without a word, sat down in a chair in the corner. He reached into the little satchel that his mother had left with him and pulled out a picture book.

Travis wondered if this was really a good idea after all. He glanced through the window. Across the way, his wife and daughter were walking down the street, and out of his life forever.

Chapter Seven

The building was low-ceilinged and un-painted. In its center was a rough-hewn plat-form on which stood a podium. A small plank table sat nearby. Scattered around the walls were a few dozen wooden chairs and some hastily built benches. Every available seat was occupied. Today it was standing room only — and the milling crowd was too angry and agitated to sit, even if there had been more chairs. The room was divided al-most evenly between the War Party and the Peace Party.

T. J. Rusk was there. He had come to Texas tracking down some men who had swindled him in a business deal. He never caught up with them, but he fell in love with the territory and decided to make it his home. Just before the siege of Béxar he had

organized his own company of volunteers —
but they did not quite make it to town in
time to take part in the fighting.

Also present was blustery Governor
Smith, a former schoolteacher who had fa-
thered nine children with three successive
wives. Despite this, or perhaps because of it,
Smith was shrill and angry.

Other members of the War Party were
James Grant and Mosley Baker, rash, ignorant men who had long been thorns in the
side of Santa Anna. Baker had been marked
for execution by the dictator but had managed to elude capture. He was there when
the other men of Gonzales shouted, "Come
and Take It!" and got this revolution off to a
noisy start, and he had helped take Béxar
back from General Cós.

Grant was a doctor who still spoke with
the sometimes impenetrable burr of his native Scotland. He had been in Texas for well
over a decade, having originally come to be
an empresario and make his fortune selling
vast stretches of land to new immigrants.
Grant was successful at his business, possibly because he so frequently skirted — and
sometimes crossed — the lines of legality.
His shady business dealings made Grant
many enemies — including Santa Anna,
who despised land speculators and ordered

many of them arrested and held in Mexican jails. Grant was on Santa Anna's arrest list but, like his bad-tempered friend Baker, had escaped capture.

On the other side of the coin, and the issue, was David Burnet. He was another one of the original empresarios who were given grants by the Mexican government to bring settlers into Texas. Burnet was the kind of man who neither swore nor drank, but carried a Bible in one pocket and a gun in the other. He could be pretty deadly with either. Back in his native New Jersey, Burnet had earned his living as an accountant. Now, with his angry shock of black hair and a severe beard that circled his massive face like a chin strap, he looked like a fire-and-brimstone evangelist. He worked the crowd like one, too.

Now, Burnet stood imperiously at the podium in the center of the room, bellowing like a preacher at his pulpit. The members of the War Party and the Peace Party sat and stood facing one another on either side of him, glaring across the chasm of their many political disagreements.

"Gentlemen!" Burnet shouted. "Over two years ago, I wrote a petition which proposed a separation of Texas from Coahuila. Many of you in this room signed that petition!"

The room, already noisy, became even louder with the supporting shouts and cheers.

Burnet leaned forward, gripping the podium with both hands, glaring at the politicians surrounding him as if they were lost souls. "But today we want more than simple separation of the states. We want independence for Texas!"

A chorus of boos came from the Peace Party. Most of them supported compromise with Mexico. They considered the desire for independence as a revolutionary act that would certainly end in terrible bloodshed.

Burnet beat on the podium with his bare hands to quiet the room. "But we will win independence only with the support of patriots. Our cause can be irreparably damaged by the wanton acts of a few opportunists who are only out to build their own fortunes at the cost of their country's freedom!"

A new wave of cheers met his statement — along with an equal number of boos.

Grant was seated beside the small plank table. He stood up and pointed at Burnet. "You want to call me an opportunist?" Grant shouted. "Hell yes, I am an opportunist! Taking Béxar changes everything.

We are in control now!"

Governor Smith stood up and attempted to shout over the cheers of the War Party, "We swore allegiance to Mexico under the Federalist constitution of 1824."

Mosley Baker stood up and interrupted, his veins nearly popping with anger. "Santa Anna tore that document up personally, did he not?" he snarled. "And named himself supreme dictator. The Centralists have changed the rules, and I for one ain't swearing allegiance to no son-of-a-bitch dictator."

On Baker's side of the room the crowd of men of the War Party clapped their hands, slapped the table or beat their canes on the floor, shouting, "Hear! Hear!" and "Me neither!"

Waving his hands to quiet the room — an impossible task — Governor Smith called out, his voice growing hoarse, "Gentlemen, are we fighting for restoration of the Mexican constitution, or for independence from Mexico?"

It was not the right question to ask this particular room. Half of the men yelled, "Independence!" or "Republic!" The other half shouted, "Constitution!" Both factions raised their voices to their highest volume until the din was nearly unbearable.

Juan Seguin elbowed his way to the front of the crowd and held his hands in the air. Most of the men in the room respected Seguin more than Smith, so they dutifully lowered the noise to a dull, steady roar.

"We can oppose the dictator Santa Anna," Seguin said, "but as loyal Mexicans."

Thompson, a charismatic but hopelessly corrupt politician from South Carolina, blustered loudly, staring at Seguin, "I ain't no Mexican!" Others around the room echoed their agreement.

Seguin raised his hand and continued. "Every man in this room became a Catholic and a Mexican citizen in order to immigrate here."

This was true, but for almost every man present, the oath had been nothing more than a formality, just a winking response to an archaic regulation. No one had any intention of living up to their new citizenship — not if there was a more profitable alternative.

Seguin said, his voice nearly overwhelmed by the squall of sound, "Sam Houston is general of the army —"

Grant interrupted loudly, "Sir, he is not the general of the men who tasted victory at Béxar!"

The War Party cheered the sentiment.

"And where is Houston, Señor Seguin?" Burnet said sneeringly. "Where is the good general . . . ?"

An empty shot glass hit the table, loudly, in the back room of Ingram's General Store and Barroom. Sam Houston stood at the bar, alone, and started to pour another shot. His hand shook so badly that he set down the bottle and prepared for another try.

Mathew Ingram, the fifteen-year-old son of the proprietor, was sweeping the main room when he noticed Houston's palsy. Mathew had silky blond hair and was small for his age. He did not realize that he was staring until Houston caught his gaze. Embarrassed, Mathew cast his eyes to the floor, carefully inspecting the place that he had just swept.

Mathew's father walked back into the bar, carrying supplies, and said to Houston, "Are you all right?"

"I have about returned to ought," Houston said with a sardonic grin, "which is a fairly good starting point, actually." He reached for the bottle again, and made another determined attempt at pouring himself a shot. He nodded at Mr. Ingram. "Obliged to you for asking."

Juan Seguin entered the barroom, taking

a moment for his eyes to adjust from the bright San Felipe street to the darkness of this dank closet. When he saw Houston standing there, he shook his head to himself. "Time to go, General," he said.

Houston ignored Seguin, concentrating hard as he poured from the bottle. He knew that the boy was still watching him surreptitiously, so he made sure Mathew noticed the steadiness of his hand. He did not spill a drop. With a certain air of pride, Houston threw back the shot. He turned to Seguin and said, "Drunk back sober is a miracle of the first order."

"General?" Seguin said again, a little more urgently.

Houston nodded. "All right, Juan, here I come." He tossed a coin onto the bar. It was engraved with the likeness of a distinguished-looking man. Under the engraving were carved the words General Antonio López de Santa Anna.

Houston and Seguin walked down the street without speaking. Houston breathed deeply, filling his lungs with the fresh air, his posture and demeanor changing with each step. Every man who saw him turned to watch him pass. Houston was physically bigger than almost any man he met. But the general impression that he was bigger than life was not solely based upon his size. He could have stood a foot shorter and still seemed to fill the street with his presence. Seguin always marveled at it, even as he felt a deep stab of frustration. He had never seen such a born leader — and had never seen a man so prone to squandering his gift of leadership with careless living.

Houston said, "Who is there?"

"Grant, Baker, some of the others," Seguin said. In as few words as possible, he summed up the general tenor of the meeting, as well as the heated arguments over how next to proceed.

"Goddam fools," Houston muttered.

Seguin continued, "Now that we have taken Béxar, they want to lead an expedition to Matamoros."

"Matamoros?" Houston said. "Why in the hell they want to capture Matamoros?"

Matamoros was a port city in Mexico. It held strategic importance because it stood at one of the main gateways to Texas from southern Mexico. It was also believed that the population of the town was opposed to Santa Anna and that there could be many new recruits there for the Texian cause. But perhaps the most compelling reason to take Matamoros was because it was a wealthy city with plenty of money, goods and weapons, all of which were openly coveted by the members of the War Party.

Seguin said to Houston, "They want to loot the port. They have the taste of blood in their mouths."

At that moment, Travis fell in step with the two men. He was closely followed by Joe, who carried saddlebags. "General Houston," Travis said, "might you spare me a moment?"

Houston paused and looked at Travis. He said nothing.

Travis was ruffled a little by the lack of response but recovered quickly and said, "Sir, would you reconsider my posting to Béxar? Now that it has been taken back . . . It is just . . . I am a cavalry officer, sir, and my abilities would be better employed outside of a town and old mission."

Travis nodded to Joe, who opened the saddlebag. Travis pulled out the uniform sketch and showed it to Houston.

"Sir," Travis said, "I have proposed a legion of cavalry. . . ."

Houston did not look at the drawing. "Place it in writing," he said.

Travis replied, "I have already done so, sir."

Joe pulled a packet of papers that he

passed to Travis. He offered them to Houston, who did not take them.

Houston looked at Travis with such intensity that it made him uncomfortable. "You are a lawyer, Travis? Are you not?" Houston said.

Travis relaxed a little. "Yes, I am," Travis said, rather proudly. "As you are, sir."

Travis looked at Houston expectantly, waiting for the rest of the question.

Houston nodded and patted Travis on the shoulder. "Well," he said, "God is surely smiling on Texas."

Travis stopped walking. He realized that he was being patronized. As Joe looked discreetly away, Travis watched as Houston and Seguin continued down the street. Then he turned and walked quietly back to his law office.

When they were a short distance away, Houston said to Seguin, "Explain to me why young men measure themselves with fights instead of yardsticks?"

Seguin said, "Why are you so hard on him?"

Houston looked at Seguin and smiled a little. "Reminds me of me," he said.

Houston and Seguin walked toward the crowd gathered outside the Public Building. "They are going to want you a bit humble,

General," Seguin said in a whisper.

The crowd spotted him and Houston hesitated, letting Seguin's comment sink in. There were some hostile stares coming from that room.

"Juan, mi amigo," Houston said, "I humble myself before God, and there the list ends."

The crowd parted to let them through.

The Public Building was in near chaos. Men huddled in groups, working over documents, arguing over details. The battle lines were clearly drawn between the Peace Party and the War Party. Burnet stalked the room, seemingly in control. He stepped up to the podium and said loudly, "The question has come to the floor whether to capture Matamoros. . . ."

Before he could finish the sentence, Burnet saw Houston walk in and lean against a wall. He continued, pointedly speaking in Houston's direction. "Discussion on the point, which is whether to capture Matamoros." Men around the room raised their hands or waved their canes, eager to argue their side of the issue or simply to hammer home a point. Burnet scanned the crowd and finally settled on Grant. He pointed at the Scotsman, who stood and gestured toward a large tactical map of Texas and Coahuila that had been nailed to the wall.

"By attacking Matamoros," Grant said, "we guarantee Texas independence. We hurl the thunder back in the very atmosphere of the enemy, dragging him — and with him, the war — out of Texas."

The War Party responded with thunderous cheers.

Governor Smith stood up, smirking. "Well, we can certainly guess who has land holdings in the Mexican interior," he said, ". . . now worthless."

Some of the men in the room made hissing sounds.

"This whole council is more corrupt than perdition," Governor Smith continued. "In war, when spoils are the object, friends and enemies share a common destiny."

The War Party side of the room erupted in a chorus of boos and catcalls aimed at Smith.

"Spoils?" interjected Baker. He stood up from his chair and stalked toward the podium. "We are talking about guts. About having enough of them to finish the task!"

There were loud cheers from most of the crowd.

Houston looked at Seguin, then took in the rest of the room, shaking his head. He slowly started to walk through its midst. All eyes went to him. Almost no one there was glad to see him, but his presence had a profound effect on the proceedings. As they watched him come forward, the boisterous group became quieter than it had been since the meeting started.

"No leadership. No training. Few supplies. Less ammunition." Houston's voice was quiet, but carried clearly to every corner of the room.

He walked over to the map, pulled his knife from its scabbard and stuck the tip to a point on the map. He held a lit cigar in his left hand.

"To march an expedition from here . . . to Matamoros . . ." — he sliced the map from San Felipe to Matamoros — "is lunacy," Houston said. "You do not split an army into vagabond militias that march off on the slightest pretext like bloodthirsty rabble."

He placed the knife back into its scabbard, puffed on the cigar and continued his walk around the room.

"Do you really believe this war is over?" Houston said. "It has not even begun, and already the scoundrels are rushing off for personal gain."

Grant and Baker exchanged insulted looks and, for a moment, the room was totally silent. Then murmurs began rising slowly — "Coward," "Quitter," "Yellow," "Drunk!" As the taunts grew louder and louder, Houston became more and more arrogant — and obstinate.

"All new lands are infested by noisy, second-rate men who favor the rash and extreme measure," he shouted. He took a long, hard look around the room. "Texas, quite obviously, is overrun with them."

The crowd, which might have started out as fifty-fifty, was now almost completely and openly against him.

From the platform, Burnet grinned down at Houston. "You opposed taking Béxar, where victory was ours," he said mockingly. "Now, you oppose taking Matamoros, where victory will be as sweet. Perhaps, sir, you simply oppose fighting?"

The crowd erupted in agreement. Many of the men jeered and laughed.

"Fighters shall lead the new country of Texas!" shouted Mosley Baker, and the men enthusiastically backed him up with their cheers.

Burnet held up his hand for order. "The council will now consider the removal of General Houston from command of the regular army. All in favor . . . a show of hands?" The majority of the room erupted with raised arms and *Hear, hears!* T. J. Rusk hesitated, then, almost sadly, raised his hand.

Governor Smith pointed to Burnet. "You, sir, do not speak for Texas," he said. "I am governor, and I hereby dissolve the council!"

Burnet turned to the crowd, clearly enjoying his role as rabble rouser. He shouted, "All in favor of impeaching Governor Smith?"

There was another rousing cheer and show of hands. All around the building were red, pinched faces, warmongers shouting, "Matamoros!" "Victory!" and "God bless Texas!"

Houston tried to speak again but this time his voice was futile against the mob. "The militias must report to the general of the army," he shouted unheard. "We must have unity of command. . . ."

Burnet put his face close to Houston's and snarled, "To whom the militias report is no longer any of your concern." Burnet turned to face the War Party and gestured toward Fannin, sitting erect like a real soldier against the wall. "The regular army shall report to Colonel James Fannin, a West Point attendee."

Fannin stood up shyly to accept the fren-

128

zied cheers of the War Party. It was true enough that Fannin had attended West Point. But what Burnet did not know — or, at least what he did not say — was that Fannin had dropped out of the academy after less than two years. He never graduated. Indeed, he never distinguished himself in any way. Of a class of eighty-six, Fannin had ranked sixtieth. Despite that, he was the only West Point man in the room, and to the angry men, who were rabid for action, he seemed to be the perfect choice to head up the army.

Houston did not know of Fannin's less-than-glittering record, but he could size up a man with a single glance, and one look told him that Fannin was not up to the job. Houston shook his head in dismay. "Amateur soldiers in the service of amateur politicians," he scoffed.

Grant shouted sarcastically to the room, pointing at Houston, "The late, great Sam Houston. Former governor of Tennessee, former general of the Texian army." His every word was met by laughter and rousing cheers.

"The fighting at Béxar has obviously produced chaos," Houston said. "The next will result in annihilation. . . ."

Grant shouted, "Coward!"

Houston looked coolly at Grant, took a puff of his cigar and responded, "Scottish catamite!"

Grant stood up. "What did you say?" he said, shocked. He had been insulted in many and various ways in his life, but this was a new low.

Houston smiled, delighted to have drawn blood. "I called you a Scottish catamite, Grant — one step down from associate pederast."

Grant drew his knife. Houston knew a theatrical moment when one presented itself. He quickly removed his silk cravat, ripped open his shirt and bared his chest. His past as an actor was coming in handy. Melodramatically, he said, "Come for me!"

Seguin sighed and stepped in behind Houston. Grant was about to make a lunge forward, when all heads around him turned.

"Any excuse to remove your clothes, right, Houston?" Jim Bowie stood just inside the door, smiling and shaking his head.

The room, for the first time that day, was absolutely hushed.

Grant, still brandishing his knife at Houston, snarled, "This ain't your concern, Mr. Bowie."

"Indeed," Houston said, mimicking

Grant's Scottish burr, "this is between me and the catamite."

Grant flinched. Bowie put a hand on his hip, letting his jacket slide open enough to expose a knife sheathed to his side, and walked toward the table. Everyone in the room knew the legend of that knife. Bowie slowly drew it out and held it, point upward. It was gigantic, so fearsome-looking that some of the men averted their eyes unconsciously. Bowie flipped the knife and tendered it to Grant, handle first.

"You want to borrow mine, Grant?" Bowie said. He leaned in closer, speaking with a low, deadly tone, "Because I will surely give it to you."

Everyone in the room stared back and forth between Bowie and Grant. Bowie dropped the knife on the table with a loud clang. He gazed coolly at Grant with a look that indicated, "Go for it." Grant would almost have rather died than humble himself before the War Party, which he hoped to lead. But he was sensible enough to realize that he would die if he carried this on much longer. He was a tolerably good knife fighter. But "tolerably good" was not quite enough to best James Bowie. After a long, awkward pause, Grant resheathed his knife.

Bowie walked over and rebuttoned Houston's shirt, making sure to show his back to Grant — and making sure everyone noticed it. His very presence seemed to calm Houston down. Looking slightly dazed, like a man who has been rudely awakened from a dream, Houston whispered to Bowie, "Buy you a drink?" Bowie smiled and placed Houston's hat on his head at a jaunty angle.

Throughout, Grant stared down at the knife in front of him but just could not work up the nerve to pick it up. The men who had been so angry and blustery only moments before now sat breathless. Thompson, the loudmouth Carolinian, stared at Bowie's knife with a kind of horrified fascination, wondering if he was about to get blood all over his nice new beaver hat. He wanted desperately to leap up and dash out the door, but he could not quite bring himself to move.

Bowie turned to the room, smiling. "You gentlemen will have to excuse Sam," he said. "He was Indian raised."

Bowie put an arm around Houston's shoulder and they walked toward the door. Bowie stopped, remembering his knife. He returned for it, slowly dragged it across the table, and placed it back in his sheath, never taking his eyes from Grant's during the entire exhibition. Everyone watched; no one breathed.

Houston and Bowie stepped out into the street. They walked along silently for a moment, and then Bowie said, "I believe you said something about buying me a drink." Houston smiled and clapped Bowie on the shoulder. Together, they walked back to Ingram's, which had not had the pleasure of Houston's business for nearly fifteen minutes.

With Houston out of the room, the War Party could continue its relentless push to organize the invasion of Matamoros, or what they were now calling the "Matamoros Expedition."

Grant said, "I propose that Colonel Fannin take charge of the expedition."

Burnet nodded and said, "All in favor?"

A chorus of "ayes" around the room passed the resolution. Fannin stood up modestly and waved at the crowd. He hoped that his face did not betray the panic he felt inside. He wanted to be a military hero, but this actually sounded dangerous.

Smith stood up in frustration. "This is absurdity," he shouted. "You will only strip much-needed supplies from our other commands and take them three hundred miles away. This expedition leaves the rest of Texas defenseless!"

The War Party shouted him down. Burnet glared down at Smith condescendingly. "If we take Matamoros, then the Mexican army has no port of entry into Texas except by land — and we can easily guard those roads. Taking Matamoros is the best way to defend Texas!" The room resounded with cheers. "As for the matter of supplies, Colonel Fannin and his men will take only whatever is necessary, leaving each post occupied with as many men as can be spared. Dr. Grant and Colonel Frank Johnson will take a hundred men to find and obtain more horses and supplies for the expedition."

Grant nodded. "Now that Béxar has been secured," he said, "the garrison there will be a bountiful source for men and weapons. John and I will leave for that place within forty-eight hours."

Men around the room nodded in agreement. This struck all of them as a foolproof plan.

Burnet looked at the War Party, then over at the Peace Party, some of whom were grudgingly beginning to see the positive aspects of the Matamoros Expedition. "The time is at hand, my brothers!" Burnet shouted. "On to Matamoros! On to victory!"

Two days later, Bowie stood in front of Ingram's, watching as the militia saddled up and rode out, hooting and cheering, certain of victory. Fannin's column headed down the road to Goliad. Grant and Johnson's men rode toward Béxar. Even though Johnson was the officer, Grant rode at the head of the column, trying desperately to position himself as their leader. Bowie shook his head in disgust and walked away.

He passed a dogtrot. It occurred to him that it was the same one in which he had been so violently ill just a few days earlier. And from the sounds emanating from it, Bowie knew that there was someone in there, carrying on his tradition. Bowie peered down the alley and saw a figure sitting on the ground at the end, against the back wall. Light from a lantern in a nearby window played over his face. It was Houston, sitting with legs splayed, head resting against the wall. His battered hat was lying nearby, as if it had fallen off unnoticed. Houston's eyes were closed and he was humming softly to himself. Bowie had been in the same condition often enough to know at a glance that Houston was dead drunk. In one hand he held an almost empty bottle. In the other, a pistol.

Bowie walked down the alley and stood before Houston. With some effort, Houston opened his eyes and peered at Bowie. There were flecks of vomit around the corners of his mouth. "Pull up a stool," he said. Bowie took a look around the alley and noticed that he was standing in the very spot where he himself had been so violently ill. He decided to squat. He said, "Oblige me and do not sleep here tonight."

Houston acted as though he did not hear. He took a long pull on the bottle. Some of the whiskey dribbled down his chin, soaking the ruffles on the front of his shirt.

Bowie said, "You are making a jackass of yourself, Sam."

Houston growled, "Vindictive sons a bitches. Sent me off to make treaty with the Cherokees." He passed the bottle to Bowie, who took a swig.

Bowie said, "The council did not know what else to do with you. You disagreed with them about Matamoros. You would certainly have been nothing but a burr under Fannin's saddle. Or Grant's."

Houston nodded and took another swig. "So they are just getting me out of the way. That is how it seems to me."

Bowie said, "Sam, look at it this way: You are going home. I know you — you are only really yourself among the Cherokee. You have told me so yourself."

Houston shrugged.

"I slept on rocks outside of Béxar for three months while that paper-collared brother-in-law of Santa Anna's lived in my home," Bowie said, "drinking up all my liquor. Everything I had is gone. Everything on paper, anyways."

Houston stared out into the darkness. He said, "Texas was a chance, a second chance, for all of us. A place to wash away our sins. That means something. Do not ever forget it."

Bowie looked sideways at Houston, who took the bottle and punctuated his point with another swig of whiskey. It seemed to Bowie that Houston was making a speech — a politician always, even when sitting in his own puke.

Houston shook his head and said sadly, "Texas is wasted on the Texians."

Bowie nodded. "The land's too good for the people," he said.

"You cannot blame the land," Houston said. They were quiet for a moment, then Houston said, "They will be back. The Mexicans. A massive, well-trained army.

Against a handful of amateurs. Only chance we have is to fight them in the open. Washington — fox and hound. 1812. Indian wars. Keep moving; burn what you leave behind." He took another swig. "Goddamn it, Jim," he said. "What is it about that damnable place?"

"What place?"

"Alamo," Houston said. "Whenever the wind blows sour in Béxar, everybody runs there and hides. Nothing but mud and a caved-in church."

"And cannon," Bowie added. "It protects my home, Sam."

Houston looked at Bowie and shook his head sadly. "You do not have a home. Any more than I do."

The statement hurt Bowie more than Houston meant to. He patted Bowie on the knee. "It is a damn shame about your wife, Jim," he said.

Bowie nodded gravely. "Damn shame about yours, too, Sam."

For the moment, they were just two men with not much left in the world, men who had every right to believe their best days were behind them. Feeling himself sinking into the pit of despair that had recently become so familiar to him, Houston forced himself to rally. With an expression that suggested he had regained his fire, he looked directly at Bowie and said, "Am I your general?"

"You know you are," Bowie said.

"All right then," Houston said, "I want you to return to Béxar, blow up the Alamo, and fetch back the cannon. Promise me you will do this?"

Bowie considered the order, then nodded. After all, it was about time for him to head for home himself.

"Promise me?" Houston urged.

"I promise, Sam," Bowie said. "Now, let us get you up out of your own filth and make you a little more presentable. Do not forget — you are an ambassador to the Cherokees. You need to show a little dignity." Bowie helped Houston to his feet.

"Well, Jim," Houston said, "I can certainly show a little dignity. Apparently very little."

The next day was bright and clear, cool and sunny. The streets of San Felipe were quiet and empty, as if things were back to normal and the town was again nothing more than a sleepy backwater. Hogs rooted in the road for something to eat. A few stray dogs did the same, more aggressively. Houston, looking worse for wear in the light of day, finished cinching Saracen, his magnificent white horse. When the saddle was secured, he wiped his cottony mouth with the back of his hand and mounted.

Mathew Ingram saw Houston through the window of his father's store. It was now or never. He stepped outside and waved at the man on the horse. "General?" Mathew said tentatively.

Houston looked straight ahead without expression, without even indicating that he had heard the boy.

"General, sir," Mathew said, "I want to fight."

Houston tipped his tricorn hat low against the light. He clicked his heels and his horse started down the street at a slow walk. Mathew trotted behind, struggling to keep up.

"It is important," Mathew said. "Tell me what I should do, sir."

Houston *whoa*'d his horse to a halt and finally looked down at Mathew. He said, "You have a mother?"

"Yes, I do," Mathew said.

"And a father?" Houston said. "You have one of those?"

The boy nodded. "Yes, sir."

"Well," Houston said, looking forward again, "go home and be with them."

Houston spurred his horse on, leaving

Mathew in the road. The boy watched him, crestfallen, then reluctantly returned to the store to resume his sweeping.

Toward the end of town Houston passed twenty men, mounted on their horses. Jim Bowie was among them. The two men stared at each other for a long moment, each pointed in a different direction. Then Bowie nodded to Houston, spurred his horse and galloped away with the others. Houston continued walking his horse out of town — one man headed away from the fray, the other toward it.

Just outside of San Felipe, Travis's men, thirty or so, waited while Travis stood on the porch steps of a tidy little house built of planks and rough bricks. A gentle couple, the Ayerses, stood in the doorway. Mrs. Ayers lightly gripped Charlie Travis by the shoulders and watched sadly as the boy prepared to say good-bye to his father. Charlie held a little cloth suitcase in his hand and stared at Travis.

Travis leaned down to his son's level and straightened the lapels on the little boy's coat. "Now you mind Mr. and Mrs. Ayers," he said. Charlie nodded. "Do not go causing any fuss. When I return we will get a home of our own. I promise."

The boy nodded again, hopeful. There

was nothing more to say. Travis, aware that his men were watching, held out his hand. "Good-bye, son."

Charlie shook his father's hand. Travis stood up and turned to return to his horse.

Charlie said, "Daddy?"

Travis stopped and turned. "What is it, Charlie?"

Charlie shrugged. "I just wanted to say it."

Travis, taken aback, could only nod. He mounted his horse and motioned for the men to ride. As he rode away, he wanted to look back, but could not. If he had not been surrounded by men, he would have wept.

Chapter Eight

The town of Zacatecas knew few luxuries, even in the best of times, but now it was a nightmare of devastation and sadness. Not long ago, despite its poverty, Zacatecas had been a town filled with hope and fervor, as federalists banded together to defeat the new dictator and his Centralist government. But it was the dictator — Antonio López de Santa Anna — who defeated the federalists. He did more than defeat them — he crushed them under his heel. Then he unleashed his army on the town, sanctioning, even encouraging a two-day orgy of pillage, plunder, rape and murder.

The Mexican army, on the march through northern Mexico, knew few luxuries either. They were under-equipped, ill fed and over-worked. They traveled without priests or physicians, and many soldados would never eat at all if they did not find, kill and cook their own food. Many of the men even brought their families with them. What choice did they have? They could be conscripted — or, as they considered it, kidnapped — into the army for ten years or more, often with no pay at all. Their families would suffer, perhaps starve without them, so they came along, becoming soldiers in a shadow army. The good thing was that it offered the men companionship and comfort. The bad thing was that it just made for more mouths to feed — and few means to feed them.

But if luxuries were lacking in the town and in the conquering army, they were plentiful in the command tent of Santa Anna. He was surrounded by finery. The floor was covered by plush carpet; the bed boasted numerous feather pillows, sheets of silk and expensive handwoven blankets of intricate design. The walls were lined with artwork and a bookshelf contained leather-bound volumes of poetry, erotica and military strategy. While his officers sometimes enjoyed whiskey or mescal, Santa Anna's liquor cabinets were filled with exquisite bottles of fine port and rare wine. At each meal, he ate delicious food from beautiful china plates and poured cream from a tiny silver pitcher. An ornate chandelier hung from the ceiling.

Santa Anna was known by his officers and aides to be vain and energetic, excessive both in fury and in intense patriotism. He was widely feared, even by those closest to him. But his personal charisma was strong. He had natural leadership qualities that led people to follow him, even when they fundamentally disagreed with his policies. He also had his special passions. Very young women — girls, really — were at the top of that list. The ancient art of cockfighting came in at a close second.

Behind the tent in Zacatecas, a cockpit had been dug in the ground, ringed by torches. A pair of handlers knelt by their gamecocks, one brown and one white. Inside, Santa Anna waited for the game to begin. He leaned back in a plush, padded chair, his feet resting comfortably upon an ornate ottoman. He held in his hand an opium box carved from onyx. As he delicately pinched a small bit of the drug to insert into his nostril, his aide, Colonel José Batres, waited, pad in hand, to take any order that His Excellency might issue, or to write down any words of wisdom that might come to his brilliant mind.

One of the handlers stepped inside. "We are ready, Excellency," he said. Santa Anna clapped his hands with satisfaction and stepped outside, followed by Batres. He gestured toward the pit, and Batres knew that he was about to receive more of Santa Anna's wisdom. "Men are like fighting cocks," Santa Anna said. "Within each lives a killer. You only have to get his blood up" — one of the handlers put the comb of his bird into his mouth, sucking blood into it so that it would stand, bright and red, like a banner of no quarter, while the other handler strapped a razor-sharp spur onto his bird's heel — "and give him the tools of destruction."

The general took his seat in a canvas field chair. Several of his officers surrounded him, waiting eagerly for the fight to begin. He gave a signal and the two roosters were released into the pit. A cacophony of squawks rose from the whirl of dust, feathers and blood. Santa Anna watched dreamily. There was nothing, he thought to himself, quite as relaxing and inspiring as a cockfight. He turned to Batres and whispered, "This . . . this mortal fury ennobles even the basest of men." Batres scribbled down each word, understanding none of it.

He stared hard at the paper, thinking that anything was better than having to actually watch this gory spectacle. Whenever he happened to glance into the pit, he quickly and squeamishly looked away.

The furious battle continued for nearly two minutes. Suddenly, with a loud screech, the brown rooster sliced the throat of the white one. Batres and Santa Anna were spritzed with blood. Santa Anna smiled broadly. Batres fought down the rising bile in his throat.

The handler announced, "The brown one wins!" Several of the officers exchanged money as the beaming handler brought the winning rooster over for Santa Anna to fondle. A private named Medrano jumped into the pit and picked up the bloody corpse of the losing cock and rushed over to where several women were plucking chickens to cook for supper. Medrano threw the rooster onto the pile and said, "Another hero for the stew."

As Santa Anna entered his tent again, invigorated by the scent of fresh blood, he found General Manuel Fernandez Castrillón waiting for him.

"Ah, General," Santa Anna said, smiling. "Have you news for me?"

Castrillón nodded. "General, we captured another group of rebels," he said.

Santa Anna picked up his opium box and held it out to show to Castrillón. "Did you know this very box belonged to Napoleon Bonaparte?"

"Yes, General," Castrillón said.

On a shelf sat an ornate bust of Napoleon. A portrait of the great French general hung on the wall. Castrillón knew very well of Santa Anna's obsession with Napoleon. He even referred to himself as the "Napoleon of the West."

Santa Anna inhaled the opium, closed his eyes and sighed deeply.

Castrillón continued, "Excellency, the citizens here are without food."

Santa Anna looked sharply at Castrillón. Normally such a statement would make him angry, but the opium was already having a calming effect. "They have rebelled against Mexico City," Santa Anna said. "Against me."

"One might contend that an act of unexpected kindness might serve to secure their loyalty," Castrillón said.

Castrillón was on shaky ground here and he knew it. But even though he had served in the military for many years, he had never found a way to disconnect his conscience.

Santa Anna stared at Castrillón for a while, smiling a little to himself. Then the president got an idea. "Do they have shoes?"

Castrillón did not expect that question. He looked to Batres, unsure where this was leading. He answered cautiously, "Some do."

Santa Anna stood and looked to Batres also. The aide knew an order was imminent, and raised his pad and pencil in readiness.

"Santa Anna declares every man, woman and child in this city will receive a new pair of sandals!"

Batres transcribed this egalitarian gem as Santa Anna walked out of the tent. Castrillón and Batres followed him into the street. Signs of the town's suffering were everywhere. Castrillón heard the moans of widows, or women about to be widowed. He heard the voices of men pleading for their lives. And everywhere, the squalor, the destruction. This was more than simply quelling a revolt, Castrillón thought; this was cruelty bordering on barbarism.

Walking swiftly, Colonel Juan Almonte approached Santa Anna and Castrillón, closely followed by a messenger. Almonte saluted and said, "Sir, there is a messenger from your brother-in-law, General Cós, sir. . . ."

Santa Anna impatiently waved them away. "Not now, Colonel."

Down the street, several Mexican soldiers were viciously beating a prisoner, dragging him back into a line of Zacatecan rebels standing before a waiting firing squad. Santa Anna gazed upon the scene with a look of benevolent calm. "Grace visits even the graceless, when they are about to die," he said. "I can feel its presence."

José Batres wrote it down. His Excellency might want to use the thought again later.

Castrillón said, "Shall we have them draw lots, your Excellency?"

Santa Anna looked sharply at Castrillón. "Why?"

"To determine which shall be executed, Excellency," Castrillón said.

Santa Anna nodded. Yes, he knew the quaint custom. He considered this for a moment, then announced, "Execute them all."

Castrillón looked as if he had been slapped in the face. Almonte passed the order along without emotion.

Castrillón said, trying to keep the pleading tone from entering his voice, "General, it is tradition that —"

"If we follow tradition," Santa Anna said, "the people in this place will remember that it was Fate that took their loved ones."

The air was filled with a deafening volley of musket fire, followed by the sounds of frantic wailing and weeping. Santa Anna smiled in satisfaction. "Instead, they will remember that it was Antonio López de Santa Anna."

Almonte returned from the firing squad and said, "Sir, the messenger from General Cós?"

Santa Anna nodded. The messenger stepped forward and announced, "General of Brigade Cós has surrendered the Alamo and retreated from San Antonio de Béxar."

Santa Anna's face darkened with anger. He clenched both hands into fists. Castrillón thought for a moment that the president was about to scream. Instead, Santa Anna muttered, "Coward! If he were not family I would slit his throat. Where is he now?"

"Heading south," the messenger replied. "Toward us."

Santa Anna turned to Castrillón and ordered, "Prepare the troops to march north." He slapped the side of his thigh and said, "If the land pirates want blood, they will drown in it."

He whirled angrily to go to his tent. He stopped abruptly, turned and pointed to the bodies of the rebels, whose blood was streaming down the cobblestone streets. Santa Anna said, "See that no one touches those bodies for a week!"

Chapter Nine

Zacatecas had been virtually decimated by battle and Santa Anna's retribution. But to the north, San Antonio de Béxar retained its graceful beauty, even if scarred from combat. Its wide plaza was lined with low buildings of adobe and stone, covered in stucco that was painted in subtle blues, purples and reds. At the center of the plaza was the imposing San Fernando church, a massive building painted a sunset pink and topped by a dome and a tall belltower. San Fernando was surrounded by a low wall. Just outside the front door was the *campo santo*, the cemetery that contained the bodies of priests, Indian workers and Béxarenos.

Directly in front of the campo santo was Soledad Street, which ran north to south. Bowie and his men, including Seguin, were riding down Soledad now. All around Béxar, the streets were bustling with Tejano families returning to their homes now that the siege was over. Most of them knew Bowie well, or at least knew of him. The Veramendis had been one of Béxar's finest and most prominent families. Even though he was only a gringo, and notorious for his violent past, James Bowie had married into the Veramendi family and deserved respect for that, if for no other reason. And many of the people of Béxar truly liked him, whatever misdeeds he might be guilty of. As he rode down the street, several Tejano children spotted him and called out, "Señor Bowie! Señor Bowie!" They ran alongside him, reaching out to touch his horse.

Bowie smiled briefly at the children, but the smile quickly faded when he spotted what lay ahead — the Veramendi House. Sergeant William Ward, a tough, sardonic Irishman and Bowie's right-hand man, noticed the look of consternation on Bowie's face. The men stopped to dismount in the plaza, but Bowie kept riding forward, toward his bullet-scarred home. The men watched him ride away but discreetly went about their work.

Ward was not quite so sensitive. "Colonel?" he called after Bowie.

Seguin shook his head and said quietly to Ward, "Leave him be."

Bowie dismounted and tied his horse to a post near the front door. He stood there, almost unwilling to step inside. Finally, he gathered the courage to push open the door and walk into his home. There were holes in the roof and walls, empty liquor bottles on the tables and on the floor, torn paper cartridges scattered everywhere. Much of the furniture was gone. What remained was battered, bruised and broken. Bowie walked through the main room and stood in the arch leading to the rear courtyard. It was a small plot of desolation — dead arbor, dirt, broken whiskey bottles. But it only took a glance to transport Bowie to another, happier, time.

Paper lanterns hang from the lush green arbor. The tables are laden with punchbowls, wine bottles, fine crystal and delicacies of all kinds. A large main table is stacked with brightly wrapped gifts. Wedding gifts. A small orchestra fills the air of the courtyard with lively music. Some of the exquisitely dressed Tejano wedding guests are dancing. Others chat excitedly as Sam, Bowie's slave, serves drinks, smiling. Bowie is impeccably dressed in his wedding clothes, a deep green velvet tailcoat with a silk vest and matching cravat.

Even though Bowie is politely chatting with Juan Seguin and his new father-in-law, Juan Martín de Veramendi, his mind is elsewhere; he can think of nothing but her. Turning, he sees the vision that he longs to see: Ursula, beautiful, eighteen years old, a dream in her long, white dress. Her hair is jet black, as are her eyes, deep and mysterious, at once innocent and knowing. Her lips are red and inviting. She smiles happily at her new husband. It is a smile that conveys an eternity of fulfillment, of ecstasy, of pride.

Ursula steps onto the patio with her sister Juana by her side. The guests applaud and she bows shyly, acknowledging the tribute of her friends and family. But she only has eyes for the man who has only minutes earlier become her husband. This is, Bowie thinks, the most precious moment of his life, a moment in which the world holds nothing but promise, the only time in his life when his spirit seems filled with pure, uncomplicated happiness.

Bowie closed his eyes, praying that the memory would last. But when he opened them he stood alone in the courtyard, the ruined arbor behind him, sadness enveloping him like a cloud.

Bowie looked out across his courtyard. There, in the distance beyond the river, stood the Alamo.

Sam stepped into the doorway and discreetly cleared his throat to alert his master to his presence. Bowie did not turn around.

"You all right, Mister James?" Sam said.

Bowie said to himself, "I have a home."

Sam did not understand that response at all. "Sir?" he said.

Bowie said, still softly, "I am sorry, Sam. I cannot blow the place up."

"Blow what up, sir?" Sam asked, confused.

Bowie turned and smiled. "Not you," he said. "I was talking to a different Sam."

Out in the plaza, William Barret Travis rode in at the head of his small cavalry unit. It was not precisely the position he would have preferred. Governor Smith had ordered Travis to take a hundred men to the aid of Colonel J. C. Neill at Béxar. Travis had tried — but all he could come up with was twenty-nine men. Humiliated at his failure, Travis had asked Smith to be relieved of his command. Smith refused. To Travis, the incident made him feel as though he were riding into San Antonio under a cloud.

Travis and his men passed shopkeepers sweeping out their stores, people rebuilding their homes and businesses, and children running through the streets, squealing and laughing. Joe rode at the rear, every bit the horseman as the white soldiers.

A mutt crossed the street to his master, Tom Waters. Waters was dressed in a rather tattered New Orleans Greys uniform, and when he saw the dog coming toward him, he opened his coat and sneaked a few scraps of meat to him. Nearby, three drunk, dissipated New Orleans Greys traded a bottle and laughed as Travis rode by. He noticed them with displeasure, but decided against taking any action for the present. There would be time soon enough for him to bring order to this rabble.

Travis brought his horse to a stop and called out an order to his first officer, John Hubbard Forsyth: "Have the quartermaster secure billeting."

The men started to dismount, but Travis continued to ride ahead.

Forsyth called out, "Where are you going, sir?"

Travis said, "I'd like to see what I am fighting for."

His horse galloped along Potrero Street, to the outskirts of the east side of town. On a

158

slight rise, Travis stopped his horse and stared straight ahead. There, less than half a mile away, was the old mission San Antonio de Valero. The Alamo. It did not look like much of a fort to Travis — a sprawling compound of low walls, some of which looked just barely patched up. But he knew that there must have been something to the place. It seemed always to be the center of trouble in this area, as if fighting men just could not stay away from it. It had to have been a hundred years old, if it was a day. But there it was. Rough, crumbling, battle scarred . . . but still standing. Waiting . . .

Chapter Ten

The Cherokee called the game "the little brother of war." And like war, the rules were variable and endlessly adaptable, depending on the number of players on each team, the size of the playing field and the character of the terrain. Each player carried two sticks with which they hit a ball carved from wood or stone, or shaped in clay and baked into smooth hardness. There were two goals, and the ultimate object of the game was to hit the ball past them. But since those goals could be a mile apart — or sometimes twenty miles — the sticks were just as frequently used on opposing players. The contestants could often endure a game that lasted for over a week and never even see the ball. The teams could consist of five men — or a thousand. Later on, the game would become known as lacrosse, but the Cherokee name for it was more apt, because of the strategy needed to win it, and the blood that was often shed in the playing of it.

As a boy, living among the Indians, Sam Houston had loved playing the game. He did not so much learn the rules as absorb them. He loved planning assaults and defenses, running players away from the goal with a beautifully orchestrated feint, or bulling straight down the field, winning the day through brute force. Today, as he rode over the hill toward the camp and saw a large group of men and boys running, shrieking and laughing across a clearing, it occurred to Houston that he was still playing the game. It was all about strategy, about winning and losing . . . surviving at any cost.

Houston had seen Indian villages that were composed of tepees and hastily constructed wood lodges. But the Cherokee had built something more stable and permanent along the Neosho River, which flowed serenely through a pine forest. Some lived in log cabins, roofed with bark. Smoke puffed from stone chimneys, and tanned hides covered the windows and doorways. Others lived in huts made from adobe, a material made through a technique learned long ago from the Indians and Mexicans of the West. At the center of the village stood a long, sedate lodge, large enough to accommodate every citizen for town meetings or, more rarely, war parties.

Except for the excitement of the game, the village was peaceful and calm. It looked like home to Houston. He reined his horse to a stop at the top of the hill and looked down on it fondly. Reaching into his coat, he pulled out a silver flask, took a nip, then quickly put it away again. A few children, hearing the hoofbeats, noticed him first. They began running toward him, squealing in delight. Some alert parents looked in the direction in which their children were running and saw Houston, too. A buzz went through the residents. Even the players on the field stopped and trained their eyes toward the top of the hill. By the time Houston rode into the village, all eyes were on him.

Talihina Rogers did not at first notice Houston, even though a day never passed that she did not gaze up the river path and hope that she would see him there, coming back to her. Intent on her beadwork, absorbed in a particularly troublesome design, Talihina was not aware of anything else until a woman sitting to her left nudged her, smiling. "The Raven is back," the woman said.

It was not Talihina's way to show her emotions to others, so she glanced at Houston and resumed her beadwork. She did not take her eyes from it, even as Houston continued riding straight for her. When she heard his horse stop only a few feet from her, she glanced up again. The entire village gathered around, wordlessly watching this little domestic drama. They all knew what neither Houston nor Talihina would reveal. Houston barely noticed that he was the object of such intense scrutiny, like an actor performing in the round. He was staring at Talihina, marveling, as always, at her beauty, her poise. Like him she was something of an outsider. Her mother was Cherokee, but her father was white. Her hair was as black as midnight, but her eyes were light gray, tinged with flecks of brilliant blue. She was taller than most of the women in the village; some of them believed that this was why she had been chosen by the Raven. He was the tallest man that most of them had ever seen. It only seemed right that he would choose a woman like Talihina as his mate.

Without a word, Talihina stood and walked into her cabin. Houston, still having not yet acknowledged anyone else, followed her inside and closed the door. The Cherokees smiled and nodded to each other and walked away, leaving the two to their reunion.

The cozy cabin was just as Houston remembered it. Hemp carpets covered the floor. Beside a wall stood a table and stools carved from the wood of the poplar. Along the opposite wall there was a broad bed covered with animal skins. As Talihina walked to the bed, she pulled her dress over her head and let it drop to the floor. She turned, facing Houston, then lay on the bed and held her arms out to him. Now he was truly home.

Afterward, Houston sat on the bed while Talihina fetched some cloth, a small bag of herbs and a basin filled with water. She returned to the bed and sat beside him. His eternal wound, just above the knee, looked worse than ever. Talihina cleaned it with the wet cloth, then applied some of the herbs and wrapped it with a white bandage. She said to him, "This has become much worse."

Houston felt uncomfortable at her ministrations and could barely allow himself to even look down at the wound.

Talihina smiled a little sardonically, "Did

not your white wife ever dress it for you?"

There was no need to respond. His white wife, Eliza, had never dressed it. Indeed, she had never comforted him in any way during their brief, maddening union. He did not know why he continued to feel so guilty about Eliza. He had not, for once in his life, been the party at fault. He had spared her good name, had taken the responsibility onto his own shoulders for the failure of the marriage. He would even have divorced her, if she would only consent to it, to allow her to find another husband. But she had not consented, and so he had not divorced Eliza. That made his marriage to Talihina, five years ago, illegal in the white world. But in the eyes of the Cherokee, they were joined together by both God and law.

Talihina was only ten years old when she first laid eyes on Houston. He was twelve. Young Sam Houston walked into the Cherokee camp with a gun in one hand, a copy of Homer's Iliad in the other and a look of frightened bravado on his face. He and Talihina became childhood friends. Later, as they became older, their friendship turned to lust, then love. They introduced each other to the sweet mysteries of the flesh, and although both of them went on to explore those mysteries with other partners,

Houston and Talihina knew that there was a bond between them that could never be eradicated. His ambition kept taking him away from her — even led to his marriage to another woman. Talihina always pictured the white wife as pale and pasty, timid and mewling; not at all the strong, capable, passionate woman that Houston needed — and deserved.

When he returned to the village in 1830, he declared that he was finished with the white world. He asked Talihina to marry him and she consented. How could she refuse? They were fated to be one, for good or bad. No matter how temporary their lives together, they were eternally bound in their hearts. Even if Houston left one day and never returned, he and Talihina would never truly part.

Each time he returned, Houston swore that he would stay for good. But Talihina knew that he was drawn by something large and powerful; something like destiny. He had been wounded in battle at Horseshoe Bend, in the fight with the British that the Americans called the War of 1812. His unhealing wound was a constant, painful reminder of his other life, a physical manifestation of where he had been and what he had undergone. Just as the leg wound would never close, neither would his dreams of greatness fade away. His other life in the white world would never release its grasp upon him.

Talihina completed bandaging Houston's leg and stood up. "I will get you some food," she said. Houston reached from the bed and grasped her arm, firmly but gently. "I am not hungry," he said.

"You have traveled a long distance," Talihina said. "You need nourishment."

"What I need," he said, pulling her toward him, "is you."

Chief Bowles sat at the head of the lodge, surrounded by leaders of the tribe. Houston sat before him, reflecting once again that Bowles looked like anything but a typical Cherokee. His mother had been a member of the tribe, but his father was Scottish. Their union had produced a hardy son with fair skin, bright red hair and a face mapped with freckles. Now eighty, Chief Bowles had been a father to Houston since the boy first arrived in the village thirty years earlier.

The council in San Felipe had sent Houston to the village to offer a treaty to Bowles — and to ensure that the Cherokee remained neutral in the coming fight against Mexico. The Texians believed that they were going to have a hard enough time fighting Santa Anna's army without constantly watching their backs against Indian attack.

Houston spoke to his mentor in Cherokee. "We expect the Texas government to be in place before the end of the year — with luck, long before that. I am here to assure you that you will retain all of your lands." He paused for emphasis. "That is over a million and a half acres."

Chief Bowles took a long draw from his pipe. "The Mexicans have treated us well," he said. "They respect our borders. They do not try to move us to ever-worse lands. The Mexican government does not consider it legal to shoot Cherokee."

Houston nodded slowly, taking a moment to gather himself. He had spent much of the day drinking, and was now concentrating as hard as he could in order to make his case in the most cogent way possible. The warriors were willing to listen to him as he made his pitch, but their faces showed that they expected little from him, especially in his current state.

"My friends," Houston said, looking around the lodge, "I realize this is not easy, to make a treaty with a country that is not yet a country, with a nation that has no real government. But that is what I have come to ask. For you, under the Texas government, life will remain the same. You can retain your own laws, live on your own land, pursue your own destiny."

Chief Bowles took his time before answering, never taking his eyes from Houston's.

"Raven," he said, finally, "we fought together in the war against the Creek. I performed the ceremony when you took your Cherokee wife. We have even been to see the Great Father in Washington together."

Houston smiled and said, "We got to bill all that whiskey to the U.S. Government."

No one in the room laughed. Houston always felt that the Cherokee did not particularly appreciate his sense of humor.

Chief Bowles said, "There will be fighting in Texas, but it is not your fight. You were Cherokee long before you were Texian. The Cherokee are already a nation. Stay with us and be a representative for our people."

Houston looked out the door of the lodge, to the peaceful village beyond. Bowles's proposition was a tempting one. The Cherokee were his family. Talihina was his wife. He understood them like no other, and could defend their rights as no one else could, or would. But Houston knew that it was impossible for him to accept the offer.

A part of him, the nervous twelve-year-old who had first come to this place and found a home here, could stay in the village happily for the rest of his life, raising a family with Talihina, living in perfect peace and contentment. But there was another part of him, the part that knew he was destined for something great, no matter how lonely or bloody was the road to that greatness. The choice was agonizing but clear. He could live a life of happiness, or he could be a ruthless conqueror.

And, God help him, he wanted to be a conqueror, wanted it more than anything in life.

Chapter Eleven

The ferry that crossed the Red River was loaded to capacity and beyond. With ten passengers, each with his own horse, as well as a large shipment of mercantile supplies, the creaky wooden craft sat several inches lower in the water than normal. As the ferry made its slow way across the river, little waves continually licked onto the deck. If it made Pasqua nervous, he did not let on. The crotchety old ferryman sat on a bench at the rear of the boat, a rudder in one hand and a bottle in the other. There was a beatific look on his face, as though this were the very life he would have chosen for himself, above all others.

David Crockett looked at Pasqua with some concern, but tried hard not to let it worry him. The opposite bank was close. If the worst happened, Crockett figured, he and his friends could swim to shore easily enough. Standing on the crowded deck with Crockett were his nephew William Patton and his friend Micajah Autry. Autry was a North Carolinian in his early forties. He had tried his hand at teaching and, like nearly every other man Crockett met — or so it seemed — lawyering. But it was Autry's poetry that drew Crockett to him. A taciturn man who seldom smiled, Autry had a surprisingly whimsical nature that only revealed itself in his writings. On their journey toward Texas, the two men had spent more than one evening sitting by the campfire, Crockett scratching out mournful airs or lively jigs on his fiddle, while Autry read his latest poem. Crockett admired literary talent; he was inordinately proud of the book that bore his own name as author . . . despite the fact that he had not exactly written it.

As the ferry pulled up to the landing, P. A. Hutton, a nosy local merchant, eyed the group of strangers curiously from where he stood on the dock. He and his hired boy Jackson began unloading mercantile supplies. Hutton spat a wad of tobacco and said to Crockett, "Welcome to Texas."

"How do," Crockett replied, carefully

avoiding Hutton's eyes. He was trying his best to remain anonymous. Often, when people realized who he was, they were so thrilled that he had to start giving speeches, shaking hands, being funny. When speaking to Autry about it, he called it "being Davy." It could be exhausting being Davy.

"Where you fellers hail from?" Hutton asked. Jackson was doing most of the work, and the sour look on his face showed that he knew it.

"Tennessee, mostly," Crockett said, tending to his supplies.

Hutton nodded wisely. "We get 'em from all parts these days," he said. He looked closely at Crockett. "Desperadoes, debtors, confidence men . . ." He watched Jackson unload a crate of rifles — by himself — and smiled. "But hell," Hutton said, spitting more tobacco juice toward the river, "now we got them Meskins outnumbered near ten to one."

Crockett nodded, clearly not interested. "That so?"

A few other locals began to gather. They were curious about the newcomers, too. Hutton said to Crockett, "What brings you fellers? Land? Prospectin'?"

"Heard there's some nice wild country left here," Crockett said. "Some buffalo

173

wanderin' loose. Some bear. Thought we'd give it a look-see."

Hutton frowned. He was disappointed. "You did not come to fight?"

Crockett laughed. "Not unless them bisons shoot back at us," he said.

The onlookers chuckled at this. Some, staring at Crockett, had begun to whisper.

"Say," Crockett said to Hutton, "what's the lodgings like around here?"

Hutton pointed up the riverbank to a rickety building made of uneven planks. "Lost Prairie Hotel" was painted unevenly on the side. "You are speakin' to the proprietor," Hutton said proudly.

Crockett nodded. He made sure his friends weren't watching, then pulled out a silver pocket watch and handed it to Hutton. "Listen," he said, "this here is real silver."

Hutton popped the watch open and read the inscription. Suspicious, he said, "How'd you come by it?"

Crockett was embarrassed and looked away. "It was . . . it was presented . . ."

A light blinked on in Hutton's eyes. "You are David Crockett?"

The cat was out of the bag. Crockett gave him a weak smile and spoke in a low voice, "Guilty."

The name rippled through the crowd. Now there were more than a dozen onlookers and Crockett could hear his name whispered more than a dozen times — *Davy Crockett . . . Davy Crockett . . . Davy Crockett . . .*

Hutton grabbed Crockett's hand and pumped it enthusiastically. "I will be damned!" he said. "I thought you was off in Washington!"

There was no getting out of it now. Crockett smiled broadly and said in a loud voice the words he had already said at several stops along the way: "Well, there was this little detail of an election back home. I told them folks, 'You do not vote me back in, you can go to hell and I will go to Texas!' "

The crowd laughed and cheered. Crockett thought he should work on the speech a little. The next time, he could add a little more detail, get a few more laughs.

When the laughter died down, Crockett said, as much to himself as to the crowd, "So, here I am. . . ."

Chapter Twelve

J. C. Neill and William Barret Travis stood
on the flat roof atop the main gate of the
Alamo. From there they had a panoramic
view of the whole rambling compound. It was
obvious that it had not been built to serve as a
fort. It was much too big, for one thing; it
spread over three acres. The long stretches of
adobe wall were strong but were totally devoid of embrasures or firing ports. Even to
Travis, who had no experience with forts, it
was immediately apparent that in order to
defend such walls, men would have to expose
themselves to enemy fire — and that was def-
initely not a good idea. Even if the walls were
defendable, Travis thought, it would take
many men to do the job — several times the
150 or so who currently occupied the place.

"It was founded as a mission over a hundred years ago," Neill said. "The Béxarenos call it the Alamo. I am not completely sure why."

Travis said, "*Alamo* means 'cottonwood' in Spanish. Maybe it was named after the tree."

Neill looked doubtful. "Maybe. But do you see any cottonwoods around here? Anyway, somebody told me it was named after Alamo de Parras — a Spanish cavalry company that occupied the place years ago. As you can see, it was not designed with military intentions."

The Alamo's flaws seemed perfectly obvious, so Travis tried to concentrate on its strengths. "The fort is well armed," Travis said.

"We have got the most cannon of any fort west of the Mississippi," Neill said, a note of pride in his voice. "General Cós left most of them behind when he skedaddled. I have placed our largest, the eighteen pounder, on the southwest wall, so it fronts the town." He pointed to the wall opposite where they stood, on the far side of the compound. "The north wall is in ruins, so I have two batteries with five cannon to defend it." Neill's arm swept to the right. He indicated a two-story structure on the east side of the fort. "What was the original *convento* is now barracks and a makeshift infirmary. We call it the long barracks." Travis nodded, taking it all in. Neill patted him on the shoulder and said, "Let us walk, shall we?"

Neill climbed down the ladder from the south gate roof and Travis followed. At the corner of the building, tall, sandy-haired Green Jameson stood cleaning his eyeglasses, watching as two men put the finishing touches on a low fence made of wooden posts that had been sharpened at the tops.

Neill said, "Colonel Travis, this is Major Jameson, our engineer. He is emplacing a palisade between the main gate and the church building here." Outside the fort, on the other side of the wooden posts was a deep ditch. It was lined with trees and brush. As a position it looked vulnerable, but Travis could tell that its appearance was deceptive. It would be difficult for the enemy to get through the sharp branches, through the deep ditch and over the sharpened posts.

Travis said, "What was there before?"

Neill shrugged. "Nothing. An indefensible flank."

Jameson said, "It is hard to explain. There are four other missions around San Antonio, and none of them has a huge gap like this. It is a major flaw in the design."

"Is it defensible?" Travis asked.

Jameson smiled. "By the time I am through with this place, it will all be defensible — even the palisade."

Neill nodded. "With some riflemen and a good cannon," he said, "this should be one of the strongest positions in the Alamo."

Travis frowned. The statement was not nearly as reassuring as Neill intended.

A New Orleans Grey passed by in a ragged uniform. Travis turned to Neill and said, "Colonel, you should know that I have a uniform on order." Neill raised his eyebrows slightly and said nothing.

"One is as one appears," Travis said.

Neill did not know exactly what to make of this. He himself was not adorned in military garb and wondered if Travis was being deliberately rude — or was simply unaware of his own pomposity.

Jameson touched his hat, bidding a subtle good day to Travis and Neill, and went back to work. At the end of the palisade was the most distinctive and interesting building in the compound, the Alamo's church.

Neill said, "The mission was established in the early seventeen hundreds, but this church was not built until almost fifty years later. From what I have been told, they had a lot of problems in the construction of it — it seems to be something of a bad-luck place."

Travis looked at the large limestone building. Even in ruins it was an imposing and beautiful structure. Its doorway was framed by spiraled columns. Between them were icon niches. Another set of niches was placed directly above them. They were originally intended to contain religious statues, and Travis was mildly intrigued to see that all four statues were still in place. It seemed an odd detail for a military site.

"Was it destroyed in battle?" Travis asked.

Neill said, "What do you mean?"

"It has no roof," Travis said.

"Oh," Neill said. "The Catholics never quite finished it. The roof and dome collapsed years ago. Cós and his men took the rubble that filled the church and built that ramp leading up to the rear." He smiled a little condescendingly and said, "I do not know how much you know about Spanish religious architecture, but the very back of the building is called the apse."

Travis nodded imperiously, as if to say of course he knew all about Spanish Catholic architecture.

"It is a good thing they built the ramp," Neill said. "In fact, we have a lot to thank Cós for. The two cannon placed there give us full coverage of the east side of the fort." He and Travis walked up the ramp and surveyed the area from the top of the church. Neill pointed to the northeast. "Back there in the corral area, we have placed another cannon. That makes this rear area quite secure, I believe." Travis looked straight ahead, toward the front of the church. A large square window was cut into the stone on the upper level. Through it, Travis could clearly see the belltower of San Fernando church in the center of Béxar.

They walked back down the ramp. There were low, dark rooms on either side of the front door. Neill pointed to one and said, "This was the baptistery and the other one is the sacristy." He glanced upward at a ragged platform above the entrance. "That is what's left of the choir loft."

Travis said with a note of profundity in his voice, "A place of worship turned into a place of war."

Neill smiled. "Well, that is true, to a point. But no one ever actually worshipped in this church, from what I have been told. Even when this was a working mission, the chapel was over there." He pointed toward the long barracks. "It is gone now, but that is where the services were held." They stepped outside and turned to look back at the grave and compelling façade of the church. "This building was never really used for anything," Neill said. "Fell in almost immediately, filled with rubble for years. I guess you could say it is a pretty useless building. At least until now. The walls are almost four feet thick — solid limestone. That makes it the strongest place in the fort."

Neill nodded to the statues on either side of the entrance. "Saints Dominic and Francis," he said. "Up above, that is St. Claire and St. Margaret. The locals tell me St. Francis had two gifts: prophecy and the ability to inspire passionate devotion."

Neill walked on. Travis hesitated for a moment, taking a long, hard look at St. Francis. It seemed to him that he would do well to acquire either of the Saint's gifts — and preferably both.

Travis caught up with Neill at the north wall. "This is the most troubling spot," Neill said. "The wall had almost crumbled to dust even when Cós held the place. He tried to shore it up with logs and mud, and Jameson has made some real strides in strengthening it — but a strong wind would blow it down." Travis leaned forward and peered over the side of the wall. The outside was propped up by timbers. Horizontal logs had been cemented to the wall — it looked to Travis like a big, helpful ladder. Beyond the wall, there was an open stretch of ground about two hundred yards long. It ended at a small forest near the river. An attack from out of those woods toward this weakened position could be catastrophic. In the weeks and months ahead, he and Neill must make this their top priority: to strengthen this wall as much as possible; to make it impregnable.

Neill had turned and was looking inside the compound. He pointed and said, "If the need arises, I recommend you take my personal quarters on the west wall. They are isolated, yet close to the primary defenses."

Travis said, "I am afraid I do not understand, sir."

"I have personal matters to attend to in Mina," Neill said. "I am leaving you in command."

Travis felt a surge of exhilaration beneath his shock — this was big news. His own command. He straightened up a bit, already feeling a little more like a real officer.

"I know you fought this posting, Travis," Neill said. "Forting up is not exactly a cavalryman's dream."

Travis saluted. Neill did not know quite what to do — no one ever saluted him.

"I will defend it with my life, sir," Travis said.

Neill smiled and said, "Your biggest task will be keeping volunteers and regulars from killing one another out of boredom."

Travis said, "Are you so certain that there is no further threat from the Mexicans?"

Neill laughed sharply. "Colonel Travis," he said, "the Mexican army would have to cover many miles in the dead of winter to get here before I return. Santa Anna may be a cruel despot, but he is not insane. Believe this: Even if they return, they will not be here until spring. And by then, the Alamo will be the strongest and best-fortified position in Texas."

Chapter Thirteen

The cantina was the brightest and loudest building in Béxar. Texians and Tejanos elbowed one another at the crowded bar. The only women in view were a few barmaids and a handful of sharp-eyed prostitutes, cagily sizing up the carousing men, timing their advances to coincide with the moment when their drunkenness made them good-natured and generous, and before it made them cantankerous and mean.

Travis knew he had to go inside, but it was not the kind of atmosphere in which he was comfortable. Drunken men were not reasonable men, and it was impossible to conduct impassioned discourse on any topic with unreasonable men. And Travis, above all, wanted to express his opinions and have them heard, understood and appreciated. It was one of the reasons he avoided strong drink. Drunkenness made his mind bleary and his ideas imprecise.

The prostitutes, however, were another story entirely. Travis often thought ruefully that his libido had gotten him into more trouble throughout his life than his political views ever had. In his younger days, he had even kept a diary, carefully listing his conquests and making cryptic notes to remind himself of exactly how each had pleased — or displeased — him in the act of love. His wandering eye had ruined his first marriage. And even now, as he looked forward to marrying his lovely Rebecca, he found it impossible to keep his mind off other women. The demure, dark-eyed Tejanas of Béxar carried a special allure for him. He remembered with great fondness his dalliances with Mexican women in San Felipe and Nacogdoches — and they, in turn, made him remember the saucy French and Cajun women of New Orleans. But the women of San Antonio de Béxar seemed more beautiful, more enticing than the others. Or perhaps it was because it had been quite a while since his last amorous experience and he was eager, even anxious to slip between the sheets with a willing and luscious Béxarena.

Travis banished the thoughts from his

mind. He had other, more crucial, matters to consider. Unpleasant matters. He peered through the door of the cantina for a moment, spying Bowie inside with several rowdy companions. He took a deep breath and walked inside.

The cantina served at once as barroom, brothel and general store. While local *vaqueros* and Texians drank whiskey from glasses, others conducted business of varying kinds. Albert Grimes, a Southerner with a neck actually red from the sun, was trying to sell a long rifle to a world-weary Tejano.

"This long tom will knock the whiskers off a hare at two hundred yards," Grimes said, his voice slightly bleary with the early stages of drunkenness. "Mwee bwayno escopayta."

The Tejano examined the rifle and said, in Spanish, "I will need shot to go with it."

Grimes looked at him, puzzled. James Butler Bonham, tall and dashing, stepped in and said, in a voice that clearly recalled his South Carolina roots, "He wants you to throw in some shot."

Grimes nodded. "Well then, you tell him them bottles of mescal better be full."

Bonham translated to the Tejano, then stepped away to let them complete the deal in their own way. He spotted Travis coming through the door.

"Will," he said, touching his hat. "Never expected to see you in a place like this. What would the folks back in Saluda think?"

Travis was incapable of responding in the same teasing tone. He had no talent for small talk or the easy, friendly insults with which men often communicate. "I am not here for a drink, Jim," Travis said gravely. "I have to see Colonel Bowie on a matter of utmost importance."

Bonham chuckled a little to himself. After all these years, it was still the same Will Travis he knew as a shirttail boy back in South Carolina. As Bonham walked out of the cantina, Bowie's slave Sam stepped over to the bar to fetch a new bottle of whiskey. Sam was a tall man, dressed in clothes that had once been fine but that were now frayed a bit around the edges. The garments had once been worn by a gentlemen — a white gentleman — and when they became too ragged, the decision had to be made whether to throw them away or to magnanimously give them to a slave like Sam. If Sam was grateful for charity such as this, he did not show it. In fact, he did not show much of anything. Sam's face was normally impassive, but those who happened to look into his eyes would see that they frequently flashed with anger. There was not much he could do to escape his lowly station in life, but he did not happily accept it. He served his master and, to a certain extent, even respected him. But give him the chance for freedom, and Sam would be gone in the blink of an eye.

The whiskey bottle in his hand, Sam walked back over to the table in the corner where Bowie was getting an earful from William Ward, the scrappy Irishman with a ruddy face and hard, angry eyes.

"At some point Texas is going to be a state," Ward was saying, "but will it lean to the North or the South? We going to have darkies working our fields, or ain't we?"

Sam poured another round, giving no indication that he heard Ward's words or cared anything about them.

Bowie took a long swig, wiped his mouth and said, "I have traded my share of flesh and I can promise you there will never be a free state that borders Louisiana."

Ward lifted his glass, as if in tribute to Bowie's sentiment. Sam stood by, carefully staring into the distance. Bowie took another drink, which brought on a fit of coughing. Recovering, teary-eyed from the spasm, he looked up to see Travis approaching.

As Travis crossed the room, he eyed the rowdy volunteers as if they were particularly unappealing animals in a zoo. No one even seemed to notice he was in the room. He spotted Bowie and walked over, Joe keeping pace several steps behind him.

Travis said, "Colonel . . ."

Bowie nodded without replying.

Now that he was this close, Travis noticed Bowie's haggard expression. "You look terrible," he said. "Almost yellow. Right around the cheeks, forehead."

Bowie did not look at Travis. "You doctoring, now?" he said in a low, annoyed voice. "Along with everything else?"

Travis realized that he was only antagonizing Bowie and decided to get right down to business. He said, "I have heard a rumor that you plan to destroy the mission and remove the cannon."

"Oh, and where'd you hear that?" Bowie said.

"Men tend to prattle on when they drink," Travis said. "Your men tend to drink."

Bowie turned briefly to scowl at Travis, then looked away.

"It would be a great mistake," Travis said.

Bowie nodded. "I agree," he said.

He certainly had not expected Bowie to agree with him. Travis's face registered his utter surprise. But before he could speak, Bowie said, "And any further discussion on the matter will be between myself and Colonel Neill."

Travis drew himself up a bit. "Colonel Neill left Béxar this morning on personal business," he said. "It is my command now."

Bowie smiled sarcastically. "My, my, this is a swift rise, Billy." He downed another shot. "You might want to break out the long britches."

Ward shared a jeering laugh with a few other Texians. Joe turned away to save Travis further embarrassment. Travis was stung by the insult, but nothing could stop him from speaking his mind — even the fear of more ridicule.

"Your men exhibit no discipline," Travis said. "If matters do not change it will become my duty, as colonel of this post to —"

Bowie corrected him. "*Lieutenant* colonel."

Travis reeled with the mockery as though from a slap. He said, desperately trying to invest his voice with authority, "Restrain your men. Or I will."

Travis wheeled away and stormed out of the cantina, followed by Joe. He passed Juan Seguin, who was entering as Travis left, but Travis was too blinded by fury to notice him. Seguin walked over to Bowie's table.

"Santiago, sentries report seeing horses outside of town," Seguin said, "in the Campo Santo."

Bowie downed his drink and rose. "Better go take a look-see," he said. He turned to Ward and the other Texians around the table. "Go get your guns, boys," he said. "We are going to take a little ride in the country."

The Campo Santo was an old cemetery, just outside of Béxar, the final resting place of many of the city's founding fathers. Because it was old, and a little remote, the graveyard was not tended very diligently. Ancient gravestones peeked out from tall, unruly grass. Some wooden crosses had rotted over time and crumbled to dust, just like the Campo Santo's permanent residents. It did not seem, to Bowie, Seguin and the men who rode with them, to be a good place to use as a campsite. Men and horses gathered there this late at night, they reasoned, could only be there for suspicious purposes.

The men tethered their horses in a copse of trees. They carefully drew their weapons and, with Bowie and Seguin leading the way, moved stealthily forward. When they heard the low whinnies of horses and the sound of men whispering, Bowie held up his hand and all the men stopped and listened.

Bowie strained to hear but could not understand what was being said. He turned to Seguin and said quietly, "Are they speaking Spanish?"

Seguin shook his head. "I cannot make it out."

Bowie saw a quick movement behind a gravestone right in front of them. In a flash, he and Seguin and the three Texians and four Tejanos with them pointed rifles and pistols in the direction of the movement. "Do not move!" Bowie called out sharply.

Just as suddenly, they heard weapons cocked right behind them. Bowie turned and found himself staring into fifteen long rifles. At his direction, his men lowered their weapons slowly to the ground. From behind a gravestone, they heard an annoyed voice: "What's a feller have to do to . . ." Then the voice shouted, "Hablo Engles, muchachos?"

Micajah Autry said calmly, "We have got 'em, David."

From behind the gravestone stepped David Crockett. He was dressed in buckskin trousers and a long woolen frock coat. Beneath it, Crockett sported a white leather vest, elaborately decorated with Indian beadwork. On his head he wore a cap made of fox fur. It was not quite the five-pound monstrosity that had sat upon the head of James Hackett, but it was clearly inspired by that fearsome headpiece. Crockett and Bowie stared at each other in the murky light.

Crockett saw that there were Texians among the group and said in a careful voice, "We are all on the same side here. Let's not start in to shootin' each other."

"What are you doing out here?" Bowie demanded.

Crockett said, "Layin' low till we figgered out if it was Texians or Mexicans raising all the ruckus in town." He held his hand out to Bowie. "David Crockett," he said.

Bowie shook his hand. "Crockett of Tennessee?" he said. Bowie had heard many stories about the legendary Crockett. His first thought upon seeing him in person was that he was not nearly as tall as Bowie would have expected him to be.

Bowie kept pumping Crockett's hand delightedly. "Davy Crockett?"

Micajah Autry turned to Bowie and said with a refined voice, "He prefers David."

By the time they got back to Béxar Plaza, word had preceded them that the famous Davy Crockett was coming to town. Excited

Texians and Béxarenos poured out into the street to see the great bear hunter and Indian fighter. Crockett took one look at the crowd, heard a few shouts of "Speech!" and shifted immediately into politician mode.

He stepped onto a bench and held his arms out to quiet the crowd. "Seems like everywhere I go," he said in a folksy drawl, "I end up givin' a speech. Now, I am not tolerable sure whether that is because people truly want to hear from me, or whether I have just acquired the habit of looking for crowds of folk and then goin' in amongst 'em."

The crowd laughed. Someone called out, "What brings you to Béxar, Davy?"

Crockett grinned his biggest coon-killing grin. He had given his speech some thought since that day back at the Red River. "Well sir," he said, "there was this little detail of a reelection back home. You see, I was voted out of office by the fine folks in my district and a 'gentleman' with a wooden leg was voted in. Between you and me, I have seen that feller drink and I am plain convinced that his leg was not only wood, it was hollow!"

More laughter.

"Yes, sir! You know what I told them folks?" Crockett said. "I told 'em, 'You elect a man with a timber toe to succeed me? Well, you can all go to hell — I am going to Texas!' "

The crowd cheered and applauded. Mial Scurlock shouted, "Davy Crockett's thrown in with Texas!" and everyone cheered again.

Crockett quieted the crowd again, still smiling. "Fellow citizens," he said, "I have come to this Texas country to aid you all that I can in your noble cause. All the honor I desire is that of defending as a private . . . well, a high private . . . the liberties of our common country!"

His speech was met with a roar of approval. It seemed to Crockett that he had come to the right place. Failure in Washington meant less than nothing out here on the far frontier. If an election were held this very night, Crockett had no doubt that he would easily be elected. He saw no reason why that fact should change when the real election time rolled around.

Crockett stepped down from his bench and moved through the crowd, shaking hands and patting small children on the head. Micajah Autry walked just behind him, enjoying Crockett's celebrity — and watching his back. Albert Grimes stepped up to Crockett with a book in his hand — a tattered, dog-eared, very well read book.

Crockett smiled a little sardonically when he saw the title: *A Narrative of the Life of David Crockett*. Grimes handed Crockett the book and a pencil. "Put your mark in it, Mr. Crockett?" he said.

Crockett took the book from his hand, signed it and handed it back to Grimes.

Scurlock said, grinning, "'I am half alligator, half snapping turtle. I can slide off a rainbow and jump the Mississippi in a single leap.' Davy . . . Tell 'em. How you can whip your weight in wildcats. I seen you on the stage. . . ."

Crockett, still smiling — although a little less so — shook his head gently and said, "That was not me."

"Why, sure it was," Scurlock said, slapping Crockett on the back.

Crockett said, "That was an actor in a play, performing a character. . . ."

"Say the lines, Davy," Scurlock interrupted. *"Lion of the West!"*

Crockett eyed the crowd with a growing uncertainty, looking for a way to change the subject.

"I dare Sant'anna to show his face now that you are here!" Grimes said.

Crockett did not like the sound of that. "I had understood the fighting was over," he said hopefully. "Ain't it . . . ?"

Chapter Fourteen

The Mexican army continued to trudge north through South Texas. The weather was frightful — freezing cold, battering rain and sleet. There was even the occasional snowstorm. Many of the conscripts, accustomed to the lush warmth of their tropical native land, had never seen snow before. The novelty frightened and thrilled them at first, then tortured them with its bone-chilling cold. Even the best-equipped soldiers were ragged and tired. Many of the peons had no shoes and wore only the light cotton work clothes in which they had been conscripted.

Jesús was one of the lucky ones. His ill-fitting uniform was warm, at least, and his feet were protected by tattered shoes. He watched as, nearby, a half-dozen peons helped to push a brass cannon on a small, ox-drawn wagon across a shallow part of the riverbed. A dozen dust-covered lancers eased their mounts into the water and rode past the peons, splashing them heedlessly. Jesús had never ridden a horse, but wished that he were on one now. It would make the journey so much easier, he thought. More important, the horseman got respect and the lowly foot soldier got none.

He carried a heavy bundle of supplies on his back, a tumpline taut across his forehead. A chain gang of leg-shackled convicts shuffled along beside him carrying similar burdens. He was told that he was a soldier, but he felt like a prisoner, a slave.

As he trudged along, his sergeant fell into step beside him. The sergeant was a hard soldier but kind in his way. Jesús was grateful that the man was sometimes willing to talk with him. It made the long hours and the rugged miles more bearable.

The sergeant looked around at the bleak and barren landscape that surrounded them. Long stretches of prairie, with sparse vegetation. No plants to eat, no animals to kill for supper. "It is a desert," he said.

"Béxar is beautiful," Jesús said. "I was born in Texas, but my father only brought us to Béxar once."

The sergeant shook his head. "It is the

end of the earth," he said.

"It sits on the banks of a river filled with fish," Jesús said, remembering the happy visit. It was only three years ago, but seemed a lifetime away. "There are great fields of corn and beans. Big, shady trees." He did not mention the lovely ladies, his favorite memory.

The sergeant shrugged. "We have all of those things in Mexico City. More," he said. They tramped on for another mile, breathing heavily. "Where is your father now?" the sergeant asked.

"My father is dead," Jesús said. "My grandfather is alone. I am going to die in a far land."

The sergeant nodded. "It is a land without God," he said.

They plodded along for a while in silence. Jesús said, "Where do you come from, Sergeant?"

"From the port of Vera Cruz," the man said, smiling faintly. "All my brothers are sailors."

"But not you?" Jesús asked.

The sergeant shook his head. "I get seasick."

They walked along for another mile, or ten. "Will we win this war, Sergeant?" Jesús said.

The sergeant looked at Jesús and patted him on the shoulder. "Santa Anna will win this war but we will not," he said.

Jesús looked at him questioningly.

The sergeant said, "We are just cannon fodder, boy. Do not be in a hurry."

At the head of the column, Santa Anna raised a hand and stopped. Everyone behind him immediately stopped, too. Santa Anna sat atop his horse alongside General Castrillón and they watched as two riders approached. Behind the riders, in the distance, was General Cós's retreating army.

With a disgusted expression on his face, Santa Anna ordered the column forward again. Castrillón could see as they neared him that General Cós was exhausted and dispirited; he doubted that Santa Anna would notice, or care. When their columns met, Cós stopped his horse and faced his president.

Santa Anna glared at Cós with a mixture of pity and fury. "My wife asks me to give her useless brother a job and what happens?" he said, his voice heavy with contempt. "I end up in this shit hole Texas again."

General Cós, miserable, said, "We were without supplies, Your Excellency. And the men were dispirited. . . ."

"Turn your horse around, General," Santa Anna said.

General Cós looked up in surprise. "I swore I would leave Tejas and never return," he said. "I gave my word. . . ."

"Turn it around!" Santa Anna shouted.

Cós, beaten down, slowly turned his horse and moved forward, back toward Béxar.

Santa Anna nodded and a trumpeter blew the signal that started the army moving north again.

Jesús's head was forced forward by the weight of his bundle and he often had trouble deciding what time of day it was. He had been marching for hours, it seemed, and had seen little but his own feet and the rough, rocky ground. Up ahead, he heard murmuring and he forced his head up to see what was happening. He saw a dozen soldiers ringed around something on the ground. When Jesús got close enough, he saw that it was the bodies of three men, stripped and mutilated, spread-eagle on the ground.

Jesús immediately clamped his hand over his nose against the horrible smell of putrefaction. His sergeant turned to Jesús and said, "This is what happens to stragglers. The Indians are always watching. Keep up, boy."

Shaking his head, the sergeant walked away.

"Sergeant," Jesús called after him.

The sergeant stopped and turned. "Yes, boy?"

"When can I go home?"

The sergeant jerked his head toward the corpses. "You want to end up like that?"

Jesús did not want to end up like those unfortunate men. But he could not shake the idea that he was more likely to end up that way if he stayed with the army than if he left. Sighing, he adjusted the bundle on his back and started walking again, in the long, long line of miserable soldados.

Chapter Fifteen

The citizens of Béxar looked for any excuse to celebrate. Tonight, partygoers crowded the cantina in Béxar Plaza, dressed in their finest clothes, dancing to the lively music of a trio of musicians who strummed guitar and sawed melodically away at violins. Officially, the fandango was in honor of George Washington's birthday. But everyone there knew who the guest of honor really was. David Crockett worked the crowd with ease, never lingering too long in any conversation, but never allowing anyone to feel neglected. Following him through the room, Micajah Autry thought wryly that if there had been any babies in attendance, Crockett would have been kissing them, campaigning for votes.

The cantina was decorated with festive lanterns and streamers. The soft golden light of dozens of candles gave the room a dreamlike glow. It was an atmosphere made for romance, and throughout the room, young men — Béxarenos and Texians — paid court to lovely señoritas, whose struggles to remain aloof and sophisticated behind their brightly colored silk fans could not quite obscure their delighted smiles.

Maria Ramona Sanchez watched the scene with an amused but alert eye. She was not here for romance — at least, not exactly. She had no doubt that her evening would end with passion — almost every one of her evenings did. But it would also end with an exchange of money. If the gentleman in question desired romance, she would bill and coo and bat her eyelids at him flirtatiously. She knew all the right words to say, to convince a man that she loved him and only him. If her client had a more pragmatic exchange in mind, without the histrionics of pretend ardor, that was all right with her, as well. Maria Ramona Sanchez was very accommodating. That was her job.

But she was not indiscriminate. She knew that there were whores in filthy jacales on the outskirts of Béxar who would rut like pigs with any man who offered them a coin. Maria Ramona looked upon those women with a mixture of pity and contempt. They were driven to that life by poverty and desperation. But Maria Ramona had chosen her profession with the cool eye of a businesswoman. She saw her body as a commodity to be bought and sold. And she knew that for her body to retain its value, she must conduct her trade with discretion and with sophistication. And that meant that she would choose her client — not the other way around. She knew that there was bound to be a young man who would appreciate her unique gifts and would be willing to pay a high price for them — higher than any other professional woman in Béxar charged. But if she did not see such a man, she would go home alone and try again tomorrow. It was not wise to offer discounts in her line of work.

Maria Ramona noticed that most eyes in the cantina were on the man called Crockett. Dressed in fine clothes, he was apparently a man of some importance. She considered making him her prey for the evening. Then she decided against it. He seemed to be the guest of honor at tonight's fandango. In such situations, there was bound to be a woman or two who would offer him for free what Maria Ramona would only share with him at great price. She stood serenely by the wall, looking around the crowd, carefully making her selection.

Nearby, Almeron and Susanna Dickinson danced. They were very much in love and thought of this fandango as a celebration of the fact that their lives were finally going well after a long stretch of hard times. When Susanna had shown up in Béxar after her ordeal in Gonzales, Almeron had feared for her safety. The siege had just ended and Cós had been run out of town, but the situation was still highly volatile, and Almeron knew that the danger was never very far away. Nevertheless, they settled in a little house just off the main plaza, where they could watch their daughter grow and dream of what their lives would be like once this war was over with. And life was good.

As they danced, Almeron watched Crockett working the crowd, shaking hands and enduring many slaps on the back. "Some of the men are speculating that he wants to be governor," he said to Susanna, "but I believe we will be declaring for a republic, in which case we will need a president."

Susanna looked at Crockett and crinkled her nose in distaste. "He seems quite . . . common," she said.

Dickinson smiled at her. "Perhaps that is

how he wants to seem," he said.

Juan Seguin and a local merchant named José Palaez stood in the corner watching the festivities. To the Texians, the fandango was a beautiful, even sophisticated, affair. But to Seguin and Palaez, it gave a very different impression. To them, their town had been invaded by a rough, uncouth bunch of land grabbers, people who had no respect for the Mexican way of life.

Palaez looked at the rowdy Anglos and grimaced. "Why are you fighting for this scum?" he said.

Seguin shrugged. "My enemy's enemy is my friend," he said. "Santa Anna has betrayed the fatherland and murdered thousands, all Mexicans."

Palaez said, "But Santa Anna only wants to rule Mexico. These . . . these want the world."

Travis passed by Seguin without acknowledging him. He moved through the crowd like a man who did not belong. No one spoke to him or offered him a drink. Travis found a spot near the back wall from which to take in the festivities. Maria Ramona noticed him at once. Yes, he seemed promising. . . . William Ward was having a drink with Bonham. When he spotted Travis he said, "Do not truck much with that feller."

Bonham smiled. "I grew up with him," he said.

Ward was surprised to hear this.

"At least until his family moved to Alabama," Bonham said. "I had not since laid eyes on him until we arrived here."

Ward glanced over at Travis again and said, "What was he like?"

Bonham settled back in his chair and smiled. "I think of Billy Travis, I think of John Duncan's birthday party," he said.

Ward looked at him with curiosity.

Bonham took a drink and said, "The Duncans threw a birthday party for John — big affair — games, tents, a little circus — all set up in a field behind their house. Only children from the finest families were invited."

"But not our Colonel Billy," Ward said.

Bonham shook his head, no. "Day of the party," he said, "I look over to the edge of the field. Off by himself, there's Billy, ragged clothes, no shoes, just standing — kind of like he is now. Party lasted all day, when it was over, sun going down, I was leaving with my parents, looked back over my shoulder."

Bonham took another sip. "Had not moved so much as an inch in five hours. Stubborn."

Ward frowned. "What in the hell was that about?"

Bonham said, "I do not know. Maybe he just wanted to tell everybody he had been to John Duncan's birthday party. I'd venture a guess if you asked him today, he would remember a hell of a lot more about it than I do."

As Crockett passed by, Travis quickly stepped forward, seeking a moment with the most popular man in the room. With a hearty smile on his face that did not seem entirely natural, he said, "Congressman Crockett, you should know that I intend to complete the necessary paperwork to make you a colonel in our volunteer forces."

Crockett, who did not stop walking, smiled a bit patronizingly at Travis. "Seems to me we got more'n enough colonels," he said. "High private suits me just fine."

The band finished its song and one of the musicians motioned to Crockett. Crockett was relieved that the moment looked spontaneous; he had asked the bandleader to invite him to play. It seemed to Crockett like a good excuse to give another little speech.

Travis walked faster to keep up with him. "I respect that," he said, "but with your reputation . . ."

Crockett held up a finger to the bandleader to indicate that he was coming in a moment, then turned to Travis, smiling an even more insincere politician's smile. "Tell you what," Crockett said. "Let us you and me have a good, long chat about this later, all right, Travers?"

Travis did not correct the mispronunciation. He just watched as Crockett walked away through the crowd, greeting every person he passed. When he reached the band, Crockett stepped onto the box, acknowledging the cheers of the crowd.

Crockett grinned and held his hands up. "Ladies and gentlemen," he said, "this is my first time at one of these Texian fandangos — and I promise to keep this speech shorter than an Irishman's temperance vow!"

The audience laughed with far more enthusiasm than the mild joke warranted.

Crockett waited for the laughter to die down, then continued. "Me and my mounted volunteers sure do 'preciate the warm hospitality we have been shown since we got here. And if this Santanner and his bunch should drop by, why, we will make it right warm for them, too!"

The crowd whooped and hollered.

Crockett's grin grew even wider. "We will

lick them like fine salt!" he shouted to even more cheers.

"Now, contrary to popular opinion," Crockett said with a self-deprecating smile, "I am not that much as a fighter. . . ."

People in the crowd laughed and some shouted, "No! Not true!" Crockett watched and smiled. Across the room, Bowie observed the performance with a straight face.

Crockett said, "And we all know I was not cut out for politics, being the only congressman that ever left Washington poorer than what he come."

More laughter from the audience.

"Fortunately," Crockett said, "I ran into my good friend Sam Houston, who said, 'Davy — David — get on down there to Texas and show them folks how "The Tennessee Grasshopper" is really played!' "

The crowd cheered. Many of them had heard about the great mountain man's prowess with a fiddle. They felt as if they were receiving a rare and precious gift just by being allowed to listen to him work his magic.

Crockett raised his fiddle to his chin, counted off, "One, two, three, four," to the leader of the band. Then he began sawing away at an infectious, upbeat rendition of "Listen to the Mocking Bird." Crockett's fiddle playing made up in enthusiasm what it lacked in technical skill, and the audience was thoroughly delighted. Many began dancing. Others stood near the stage, clapping in time to the music.

Jim Bowie was not quite as excited as the others. With a dour look on his face, he turned to Crisp, the man standing next to him, and said, "Bear hunter wanders into town, you would think it is the second coming."

As Crockett continued to fiddle, Ward walked up to Bowie and whispered in his ear. Bowie's face registered disbelief, then anger. Spotting Travis leaning against the wall on the other side of the room, Bowie forged through the crowd and grabbed Travis's shoulder, spinning him around until the two men were nose to nose.

Bowie snarled, "You do not have the sand to talk to two of my men, much less arrest them!"

A flash of fear showed on Travis's face. He tried to cover it with a look of indignation. "I told you I intended to restore order!"

Furious, Bowie said, "You have no command over my volunteers!"

"I have *absolute* command!" Travis shouted.

A crowd had gathered, surrounding the

two. Crockett noticed the commotion and jumped down from the box. The music stopped.

Bowie said in a low voice, "It'll be a cold day in hell when I take orders from a debtor who leaves a pregnant wife in the dead of night!"

Travis said, "Or I from a land swindler who marries a girl — rest her soul — for her family's money!"

Bowie tossed off his coat and pulled his knife from the scabbard. Travis now feared for his life and could not manage to come up with another expression to hide it. He took two quick steps backward to put some distance between him and the legendary knife fighter. Crockett jumped between them.

"Whoa, fellers!" he said. "Just 'cause we got nobody to fight does not mean we start looking to our right and left."

Bowie continued to stare at Travis, refusing to back down. Travis sized up the situation, desperately looking for a way to save face.

"Congressman Crockett has a point," Travis said. "We should do this democratically. A vote."

Bowie relaxed a bit and almost smiled.

Scurlock shouted, "Crockett! We want Crockett!"

Bowie's smile dropped.

Crockett grinned modestly. "Naw, naw," he said, shaking his head. "I am with you boys, not over you."

Bowie looked around the room, now hushed. He said, "All for the lieutenant colonel raise your hands!"

Three men raised their hands. Travis tried to read the situation, looking around, seeing no sign of support anywhere. After a few seconds he said, "Come on, men. No repercussions. All in favor of me commanding?"

Slowly, a few more hands raised, but not many. In the corner, Joe looked left and right, hoping for more votes.

Bowie smiled with satisfaction. He said, "All for me?"

A majority of hands raised, including most of Travis's men. Travis, humiliated, looked to Crockett, who held up two palms. "The gentleman from Tennessee respectfully abstains," he said.

Bowie grinned. The crowd reacted, slapping backs as Bowie put his jacket back on. But Travis could not take it. He pointed at Bowie and said, "You can command the militia only. The regulars cannot be led by a volunteer. It is illegal."

Even Travis knew how lame this sounded. All around him men scoffed and jeered.

Bowie said, "You don't like the outcome, so you change the rules. Is that it, Buck?"

Ward said, "Do not fret about it, Jim. We all know who is in charge."

There was a murmur of agreement around the room. Bowie thought for a moment, then issued his first official order. He said to Travis, "Release my men!"

There was no way out. Travis slowly nodded to one of his men, John Forsyth, who went off to let Bowie's two drunkards out of jail. Then, tail between his legs, Travis walked through the crowd and into the night. He had come to Béxar to take command of all the force, but how could he command men who did not respect him?

As Travis walked down the street, away from his humiliation, he noticed a lovely woman standing in the shadows. Maria Ramona Sanchez had made her choice.

The confrontation had brought the fandango to a pause, but not to a full stop. Bowie and his men settled in with numerous bottles to celebrate the happy outcome of the election, while Crockett divided his time between playing his fiddle and working the crowd. He and his Tennessee friends were not nearly the prodigious drinkers that Bowie and his men were, but they held their own as the evening wore on. When the fandango finally came to an end, some hours later, Crockett was even slightly surprised that he could still walk. As he, Autry and a few others, all a little worse for wear, wove down the street on foot, they talked about their bright future in Texas.

Crockett said, "I will put in for that parcel on the Red River. The one we passed on the way here. The one with that blue hole at the elbow."

The men nodded and grunted agreement. Even those who were not quite sure what Crockett had just said.

Autry said, "Don't know why we had to tent up outside of town when there are so many fine houses with big cornhusk beds just sitting empty."

Crockett peered from house to house. "Why are they empty?" he asked.

Autry said, "Folks hereabout believe the Mexicans are comin' back."

Crockett looked concerned. "Is that a fact?" he said.

"Yes, sir," said Autry. "But most of the boys think they will not be here till late spring, if they come at all."

Crockett and his party passed a small house with door and windows open wide. Inside, Ana and Gregorio Esparza were burying silver in a hole in the dirt floor.

Their little son, Enrique, sat on the floor, playing with a top, gazing dreamily out into the night. Crockett stopped and watched with some trepidation. Enrique's attention was caught by the kindly face of the tall Anglo. He stared at Crockett, ignoring his top for a moment. Behind him, his father spoke quietly, but urgently.

"Enrique," Gregorio said, "close the door, son." Enrique got up and closed the door, staring at the strange Americanos all the while.

Crockett stared at the closed door for a moment, then turned to Autry and said, "Figger they know something that we do not?"

Travis's bedroom was nearly dark, illuminated only by the soft, flickering light of a single candle. Travis, without a shirt, sat on the edge of his bed, staring into the darkness. Maria Ramona lay sleeping behind him. She had seen what happened in the cantina and had felt sorry for the young man. She almost considered sharing her company with him at no charge, then decided against it. Pity, she told herself, did not put food on the table. Even so, Maria Ramona had decided to give Travis extra effort and care. Even if only for a few moments, he could forget his troubles. The thought made her feel generous and kind. She even consented to sleep in his bed, a gift she rarely gave to men. She hoped that the young man appreciated how special this evening had been.

Travis stared straight ahead. Slowly, his face started to change from defeated to determined. He licked his thumb and put out the candle. It sputtered, leaving the room dark. He lay back on the bed and wrapped his arms around the beautiful stranger and quickly fell into a dreamless sleep.

Chapter Sixteen

A Mexican dragoon crested a hill on his horse, stopped and smiled at what he saw. There in the distance were the lights of Béxar. Behind the dragoon were dozens more like him, followed by hundreds of exhausted foot soldiers and scores of *soldaderas* — camp followers, wives and prostitutes. The lines stretched back over a mile. The Mexican army had endured an impossible march, hundreds of miles all the way up to Béxar. They had suffered, frozen, fought, bled and died. But now the journey was at an end. They were here. Glory was at hand.

In Béxar, the first pink and orange streaks of dawn were beginning to color the sky. The fandango had left the streets quiet. Except for a few shopkeepers and some industrious businessmen, almost everyone in town was still in bed, sleeping it off.

Up in the belltower of San Fernando church, Daniel Cloud fought to stay awake. He had not had as much to drink as some of the men, but the night had taken its toll on him, nonetheless. He and beautiful seventeen-year-old Isabella had found a quiet spot in a stable near Soledad Street, a place where her suspicious father would never think to look. She was ashamed at having to deceive her parents, but they distrusted the gringos. They did not understand. One day, she believed, they would. Cloud would prove himself worthy of their daughter and they would welcome him into their family. But that day might be a long time in coming. In the meantime, Cloud and Isabella had to take advantage of whatever opportunities presented themselves. He worried that she felt cheapened by secretiveness, by giving herself to him in a stable or behind the protective cover of trees by the river. But this, too, he would make up to her one day, when this terrible war was over.

It was so tempting to close his eyes, to relive every thrilling moment of the night before, but Cloud fought to stay alert. The countryside was beautiful in the silence of early morning. Already, the grass was growing in green as the long winter was coming to a close. The distinctive blue flowers he had encountered all across Texas were beginning to peek through the underbrush, spreading a lush carpet of color across the plain. And in the distance a flash of silver . . . Silver?!

Cloud leaned forward and peered into the distance. Helmets! Horses! Lances! They were here . . . the Mexican army was here!

He grabbed the rope and began pulling furiously. The bell pealed out again and again. People began to emerge from the houses, looking up at him. Some had fearful expressions on their faces. Others just looked angry at being awakened at this ungodly hour.

Cloud looked down and saw Travis sprinting across the plaza toward the entrance of the church. Travis took the stairs two at a time until he reached the top. As he arrived, the ringing slowly died out. Daniel Cloud stared into the distance, confused. He turned to Travis and said, "I saw glints of metal. Horses. That way." He pointed. "I know I did." Cloud shook his head, as if he had been dreaming. "Then I looked again and did not see nothin'."

Travis left the cupola and walked across the church roof to the west end, followed by Cloud. He stopped and squinted. There, in the far distance, he saw it, too. He could not tell if it was two or five miles away, but there they were — the Mexican army cresting a hill. It looked to Travis like an army of ants — endless.

Bowie raced up, coughing from the exertion. He stood beside Travis and looked in the same direction. He saw it, too, and grew stoic.

Bowie coughed again and said, "On the plus side of the ledger, Buck, I just found the miracle cure for a hangover."

Travis looked at the army. It seemed to be composed of thousands upon thousands of men. He found it horribly fascinating. "We will never be able to defend the town," Travis said. He looked down into the plaza. Nearly all of the Texians were there, wondering what was going on. Travis called down, "Get your belongings and make your way to the Alamo. The Mexicans are in sight!"

For some reason, he had expected them to calmly walk back to their quarters, gather their things and start out for the mission. Instead, the plaza exploded into bedlam. Soldiers and civilians scurried about in disarray, panicking, rushing back and forth. Travis and Bowie ran down the tower stairs and headed for their own homes. When

Travis burst into his bedroom, Maria Ramona was already gone. He called for Joe to start packing their things.

Moments later, Travis and Joe rode through the mob on horseback, calling for calm, trying to get people to listen. "Orderly withdrawal," he called out. "Orderly withdrawal to the Alamo! We will proceed in an orderly withdrawal."

Nobody listened to him. Behind Travis and Joe, a small herd of longhorns was being driven through the plaza by Crockett's men. Crockett and Autry were on foot. "Keep them beeves out of the buildin's!" Crockett shouted. "Go, go, keep 'em movin'!" He noticed a Tejano woman cowering against a wall and nodded politely to her. "We be out of your path directly, ma'am," he said, smiling. "Mind them horns."

Grimes was not concerned with cattle. He was trying to wrestle his rifle back from the local he had just sold it to. "I know I sold it," Grimes said to the man, who did not understand a word he was saying. "But now I need it back."

Almeron Dickinson saddled his horse and mounted, holding his hand out to Susanna. "Colonel Travis said it would be weeks before they got here!" Susanna said pleadingly.

Almeron smiled down at her. "They see our cannon," he said, "and they will think twice about charging in. Come on."

Susanna wanted to swing herself up into the saddle behind her husband, but could not manage to do that and keep little Angelina in her arms. Joe pitched in to help her hand the baby to Almeron, then helped Susanna into her spot. Susanna smiled her thanks to Joe, then Almeron spurred the horse to a trot in the direction of the Alamo.

Travis was stunned by the chaos and continued to make pleas for order. "Orderly withdrawal . . ." he said over and over. "Orderly withdrawal . . ."

Tom Waters passed Travis chasing his mutt, who was spooked by all the noise and activity. "Come here, Jake," Waters called. "Come here, boy!"

Seguin and his men were loading bags of corn from a warehouse onto wagons.

Travis rode through the crowd toward him. "Captain Seguin," he shouted. "Get your men into the Alamo!"

Seguin kept loading and said, calmly, "You can starve by yourself, Colonel, but I am bringing the corn."

Travis rode on, followed by Joe. They passed a Tejano woman holding the hand of a little girl. The two of them watched the

Anglos stream to the Alamo. The little girl tilted her head toward her mother's. "Are they going to die, Mama?" she asked.

The woman nodded sadly. "Yes, child. Every one of them."

At the Veramendi House, Sam tossed food and utensils into a cart. Bowie was loading the cart, too, but he had to stop frequently when uncontrollable coughing overcame him. He wiped his mouth with a cloth and Juana, his sister-in-law, saw that it was red with blood. He said to her in Spanish, "There's a shotgun hidden in the commune." She ran inside to fetch it.

Sam stepped forward and said, "Are you all right, Mister James?"

Bowie waved him away and kept working. *Fine,* Sam thought. *Let him die. The sooner the better.*

The men herded cattle through the shallowest part of the river, just below the footbridge, carefully guiding them through the narrow entrance of the half-moon-shaped lunette that guarded the Alamo's main gate, and then into the Alamo courtyard itself. The steers were followed by frantic people and animals, by Texians carrying guns and supplies through the main gate, by Tejanos, anxiously looking after their families. Gregorio Esparza escorted Ana and his children inside. Little Enrique was terrified. His mother looked uneasily at the disorganized Texians and crossed herself. It was not the first time that the thought, Are we on the wrong side? crossed her mind.

Almeron Dickinson led his wife, baby and several women inside the Alamo church to the baptistery, just inside the front door. "Thick walls," he said to Susanna. "You will be safe here." Almeron and Susanna looked deeply into each other's eyes. He kissed her and the baby, then ran over to Bowie to find out what his orders were.

All across the Alamo courtyard, there was confusion among the regulars and the volunteers. Forsyth shouted to a group of men who were standing still, looking dazed. "Get up there," he called, pointing. "Get over there. I do not care where you get, but get."

Ward answered indignantly, "I answer to Bowie!" He added to himself, "Wherever he is."

Bowie was at the Alamo's main gate. He, Green Jameson and Seguin stood by while animals and people streamed by. Seguin wrote furiously on a scrap of paper while Bowie dictated, ". . . under guarantee of a white flag which I believe will be respected by you and your forces."

Seguin was writing the message in Spanish.

Bowie said, "Sign it, 'God and Mexico . . .' "

He reconsidered, grabbed the paper and drew lines through something. "Make that 'God and Texas,' " he said. He looked at Seguin and said, "Ah hell, when was there somebody I could not talk to?" Bowie turned to Jameson. "Find something white."

In his headquarters, Travis sat at his desk writing a letter:

The enemy in large force are in sight. We want men and provisions. Send them to us. We have men and are determined to defend the Alamo to the last.

Ward and Grimes and a few other Texians hustled past Travis's office. Ward looked at the closed door contemptuously. "We are under attack," he said, "and yore majesty locks hisself in his room."

Travis sealed the letter, then grabbed another sheet and began to write. This letter was addressed to Fannin at Goliad.

We have removed all our men into the Alamo, where we will make such resistance as is due to our honour, and that of the country, until we can get assistance from you, which we expect you to forward immediately. In this extremity, we hope you will send us all the men you can spare promptly. We have one hundred and forty-six men, who are determined never to retreat. We have but little provisions, but enough to serve us till you and your men arrive. We deem it unnecessary to repeat to a brave officer who knows his duty, that we call on him for assistance.

As Travis wrote, Joe paced nervously behind him.

"Joe," Travis said without looking at him, "sit down before that terror catches." He wondered if Fannin would detect the sarcasm in the last line — "We deem it unnecessary to repeat to a brave officer who knows his duty . . ." — as if that tin soldier would know his duty from a hole in the wall.

There was a knock on the door and Crockett stepped into the room. "Colonel?" he said.

Travis looked up, quill still in hand, dripping ink onto the desk below. To Crockett, he seemed more than a little dazed.

"Do not mean to disturb ya, Colonel," Crockett said, "but we got a mare's nest out here."

Travis said, "I have to get couriers out while there's still time." Crockett nodded and started to withdraw. "By the way," Travis said. Crockett stopped and turned. "I want you and your men to take a position at the palisade."

Crockett cocked his head to the left. "That little old wood fence?"

Travis said, "You prefer a different assignment?"

Crockett smiled. "Naw, that is precisely the one I was going to put in for."

Travis nodded. "If you could oversee manning the walls it would be a help."

Crockett said, "Yes, sir."

"We should have six men to a cannon," Travis said. "Eighteen tubes, which works out to . . ."

"Hundred and eight men," Crockett said quickly.

Travis looked at him with some surprise.

Crockett smiled modestly. "Even bear hunters have to do a little figgerin' from time to time."

Travis smiled and continued, "And we should have a man with a musket every four feet of wall."

Calculating rapidly in his head, Crockett knew they were in trouble. "Colonel Travis," he said, "we are going to need more men."

Chapter Seventeen

A footsore troop of several hundred Texians trudged into the courtyard of La Bahía Mission near Goliad. It was a younger mission than the Alamo, built in 1779, and, to the eyes of the men who had seen both places, seemed to be the stronger of the two. The large and ornate church was in good repair, as were the officers' quarters and barracks. The entire compound was surrounded by sturdy walls, eight feet high.

The Texians who had just arrived to occupy La Bahía, however, were not impressed with it. At the moment, nothing mattered much to them except food and sleep. They had been marching for hours, urged along by their curiously prim and hesitant leader, Colonel James Walker Fannin. Marching through the gate, the men looked around, tired, hungry and disgusted. A low groan rumbled through the group when Fannin stepped in front of the church and raised an arm to get their attention.

"Men," he said politely. "Men, if I could please ask for your attention . . ."

"God in heaven," muttered an Englishman named Huberman, "he's going to give us another speech."

The Texians threw their packs and rifles down and flopped into the dirt of the courtyard. No one was paying much attention to Fannin. Few of them even looked at him.

Fannin raised his voice slightly. "I understand that you might be rather disappointed that we have, um, postponed our assault on Matamoros . . ." he said. His voice still carried the lilt from his childhood in Georgia. He was not a fiery Southerner like Bowie or Travis, but of the more refined plantation variety.

Fannin continued, ". . . but discretion being the better part of valor, I have decided that we will remain here in Goliad." He braced himself for a protest, but the men said nothing. Most of them were simply happy that they did not have to walk any farther.

"We will stay here awaiting resupply and further orders from . . ." Fannin tried to give his voice an edge, but could not manage it, ". . . from whomever is now in *charge* back in San Felipe."

The men grumbled a little. It was those buffoons back in San Felipe who had gotten them into this mess in the first place. They thought they were headed for riches and heady victory in Matamoros. Instead, they had marched for days, only to wind up stuck in this little colony in the back end of nowhere, whose only importance was its strategic position on the map. There were, they knew, basically two roads that led into Texas from Mexico. One came in from the west, through Coahuila and across the Rio Grande. That road led straight into San Antonio de Béxar and on to Bastrop and Washington-on-the-Brazos. The other came up directly from the south, through Matamoros. Winding northward, the road went through Agua Dulce, San Patricio, Refugio and straight into Goliad. Leaving either Béxar or Goliad unguarded simply opened the door to Texas to Santa Anna's army.

Fannin continued, "Since we may be here for some time, I'd like to christen this garrison Fort Defiance!"

One of the Texians groaned. Nobody else responded. Nobody else cared.

Fannin took the non-response as a rejection of his idea. Growing a little desperate he said, "Unless you all would like to vote on a name . . ."

It seemed to the men watching from the walls of the Alamo that the Mexican army swept into Béxar like a majestic sea: officers in red-breasted coats braided with gold; dragoons on horseback whose silver helmets glinted in the sun as if they were garbed in lightning; presidial troopers bearing lances. And behind them, soldados in blue coats and white trousers and, on their heads, tall shakos topped with pompons. There were hundreds of them, marching through the streets in perfect formation. Although many like Jesús were unwilling — even terrorized — conscripts, they looked like a formidable war machine to the Texians.

Before this vast army rode Santa Anna, front and center. Slightly behind him, his aide, Colonel José Batres, struggled to stay close enough to the general to respond to any orders while, at the same time, keeping a respectable distance.

Santa Anna watched with amusement as the citizens of Béxar rushed to escape his view, peered warily at him from windows or doorways or tried to ingratiate themselves by cheering loudly as he passed. "They scatter like frightened children," he said.

Batres, not knowing if this statement required a response, simply said, "Yes, General."

A Tejano woman leaned down to her six-year-old daughter and urged in a loud whisper, "Say it, say it, just like we practiced!"

The little girl waved her right arm in the air and called out, "Viva Santa Anna! Viva Mexico!" At her mother's urging, the girl ran alongside Santa Anna's horse, shouting it over and over, in a rehearsed monotone, *"Viva Santa Anna! Viva Mexico!"*

Santa Anna glanced down at the girl, nodded and touched his hat. At the acknowledgment, she stopped immediately and walked back to her mother, hoping for a reward for doing her task so well. But Santa Anna's look only lingered on the little girl for an instant. Almost immediately, his attention was caught by a stunning young Tejana standing in a doorway. She was slight, with high, rounded breasts and hair as dark as the night sky. Her eyes were large and brown; they widened with awe as the girl watched the procession pass her house. Naturally, the general felt that he himself must be the source of that awe, and smiled at her. The girl barely had time to cast her eyes shyly toward the ground before her mother grabbed both of her shoulders, dragged her inside and closed the door.

Santa Anna glanced over at Batres. The aide had seen that look before — many times. Batres nodded at his general — message received. It was the part of his job he found most disturbing, procuring women for Santa Anna. But most of them were happy to be procured. And the ones who were not willing . . . well, they could always be persuaded, one way or another.

Castrillón and Almonte stopped in the pleasant shade of a house owned by the Yturri family. It stood on the northeast corner of the plaza, just across from San Fernando church. They had already arranged with the owner — who was, at the moment, an ardent supporter of His Excellency — to occupy the house as Santa Anna's headquarters. Yturri, his wife and four children hurriedly collected a few belongings and prepared to exit through the back door while Castrillón and Almonte sat out front, watching Santa Anna admiringly as he rode toward them.

"What other man could have made this march?" Castrillón asked. "Every time I question him I am reminded of his greatness."

Santa Anna rode up beside them. Batres swung himself off his horse and helped the general to dismount.

Approaching Castrillón and Almonte, he said, "Are the advance troops encamped?"

Castrillón nodded. "Yes, sir."

Santa Anna looked around the plaza, still a swirl of activity as the army continued to enter the town, column after column. "Is the battery placement spotted?"

Castrillón replied, "Yes, Your Excellency, but it may not be necessary."

Santa Anna looked sharply at him.

"It appears the Texians may desire a parley," Castrillón continued. "We should respond with terms."

Santa Anna looked at Castrillón with disgust. He was a fine general, was Castrillón, but Santa Anna often had cause to wonder if he had the ruthless ambition required to win wars, to conquer territories and people. Castrillón was brave, strong and wise. But his misplaced humanitarianism would be his downfall.

For his part, Castrillón knew that every time he said anything that conflicted with Santa Anna's ruthless theories of total submission of the enemy, he put his life on the line. Even so, he could not abandon his principles just to please his general — even though he knew many other officers who had, willingly.

Castrillón pretended that he did not see Santa Anna's negative reaction. He hoped that this conflict could still be resolved without violence. So he asked again, hopefully, "What are your terms, General?"

Inside the Alamo, Green Jameson said to Jim Bowie, "I wonder what his terms will be."

"Santa Anna can be a hard man," Bowie said. "But he has to know that he's bit off more than he can chew."

Jameson looked toward Béxar. "Yes, sir, they got us outmanned, but by God, we got 'em outgunned. We can beat those Mexicans ten to one with the artillery in this place."

Bowie smiled. "No reason it has to come to that. Let us go talk some sense to those gentlemen."

Jameson hoisted the white flag and the two men walked out the gate, through the lunette and toward the river bridge. They stopped there, awaiting the approach of two Mexican riders. Bowie brightened when he recognized Castrillón, riding alongside Almonte. He knew the general to be a good man. More important, he was a smart man, unwilling to shed blood needlessly.

Even before Castrillón and Almonte came to a stop at the bridge, Bowie smiled broadly and called to Castrillón, "Manuel, how many times we going to trade this old church back and forth before this war is over?"

Castrillón cast his eyes downward. He could barely stand to look Bowie in the eye.

Bowie noticed Castrillón's odd manner and glanced nervously at Jameson. Perhaps, he thought, Castrillón was uncomfortable with exhibiting this kind of informality before General Almonte. Bowie decided to approach the issue with a bit more formality. He said, "I have come out to see if your commander would be willing to parley out of this unfortunate situation."

Castrillón still avoided Bowie's eyes and said nothing. Almonte dismounted and handed Bowie a piece of paper. "From General Santa Anna himself," Almonte said in English.

Bowie opened the note and started to read.

Travis was in his quarters, seated at his desk. At the doorway stood Colorado Smith and Launcelot Smither. Travis handed a letter to Smither and said, "Gonzales." He handed the other to Colorado Smith, saying, ". . . and to Colonel Fannin at Goliad. Godspeed."

They turned to go for their horses. Just outside Travis's quarters, Susanna Dickinson waited, holding Angelina in her arms. "Mr. Smither," she said. He stopped and removed his hat. "Ma'am," he said.

Susanna touched his arm. "I do not believe that I ever properly thanked you for your help in Gonzales."

Smither looked at the ground. He had always lived alone, and even talking to women made him uneasy. "Glad to do it, ma'am," he said.

"You saved my life, Mr. Smither, and the life of my daughter," Susanna said. "I cannot thank you enough."

He nodded, still not looking at her.

Susanna said, "And with this trip, you may just be saving our lives all over again. Please keep yourself safe."

"Ma'am," Smither said, "I have often had occasion to wonder . . . that is, I do not know if you owe me any thanks."

"What do you mean?" Susanna said.

Smither said, "I am the one that brung you to Béxar. Seems to me I pulled you out of the fryin' pan, and flung you into the fire."

Susanna smiled. "You reunited me with my husband, Mr. Smither. That is the most important thing. Whatever happens now, we are together."

Smither touched the brim of his hat and walked away.

As he turned, Smither nearly bumped into Captain John Forsyth, who was rushing toward Travis's door. "Colonel," Forsyth said in an accent that betrayed his New York birthplace, "I think you should see this."

Travis followed the captain out of his quarters, to the southwest wall ramp. They trotted up the ramp to the eighteen-pound cannon, aimed straight at Béxar. It seemed that everywhere Travis looked, he saw the Mexican army, putting up tents, erecting cannon placements. The lancers and dragoons moved to and fro on horseback, fanning out to make sure that every angle of the Alamo was under their guard. There were only two thousand soldiers in view, but to Travis, watching them spread out around the fort, it seemed as if the army contained multitudes. He thought to himself that he had never seen so many people in one place. It was thrilling — even beautiful in a way — even as it frightened him out of his wits. Anxious not to let the men see the fear on his face, Travis struggled to keep from sweating or trembling or turning away as he tried to take in the awesome and terrifying sight.

Travis was so absorbed in the sight that he did not at first notice that Crockett also had climbed the ramp and was standing beside him, in awe as well.

"Colonel Travis," Crockett said, "I have said it before, but I will say it again: We are going to need a lot more men."

Travis did not seem to hear him. He said, almost to himself, "Now, that is a handsome army."

Suddenly, he saw something else besides the horrible majesty of the Mexican army. He saw Bowie and Jameson on the river bridge, conferring with two enemy officers.

Outraged, Travis said, to no one in particular, "What is Colonel Bowie doing on the bridge?"

William Ward, the feisty Irishman — and one of Bowie's volunteers — replied smugly, "Trying to get us out of this mess."

Daniel Cloud cocked his flintlock and aimed it directly at Almonte's chest. "I could nail him right here," he said, squinting one eye as he peered down the sight. "Right between them pretty buttons."

Crockett patted Cloud on the shoulder. "Do not make me nervous, son. That feller might be our ticket out of this mess."

Travis continued to stare at Bowie with open animosity. Without looking away, he said, "Fire the eighteen pounder."

No one moved. No one was quite sure if they had heard what they thought they had.

Travis said, louder and angrier, "You heard me. Fire the cannon."

Almeron Dickinson and his cannon crew quickly prepared the cannon with powder and shot. At Travis's nod, Dickinson sparked the primer.

On the bridge Bowie finished reading the letter for the second time. It was bad news.

". . . the Mexican Army," it read, "cannot come to terms under any conditions with rebellious foreigners to whom there is no other recourse left, if they wish to save their lives, than to place themselves immediately at the disposal of the Supreme Government from whom alone they may expect clemency after some considerations are taken up." It was not even signed by Santa Anna, but by his aide, Batres.

Bowie looked at Castrillón with shock in his eyes.

Castrillón said in English, "I am sorry, Jim."

From the walls of the Alamo, the blast of a cannon shook the ground. Bowie, Jameson,

Castrillón and Almonte whirled toward the fort, staring in disbelief.

In Béxar, Santa Anna barely flinched at the sound and watched calmly as the cannonball smashed into a small house east of town. Santa Anna turned to Batres and commanded, "Raise the flag!"

"Which one, General?" Batres said.

On the bridge, Castrillón and Almonte steadied their horses, spooked from the blast.

"Goddamn! Manuel," Bowie said. Then switching to Spanish, he continued. "I had nothing to do with that!"

Without a word, Castrillón and Almonte turned their horses and galloped back toward town. Bowie stalked angrily back to the Alamo, followed by Jameson, who struggled to keep up. He carried the now useless white flag down by his side.

Back at the southwest wall, Crockett looked toward the belltower of San Fernando and said, "Lookee there, Colonel." Travis followed Crockett's gaze with dread. Slowly rising over the highest point in the town was a flag. It was not a flag that any man in the Alamo had ever seen before, but not a one of them had any trouble deciphering its meaning. It was blood red in color, with a skull and crossbones design at dead center. As a Mexican soldier secured the flag in place, still more troops came marching into town in the background. Crockett said, "Well, sir, that cannot be a good sign."

Bowie stormed in through the main gate and raced up the ramp to where Travis stood. Both fists clenched, his face was just inches from Travis's. "Are you a fool?" Bowie snarled. "I was trying to get us a truce!"

Travis responded loudly, his voice cracking with anger. "If we broker a cessation," he said, "we will do so from a position of strength, not weakness. We do not turn belly up and beg. Otherwise we have said nothing and this conflict means nothing!"

Bowie, fighting to control his rage, said in a low, strangled voice, "Dying for nothing means shit to me."

Travis eyed the letter in Bowie's hand. "Their response?"

Bowie stuck it out. Travis took it from him, read it, and looked up. ". . . Surrender at discretion . . ." He almost smiled. "Discretion means they can do anything to us that they please. Perhaps, Colonel, they will only execute officers?"

Crockett pointed to the skull and crossbones flying above the San Fernando church belltower. "Looks like we all just got promoted."

In the courtyard of the Alamo, the Tejanos gathered in a small group. "I saw General Cós," said Gregorio Esparza. "He has broken his promise not to return."

Seguin scowled. Cós was a coward, and that, Seguin could almost accept. But he was also a liar, and that stabbed at the very heart of Seguin's principles. "A man should keep his word," he said. He thought of something even more troubling and said to Esparza, "Is your brother with them?"

Esparza looked sadly toward the town. He and his brother Francisco had argued bitterly about the future of Texas. Francisco was ruled by his country. Gregorio was ruled by his conscience. "Maybe he raised the flag," Gregorio said.

Up in the southwest battery, the angry confrontation between Travis and Bowie had cooled into something like an impromptu council of war. Bowie and Crockett looked at each other, and then both turned their gaze toward Travis. It was a look that said, *Well, now what?*

Travis said, "We wait for reinforcements. Within a few days all of Texas will know our situation."

Bowie sneered, "Tell me, Buck, in Alabama, precisely how many is a few?"

Travis ignored the remark. "Gentlemen," he said, "I suggest we man our posts and prepare for a response not made of cloth." He walked away, the very picture of the in-control commander. Bowie and Crockett looked at each other skeptically. Crockett said, "You figger that fancy talk just comes off the top of his head?"

"I have never been too fond of the heroic gesture," Bowie said.

Suddenly they heard the roar of a Mexican cannon. The men in the Alamo saw the puff of smoke from an enemy position and braced themselves for the hit. A pitch black cannonball cleared the wall, traveling slowly enough to be clearly visible to the men, but fast and powerful enough to blast into the long barracks and leave an angry ragged crater in the wall. In the baptistery of the church, only a few yards away, little Angelina Dickinson wailed with terror. Her mother tried to comfort her, but felt on the verge of screaming herself. The other women held their children close and kept their heads low as dust swirled all around them. "There, there, baby," said Susanna, because she could not think of anything else to say. "Go to sleep. . . . Go to sleep. . . ."

Chapter Eighteen

At the Yturri house, Santa Anna called for a war council. As his generals gathered there, Mexican soldiers, Jesús among them, were unloading Santa Anna's belongings from a cart and carrying them into the house. It was Batres's job to oversee them. Since he had no idea what it actually took to do any task, the only supervisory method he could come up with was a combination of threats and warnings. "Careful with the general's crystal!" he shouted officiously. "Broken bones for broken glass!"

The soldados knew that this was no idle threat, so they handled the crates carefully. Jesús grasped his end of a long wooden box tightly, walking backward into the house, taking tiny, cautious steps.

Inside, Jesús was overwhelmed by the

splendor. The home was like no other he had ever seen, as unlike the jacale in which he lived with his grandfather as a mighty river is from a dribble of spit. The main room of the Yturri house was richly painted in shades of burnt umber and orange. Delicate mosaic tiles framed the entrance. Santa Anna sat at the head of an oblong mahogany table, which was polished to a mirror-like shine. Likewise glossy black stones of the floor reflected the flames in the ornate fireplace in the corner and the tinier flickers from the candelabra, making it seem as though the generals were standing in a shallow lake of fire.

Generals Castrillón, Almonte, Sesma, Cós and Caro gathered around the table. Castrillón and Almonte sat; the others stood behind them. All awaited the words of their president. For the moment, Santa Anna was not speaking. He was sipping coffee poured by his manservant, Ben, a free man of color who had found a more congenial home in Mexico than in his native America.

Santa Anna placed the fine china cup in its delicate saucer and dabbed at his lips with a napkin. "Is Houston with them?" he asked.

"No," Almonte replied.

Santa Anna thought about this for a moment and nearly smiled. He took another sip of his coffee. "I heard that his young wife deserted him," he said. "Because he has a wound that never heals."

"He left office rather than answer to the scandal," Almonte offered.

Santa Anna found the idea baffling. "What kind of man gives up power for a woman?" he asked. Then he smiled again. "He will come — if only to salvage his reputation."

Santa Anna took another sip of coffee. "What of Jim Bowie, the knife fighter?"

Almonte said, proud to be the source of so much good information, "Inside the mission. And someone else of worth . . . Davy Crockett."

Santa Anna looked delighted. "Crockett? The great bear killer?"

Almonte nodded.

"He is a real person?" Santa Anna said.

"Yes, Your Excellency," Almonte said. "He recently served in the United States Congress."

This was another puzzling idea to Santa Anna. "Congress?" he asked. "Are you sure it is the same Crockett?"

Almonte nodded, "The very same. He sometimes wears an animal on his head, or so I have heard."

Santa Anna smiled. "How extraordinary," he said.

"They are disorganized and outmanned," Almonte continued. "We should take advantage immediately."

Castrillón knew that he was about to incur the wrath of the president once again, but he felt compelled to offer a few rational words. "We have heavy cannon arriving in a few days," he said. "They are not going anywhere."

Almonte shook his head and scowled. "There are more rebels less than a week's march from here, at Goliad, under Colonel Fannin." He looked to Santa Anna for approval.

But Santa Anna had little reaction to either general. He seemed calm, as though everything were going exactly as it ought to. "Houston, Fannin — more meat for the spit," he said. "We wait. But we will make the dark a nightmare to remind them of the truth yet to come."

Travis walked the north wall battery. He had chosen this spot as his command post, since it was arguably the weakest position in the fort. Crockett and the Tennesseans were over at the palisade. To the naked eye, that wooden fence would seem to be the Alamo's most vulnerable spot. But the sharp timbers and the trench outside, lined with ragged cut trees, combined to make it a formidable place to attack and a rather easy one to defend.

But the north wall worried Travis. Cós had done some work on it back when he and his army occupied the Alamo in the fall, and Jameson had been working on it ever since, shoring it up as best he could. Yet it remained a crumbling patchwork of stone, logs and adobe. A couple of good cannon blasts would turn it into a sieve. And if the Mexicans attacked, there were hand- and footholds aplenty. They would not even need ladders to get over this wall — they could simply climb right in.

Right now, however, it did not look like the Mexican army had any intention of attacking. They were slowly and methodically going about setting up for a siege. This could be bad, Travis thought, but it meant more time. The longer they laid siege to the Alamo, the more chance he had of getting help. Travis was nervous, but hopeful. Houston would come, and Fannin. This might all turn out just fine.

At the palisade, Micajah Autry fought the boredom by cleaning his rifles. Again. He said to Crockett, "Personally, I'd just as soon take my chances fighting out there in the open."

Crockett nodded. "I do not like being hemmed in any more'n you," he said. "But here we sit."

Bowie walked toward them, eyeing the ridge. Already Powder House Hill was dotted with tents — dozens of them. He seemed to be about to say something when he was overcome by a fit of coughing. He steadied himself with one hand against the wall until the attack was over.

Crockett said in a kindly voice, "If it ain't getting too personal, what ails you, Jim, exactly?"

Bowie shrugged. "Consumption. Typhoid. Pneumonia. One or all. Exactly."

Crockett spotted Bowie's famous knife and eyed the hilt with fascination. Bowie noticed his interest, pulled back his coat and slipped it out without even looking. He offered it to Crockett, who held it a little like a religious artifact. Crockett whistled softly, impressed at the size and heft of it but, more important, at the knife's history.

"That knife fight you was in, at that sandbar in Natchez," Crockett said, "the one that got written up. . . . Was all that true?"

Bowie smiled slightly. Everybody always

wanted to know about the sandbar fight. It was a story he had told a thousand times, and could have told ten thousand times, if he complied every time somebody asked. It amused him that the legendary David Crockett seemed just as impressed with the Bowie legend as anybody.

It was not even supposed to be his fight. He was just acting as a second in a duel between Samuel Wells and Dr. Thomas H. Maddox. One of Maddox's seconds, Norris Wright, was an old enemy of Bowie's — a banker, a sheriff, a scoundrel. Hell, it wasn't even that much of a duel — both men missed. They stepped forward to shake hands, but there was too much bad blood among the seconds for things to end there. Sam Cuny, another of Wells's seconds, decided to use the opportunity to settle a score with Col. Robert Crain, who was with Maddox. Nobody said a word. . . . Nobody had to. Cuny and Crain pulled out their pistols. Bowie pulled out his, too. Crain fired. Bowie fired back, clipping Crain's cravat but not hurting him. Crain drew his second pistol and fired, hitting Cuny in the thigh. The blood spurted from it as if from a spigot.

Crain started to run back toward the trees, but Bowie drew his huge knife from its scabbard and chased him. Crain whirled and threw his empty pistol full force at Bowie, smacking him square in the forehead. Bowie staggered and fell back against the upended trunk of a driftwood tree. Dr. James Denny, one of Wells's party, came to Bowie's aid, helping him up. But now Wright was there, firing his pistol. The ball blew two of Denny's fingers off and passed with a thud into Bowie's lung.

Bowie was like a maddened bull now. He lunged toward Wright, who ran away. Two of Maddox's party, the Blanchard brothers, fired their pistols at Bowie. One shot hit him in the thigh, bringing him down. Wright turned, pulling the tip of his sword cane to reveal its sharp blade. He began to stab Bowie on the ground, joined by Alfred Blanchard with his sword cane.

Bowie, stabbed repeatedly, flailed with his legs and knife, nicking his assailants several times.

Finally, Bowie managed to sit up, grabbing Wright by the collar. When Wright straightened, he pulled Bowie to his feet, and Bowie thrust his knife deep into Wright's chest. It was a frozen moment — two old enemies staring into each other's eyes, Wright's wide in shock, Bowie's hard with rage.

Bowie twisted the knife sideways. Blood spurted into Bowie's face, covering him with gore. Wright's eyes were still wide, but now they saw nothing. He crumpled to the ground. Blood pulsed from his chest for a brief moment, and then all was still.

"It was him or me," Bowie said to Crockett.

Crockett smiled. "Yeah, but 'him' had already put a sword cane and two shots in you. . . . Least that is the way I heard it."

"I do not recall, rightly," Bowie said quietly. "I was too busy killing the man."

Crockett and Bowie looked back to the ridge. There were no cannon up there yet, but it was only a matter of time. Mexican soldiers swarmed over the hill like fire ants.

"They are in no hurry," Bowie said. He scanned the horizon. The sun was setting, casting the venerable face of the Alamo church — and Crockett and Bowie before it — in a soft glow of crimson and gold.

Autry shook his head. "Why do they not simply attack us?"

Bowie looked at Autry, then at Crockett. He said, "I have seen vaqueros spend all day killing one bull."

Crockett said, "You can spoil the meat, worrying the animal like that."

Suddenly, the air was filled by the strident sounds of a bugle call. It was not a pleasant tune, and all around the wall, the men of the

Alamo looked in the direction of the sound. Ward said, to no one in particular, "You bring a band, you are counting on having something to celebrate."

Crockett joined Travis at the southwest battery and looked toward Béxar. "Mighty nice of them to serenade us like this," he said. "Now, that ain't a 'charge,' is it?"

Travis shook his head. "It is a cavalry march, but I am told Santa Anna fancies it for other uses. He borrowed it from the Spaniards, the Spaniards from the Moors. It is called *Deguello*."

Crockett said, "Kinda catchy."

Travis smiled grimly. "Deguello means 'Slit. Throat,' " he said.

Crockett's own smile faded. "Well, it ain't that catchy."

Abruptly, the music ended. There was a long, ominous silence all around the courtyard. Instinctively, the men knew this was not a good sign. Suddenly, Mexican cannon began firing from every emplacement. Cannonballs hit the north wall, splintering one of the timbers holding it up. Another followed close behind and punched a hole almost through to the other side. Other cannonballs landed in the river, just short of the west wall. The men on that side of the fort could feel a spray of water from the blasts.

Then a cannonball vaulted over the wall and rolled across the courtyard. The men were shocked to see that its fuse was still burning. Panicked, they flung themselves toward cover. There was an eternity of anticipation — all eyes on the bomb. Just when they thought it might be dead, it exploded with a deafening roar, sending shrapnel in all directions. Pieces of metal blasted into walls and doorways. The men crouched lower, holding their arms over their heads, finding whatever protection they could. Waters grabbed his mutt and dove for cover. Men, women, children cowered at the walls, in the baptistery, in the long barracks. In Travis's quarters, Joe huddled in a corner of the room, his hands over his ears, his face in a grimace of terror.

It was no easier on the Mexican side. Jesús was completely unnerved by the noise, the acrid smoke, the chaos. His task was to throw water on each cannon after it was fired. Between shots he slumped to the ground, crying and screaming.

There were screams in the Alamo baptistery as well. Angelina Dickinson wailed loudly, squirming as if desperate to free herself from her mother's arms and run away from the horror. But as dawn broke over the placid Texas countryside, the bombardment abruptly ceased and, within moments, so did the cries of little Angelina. Exhausted, she nestled against her mother's breast and quieted down. In moments, she was asleep.

The other women exchanged glances. Was it over? Nervously, they arose from their hiding places and peered outside into the courtyard. At first, it was completely empty; the silence was deafening. And then one by one, two by two, others began to emerge from their cubbyholes and step into the light. It was over. For now.

Green Jameson ran through the compound, pointing at men to follow him to the north wall. The fort's weakest point was now considerably weaker than it had been the night before. There was not much to work with, except mud and scraps of wood, but Jameson and his crew worked diligently at patching the crumbling section. Above them, Ward and five other riflemen aimed out at the cannon placement on the north side, covering the working men as best they could, knowing that if the Mexicans opened fire with the cannon right now, they would all be wiped out.

Ward peered into the distance. Dolphin Floyd, a farmer from North Carolina, stood beside him, his flintlock shaking mightily in his trembling hands.

"Notice anything different about them cannon?" Ward asked quietly.

Floyd did not say a word. He was afraid if he opened his mouth, he would just start screaming. He simply shook his head no.

Ward nodded in the direction of the gun emplacements. "They moved 'em closer last night."

Floyd closed his eyes tight and tried to think of North Carolina, of his small farm and his wife, Emily, prettiest girl in the county. At least she had been when they met, before the fever took her. But none of those pictures of past beauty and peace would come into focus. In his mind's eye, all Floyd could see were images of himself being torn limb from limb by a Mexican cannonball. When he opened his eyes again, he could see that Ward was right. The mound of dirt protecting the cannon placements had advanced. Closer and closer, heading straight for the walls of the Alamo.

Chapter Nineteen

Travis pulled his saber from its scabbard and drew a line in the sand.

"There," he said. "That would be the spot."

Sam and Joe were standing in the middle of the courtyard, holding shovels and looking at the slash that Travis had just made in the ground.

"As our well is drying," Travis said to them, "any day you find yourself not busy with other matters, you need to be digging a new one here."

Both men nodded and Joe softly said, "Yes, sir." Travis walked away to check on Jameson's progress on the north wall. When he was out of earshot, Sam said with disgust in his voice, "Ain't bad enuf we got to fetch 'em the water, now we got to find it, too."

Joe had already begun digging in earnest and Sam shook his head. "Don't work so hard," he said.

Joe kept shoveling. "Sooner I get down this hole," he replied, "sooner my head don't get taken off."

Sam said, "Sooner you get a bunch of white men they drinkin' water, sooner you get a pat on the head."

Joe looked at him as if he had been slapped. Then he resumed his digging.

Sam joined him and dug for a while, half-heartedly. He noticed that no one in the compound was paying much attention to them, so it did not really seem to matter if they worked hard or not. Joe dug with purpose, however, obviously trying hard to do a good job for his master. Sam looked at him with a tinge of pity.

"He had you long?" Sam asked.

Joe paused in his digging for a moment and said, "Mister Simon White down at Brazoria hold my contrack, an' he hire me out to Mister William last July."

Both men continued to shovel in silence for a few moments. When Sam spoke again, it was quietly — so quietly that Joe could barely hear his voice over the scrapes of the shovels. "I knowed a man name Nemo belong to Simon White —

run off for Saltillo," he said.

"Did he make it?" Joe asked.

Sam shook his head. "I wish I knew, but I don't."

Travis, satisfied with Jameson's progress, walked the perimeter of the compound, checking fortifications, making mental notes for new plans of defense. Several of the New Orleans Greys were in the long barracks, digging trenches that could be used as a retreat point.

"Men," Travis said, "bag some of that dirt and stack it against the walls. That will double the thickness, make it better protection."

The men, who were already planning to do just that, nodded at Travis and waited for him to leave.

Louis Dewall was working at a forge, chopping up horseshoes, chains — anything that could be used as cannon shot. Dewall had owned a smithy back in New York. There was not much call for blacksmithing in the Alamo, but he was resourceful and eager to help in any way he could. When he had reduced to shrapnel whatever metal piece he started with, he threw the red-hot chunks into a bucket of water to cool. His friend Daniel Cloud retrieved the pieces from the bucket and placed them by the handful in canvas bags.

Travis paused to watch them work for a moment, then said, "There are two leaden troughs in the horse pens. Should make fine cannon shot."

And then he was gone.

Cloud watched Travis walk away. He said to Dewall, "What in the hell are we saving our cannonballs for?" Dewall shrugged and went back to his forge.

Travis headed back to his quarters when he heard the familiar noise of rough, hacking coughs. Travis followed the sound to find Bowie leaning weakly against a wall, nearly helpless with coughing. Bowie slapped the wall in disgust over his condition. Travis gave Bowie a moment to compose himself, then walked over.

Bowie looked at him, spat some blood onto the ground and wiped his mouth. "Notice how you don't really hear it until it stops?" he said.

Travis was silent for a while, then said, "I have never been in a cannon battle before. Not of this magnitude."

Bowie realized that Travis was offering him an olive branch of sorts. He was not such a bad man. A little full of himself, but he was young. He would grow out of it.

Bowie was just about to reply when Travis spoke again.

"Until they decide to attack," he said, "I suspect we will be bombarded on a nightly basis. Deprive us of sleep."

Bowie nodded, still holding his bloody handkerchief to his mouth. "Till we start seeing ghosts everywhere."

Travis said in a soft voice, "Colonel, I became a little heated with you in front of your men. It was ill advised and not terribly professional."

Bowie waved off the apology. "Forget it," he said. "Most of 'em didn't understand what you were saying anyway."

"It is important that you and I agree," Travis said. "For me, though we are poorly supplied, surrender is not an option. I submit that we engage and delay until reinforcements arrive."

Bowie nodded in agreement. "I feel the same way," he said. With more than a little sense of amazement, Travis nodded back. They had actually reached a consensus.

Bowie said, "Sometimes it's just the way you say things, Travis. That's all, I swear to God." He walked away, coughing as he did. Travis watched him go. He was sorry for Bowie's illness, but could hardly help a surge of elation when he considered that

Bowie's condition placed Travis in absolute command of the Alamo. All their votes, all the warring factions made no difference now. Bowie was no longer fit to lead. Travis frowned and shook his head, trying to rid himself of such unworthy thoughts. He had no time to gloat, only to command.

He walked into his office and sat down at the little drop-leaf desk that had followed him from Alabama to New Orleans to Nacogdoches to Anahuac and finally to Béxar. He had written love letters on this desk, made steamy, secret entries in his diary, and signed divorce papers. And now, he must write a letter that would bring aid from all corners of Texas. Once Houston, Fannin and all the others truly understood how dire his circumstances were, they would come to him in multitudes, driving Santa Anna back over the Rio Grande toward Mexico City. This war could still be won.

He unfolded and smoothed a piece of brown wrapping paper, dipped his quill in ink and began to write:

Commandancy of the Alamo —
Bejar Fby. 24th 1836
To the People of Texas & all Americans in
the world —

266

Fellow citizens & compatriots —

I am besieged, by a thousand or more of the Mexicans under Santa Anna — I have sustained a continual Bombardment & cannonade for 24 hours & have not lost a man — The enemy has demanded a Surrender at discretion, otherwise, the garrison are to be put to the sword, if the fort is taken — I have answered the demand with a cannon shot, & our flag still waves proudly from the wall — I shall never Surrender or retreat. Then, I call on you in the name of Liberty, of patriotism & every thing dear to the American character, to come to our aid with all dispatch — The enemy is receiving reinforcements daily & will no doubt increase to three or four thousand in four or five days. If this call is neglected, I am determined to sustain myself as long as possible & die like a soldier who never forgets what is due to his own honor & that of his country

Victory or Death!
William Barret Travis
Lt. Col. Comdt

He started to fold the letter, then thought that he should offer some heartening news, to indicate the resourcefulness and resolve of his men.

P.S. The lord is on our side — When the enemy appeared in sight we had not three bushels of corn — We have since found in deserted houses 80 or 90 bushels & got into the walls 20 or 30 head of Beeves — Travis

Travis read the letter over. He thought of a few high-flown phrases to add, but there was no time. This letter, as hastily written and crude as it was, would simply have to do. The readers would have to forgive its literary failings.

Travis turned to Joe, who had tired of digging and returned to their quarters. While Travis was immersed in the composition of his letter, Joe had been sitting patiently on a stool by the door. "Joe," Travis said, "go get Captain Martin and tell him to report to me immediately."

"Yes, sir," Joe said, and bolted out the door.

In just a moment, Albert Martin stepped in. "Sir."

"Captain Martin," Travis said, "I want you to take this message to Gonzales."

"Yes, sir," Martin said.

Travis handed the note to Martin. "Bring back every able-bodied man you can find," he said. "And have this message relayed on by someone there. Colorado Smith and Mr.

Smither rode out yesterday. Perhaps you will see one of them to hand this off to."

Martin nodded and ran out to prepare his horse. Travis sat at his desk. Now for the hardest part: waiting.

At dusk, just as Albert Martin rode out of the Alamo and found the road to Gonzales, the bitter sound of the Deguello came blasting at the Alamo from the Mexican army band in Béxar. All around the fort, the men grimaced and started looking for cover. They knew what was coming. And, the moment the nightmare call ended, the bombardment began again. The men of the Alamo crouched and covered themselves and prayed that a shell would not find them in the dark.

Chapter Twenty

James Walker Fannin set up his headquarters in the chapel of La Bahía Mission or, as he preferred to call it, Fort Defiance. He liked his office because it made him appear very much the commander, seated behind his large desk, facing the door. Men entered, hat in hand, to ask his advice or to await his orders, and he, with his wealth of military experience, gave them the answers they needed.

At least, that is the way he saw it. His men barely gave Fannin a second thought. When he did come up in their conversation, they snickered and joked about how he hid in his quarters all day, not only avoiding the fight at hand, but also avoiding any kind of action at all. One wag suggested that his men should start calling him "Faintin'." It was not much of a joke, but the men of Fort Defiance found it hilarious.

While the men of the Alamo spent their days shoring up their crumbling defenses, the garrison at La Bahía had far fewer responsibilities. The walls were tall and solid, the cannon well placed, and the supplies more than adequate. Day to day, there was little for them to do but wait for something to happen. When they saw Colorado Smith galloping furiously toward the fort with Travis's most recent message, the men thought that their wait was over.

Many of the Texians at Fort Defiance knew Smith and greeted him enthusiastically as he rode through the gates. "Where's Fannin at?" Smith yelled to no one in particular. Jack Davis, a Pennsylvania boy, paused at his whittling long enough to point toward headquarters. Corporal Zaboly ran to Smith as he dismounted, then quickly ushered him into Fannin's presence.

Fannin read Travis's letter, frowning all the while. Smith refused his offer of a seat. He was eager to be on his way again and paced restlessly as Fannin read. "When did you leave the Alamo?" Fannin asked.

"Two days ago," Smith said.

Fannin leaned back in his chair and stroked his chin. He believed it made him look thoughtful. "So there's no way of knowing," he said to Smith, "by now, the garrison might have surrendered."

Colorado Smith smiled in amazement. "Jim Bowie?" he said incredulously. "Surrender?"

Fannin said, "Or perhaps they have been overrun."

Smith shook his head. "I do not believe that Santa Anna was ready to attack," he said. "It looked to me like the Mexicans were setting up for a siege."

Fannin sighed and stood up. He began to pace around the room. He looked very much like an officer with strategy on his mind.

"Fort Defiance," he said importantly, "where we sit, is equally important, strategically."

"Those men are in a desperate situation, sir," Smith said.

Fannin waved him away impatiently. "I understand that," he said. "But our supplies are low. And to risk the main force of our army in the open like that . . ."

He shook his head. Fannin saw that Smith was looking at him with a kind of disgust on his face. He straightened a little and said, "I will . . . consider this action, of course. The stand that Bowie and Colonel Travis have taken is very courageous."

Smith's expression changed from disgust to hopelessness. He realized that Fannin was not going to rush into anything. He suspected that Fannin was not actually going to do anything at all.

"Courageous," Fannin said, "but, if I may say so, ill advised."

Two arrows lay on the ground. One arrowhead was barbed, the other was smooth. Sam Houston, squatting and drinking from a bottle, watched two six-year-old Cherokee boys examine them.

"This one is for birds?" one asked.

"That is right," Houston replied in the boy's language.

The other boy picked up the smooth arrowhead. "And this one is for fishing."

Houston shook his head. "No."

"Is it for very big birds?" the boy asked.

Houston said, "It is for men."

The boys looked at the arrow with a new kind of respect. Houston looked up, his eyes squinting in the bright sunlight. A dark bird circled lazily in the sky above. Casually, Houston picked up the bird arrow and drew it back on a bow. At first glance the bird appeared to be a crow or perhaps a buzzard. But now Houston could see that the bird was a raven. Arrow pointed upward,

Houston stared at the bird for several seconds. Then he slowly lowered the bow.

Neither boy understood his reluctance to shoot the bird — it seemed to be a very easy shot, especially to a great hunter like Houston.

The sound of galloping hooves made Houston and the boys turn around and look down the trail. Deaf Smith was riding toward him. Smith had a stern look on his face, but that was not very unusual. It occurred to Houston that he had never actually seen the man smile.

"Deef," called Houston loudly.

Smith dismounted and held out his hand to Houston. "Sam." Houston shook his hand. He still held the bow and arrow in his left hand.

Houston said, "Well, I suppose that you have ridden all the way out here to give me some delightful news. I can tell by your sunny disposition."

Most men would have responded in kind, but Smith never engaged in verbal pleasantries. It was if he never had the time to joke. And he never seemed to understand that anybody else was joking. To Houston's greeting, he shook his head mournfully.

"No, sir, I got no good news at all. Far from it," Smith said.

Houston's face darkened. "Tell me," he said.

"The Matamoros Expedition, for one thing," Smith said. "It is a disaster. They are split up, probably dead by now. Johnson and Grant off one way, Fannin off t'other."

"Those damn fools. Those goddamned fools," Houston said. He flung the bow and arrow to the ground angrily. "I would say that they deserve what they get, but we need those men. What a stupid waste."

Deaf Smith nodded gravely. "Yes, sir," he said. Houston could tell from the agitated look on Smith's face that the bad news had not ended yet.

"What?" he said.

"Well, sir," Smith said, "there is another matter. Santa Anna has captured Béxar."

The news was not exactly unexpected, but it seemed too soon. How in the hell, he wondered, did Santa Anna get his army all the way up from Mexico City in the dead of winter? He always figured that the dictator was not quite human, but he always assumed that the men in the Mexican army were.

"When did this happen?" Houston said.

"Three days ago," said Smith. "Our troops are forted up in the Alamo."

The Alamo. Why did everybody who

came within a hundred miles of that place seem to fall under its spell? Every military man who saw it thought that it would make a fine, strong fort. And so far, they had all been terribly wrong. The place had meant nothing but defeat for everyone who ever occupied it. The men inside the Alamo now would be no exception.

Chief Bowles sat staring at the river. He had seen Houston talking with the other white man and could tell by the look on Houston's face that something big had happened outside. Houston had talked to him often about staying here, making a home with Talihina, finding contentment among the Cherokee. Chief Bowles knew this was just talk. Houston had a destiny. Perhaps it was a dark destiny, but it could not be denied. He would be leaving soon. Today, perhaps. He would never come back.

Houston asked Smith, "Do you have paper and a pencil?"

Smith nodded and dug through the ragged pack that he kept hanging over his shoulder. He produced an old envelope and a stub of a pencil and handed them to Houston.

As Houston scribbled, he said, "Take this back to Governor Smith. If Burnet and those other fools do not go off half-cocked, maybe we can still rally before this whole thing turns into a disaster."

Smith pocketed the note. "Where are you goin' to be, sir?" he said.

Houston looked around the village. With a stab of pain, he knew what he had to do. "I'll be along," he said. "Tell 'em all that I will be along directly."

Deaf Smith remounted. "You ought to get yourself something to eat before you leave, Deef," Houston said.

Smith shook his head. "Got some fatback and bread in my pack. I can eat in the saddle." He slapped his horse's flank and waved at Houston as he rode away.

"I will see you soon, Deef," Houston called, but he doubted that Smith heard him.

Chief Bowles felt Houston approach but did not turn around. When Houston sat beside him on the riverbank, the chief noted that he had changed into his white man's clothes — the long frock coat, the rough buckskin breeches and his odd tricorn hat.

The two men sat in silence for a moment, then Houston said in Cherokee, "How did I come by my Indian name?"

"The Raven is proud and dark," Chief Bowles replied. "And alone. That was you as a boy, when you first came to us."

"And now?" Houston asked in English.

Chief Bowles answered in English. "Now they have another name for you . . . 'Ootstetee Ardeetahskee.' "

"Ootstetee Ardeetahskee," Houston repeated, almost to himself. "The Big Drunk." He shook his head sadly.

Chief Bowles said, "In the stories, the Raven is often cursed. He is beaten and crushed and left for dead. But in the end he outwits his enemy."

Houston glanced over at Chief Bowles, but the old man did not take his eyes from the river. Houston knew he was trying to tell him something. But what?

"Of course, that is only in stories," Chief Bowles continued. "And you are the Raven no more."

Houston felt a touch on his shoulder. Talihina stood behind him. Her mouth looked set, determined, but there was deep sadness in her eyes. "Come," she said. "Come to my bed."

They had made love many times before, in the smoky closeness of a lodge, under the lush canopy of the forest, on the banks of the river, serenaded by its many songs. Talihina approached the act in a way completely unlike that of any of the Anglo women Houston had known — even those professionals for whom enthusiasm should have been a stock in trade. Talihina expressed her passion with total abandon, without shame, without the coy inhibitions that East Coast women seemed to think was essential to their mystique. Houston often felt like an animal in her embrace — powerful, free; not thinking, just feeling. Sometimes both would shout their pleasure to the skies, roaring like beasts, gasping and moaning with the intensity of the experience.

But today, their lovemaking was slow and tender. Talihina lay upon her back and gently guided him into her. As he thrust forward and established an easy rhythm, she never took her eyes from his. They did not say a word, nor did they make a sound, until the sad pleasure of the ending brought forth sighs and shudders.

Nor did they speak as they washed and dressed, and walked toward Houston's horse. He mounted and looked down at Talihina. If she asked him to stay, he did not know what he would do. Texas be damned. How could he live his life without this woman?

She spoke softly, in Cherokee, "Do not return here. Your pride has chosen for you."

Houston almost smiled; he was released.

Dreading the moment, he thought that he would be heartbroken. But he was not — he was relieved. Now, Houston could devote himself completely to the cause of Texas, the only mistress to whom he could ever truly give his heart.

Without a word, Houston slowly walked his horse away. The walk turned into a lope, then into a gallop as he disappeared down the trail. When she knew he was out of sight and beyond earshot, Talihina crumpled to the ground and wailed with grief.

Chapter Twenty-one

Margarita Fernandez was an old woman, widowed for over twenty years. Now that her children were grown — with children of their own — and she had no husband to take care of, Margarita had a lot of time on her hands. Her daughters cooked for her and cleaned her jacale and she was required to do little in return. She loved to watch after her grandchildren, and weave quilts and gossip with her friends in Béxar Plaza. But she could do these things, or not do them, as the spirit took her. Sometimes, she liked to spend her afternoons alone, just walking on the outskirts of town, where the countryside, and even some of the few buildings, had changed little since she was a girl.

As a child, Margarita had attended church services at the old mission across the river. She received her first communion in a little adobe chapel that had since been torn down. It had stood beside the old church, the building that her parents always forbade her to enter. It stood in ruins, filled with debris. Margarita and all her friends were convinced that the ancient limestone church was haunted, and they loved to sneak over at night and listen for the howls of departed souls that they knew must be trapped there. Sometimes, swarms of bats would fly from the church building, darkening the sky for a few moments with their numbers. "You see?" Margarita would tell the other children in a sepulchral voice. "Those are the spirits that haunt the mission. They take the form of bats and roam the countryside looking for living bodies to inhabit." She would point her finger at them, as if trying to settle on one particular child. "A living body . . . like . . . YOU!" she would shout, jabbing one of the children, who would then scream in terror.

Today, Margarita still enjoyed strolling over there in the afternoon, sitting in the shade of the old walls, remembering when it was a place filled with life, instead of by men who sought death. Every once in a while she would stay there until dusk, waiting for the bats to emerge. They no longer frightened her. Now they just made her sad for her lost youth.

There were no longer bats in the Alamo. They had been driven out by war. The silly, harmless terrors of her childhood had been supplanted by the all-too-real horrors of bloodshed and death. Margarita knew there were Béxarenos inside the old mission now, squared off against their own brothers in the brightly dressed army that occupied Béxar. It all seemed futile to her, and slightly ridiculous. All of this sword rattling, all of those threats. For what? All Margarita wanted was for Béxar to be like it was when she was a girl, a sleepy, peaceful town where nature shared its bounty and God had bestowed a surfeit of beauty and charm. But that was not to be, she thought. Men crave war like babies need milk, and there would only be peace again when they had all killed each other off and left the land to its own peaceful devices.

As she strolled over the bridge toward the mission, she saw some of the men on the walls glance at her, then look away. She was not important to them. She was not important to anybody. Margarita Fernandez did not worry much about that. She had lived too long and had seen too much pain and sorrow to worry too much about anything.

Seguin, Esparza and a few other Tejanos from Seguin's company were gathered on the west wall, staring out toward Béxar. When Margarita Fernandez walked by, Seguin called out to her. "Mother," he said.

Margarita looked up at him, shielding the sun from her eyes by holding her hand to her forehead. "I am not your mother," she said.

The Tejanos laughed. Seguin said, "They let you come and go as you please?"

"I am too old to matter," Margarita said. "Four months ago they were here and you were there." She pointed behind her to Béxar. "Then they left here and you were still there. Now they are there and you are here. I am too old to care anymore."

Scurlock stepped up behind Seguin and said, "Ask her what in hell they are waiting for."

Seguin leaned over the wall and said to Margarita, "Do you see any preparations for attack? What are they doing?"

The old woman shrugged. "The generals eat, the army starves."

Seguin looked at Scurlock and shrugged. Antsy and nervous, Scurlock had been cooped up long enough. He shouted toward Béxar, "Come on! Fight! We are waiting!" The Tejanos shook their heads. "Yer yeller!" Scurlock yelled. "Every Meskin is yeller!"

Suddenly, Scurlock realized what he had said. He turned sheepishly to Seguin's men and shook his head in silent apology.

Seguin put his hand on Scurlock's shoulder. "We are all Mexicans, Scurlock. Remember well the oath you took." Seguin looked back over the wall and said to Margarita, "Next time bring tortillas!"

Margarita Fernandez smiled and walked away, back toward the bridge. From the looks of the army in Béxar, these poor men would not be here long enough to enjoy any tortillas she might bring.

Scurlock sat down and shook his head. "This is one crazy mess," he said.

Across the way, in Béxar, Batres made his way across the plaza, passing carts, stepping around little flocks of chickens, pushing past locals. He adjusted his jacket and walked up to the door of a house and knocked. The woman who opened the door was the mother of the stunning Tejana who had caught Santa Anna's eye when he rode into town. The girl was standing behind her mother, peering at Batres shyly.

Batres removed his hat and bowed. "Madam," he said to the woman, "she is even more beautiful upon inspection."

The woman opened the door wider. "Come in, señor," she said. "We have much to discuss."

An hour later, Santa Anna rode with Batres down Potrero Street, toward the front lines. "Her father is dead, Excellency," Batres said, "and her mother will not let her daughter see you. Unless . . ."

Santa Anna said, "Unless?"

Batres shook his head sadly, "Unless you marry her first. Unfortunate."

Santa Anna smiled. "I think the ceremony should be simple. Do you agree?"

"But, General," Batres said, "by your order we brought no priests with us . . . and anyway . . ."

Santa Anna glared at Batres and the aide immediately understood.

"A simple ceremony," he said. "Yes."

Santa Anna gestured toward his soldiers. He said, "The men will be happy to see me."

In the Alamo, Juan Seguin stood beside Crockett. They were both peering over the palisade into the distance. "Look to the ridge, David," Seguin said. Crockett looked at him questioningly. "You said you wanted to see him," Seguin said. He pointed up the hill. Crockett squinted. Sure enough, Santa Anna and Batres were approaching a cannon placement on horseback.

Crockett said to Seguin, "That is Santa Anna?"

Seguin nodded.

"Quite the peacock," Crockett said. "Is he more politician or soldier?"

Seguin said, "Whichever is appropriate at the time." He smiled to Crockett. Crockett smiled back, understanding that Seguin was speaking not only of Santa Anna.

"When General Iturbide betrayed the fatherland, he made himself emperor," Seguin said. "So what did the young Santa Anna do to gain favor? He courted the emperor's sister."

Crockett laughed. "Heck, a man's got to get along in life. I was pretty ambitious as a young feller myself."

Seguin said, "She was sixty years old. . . ."

Crockett stopped laughing and glanced back over at Santa Anna on the hill. "I was never that ambitious."

Santa Anna and Batres rode casually along the front line, inspecting each cannon placement. They arrived at Jesús's regiment; Santa Anna proudly reviewed his forces. "It is a beautiful day," the general said. "A beautiful day."

The very presence of Santa Anna made the soldados nervous. Each tried to avoid his gaze, as if he were some deadly form of snake. Santa Anna spied Jesús, almost hiding behind the older men. He summoned the boy to him.

"Soldier!" Santa Anna snapped. Jesús stepped out and stood before him. Santa Anna said approvingly to Batres, "A boy fighting on the front, like a man." Turning to Jesús he said, "You are very brave. I wager your grandfather fought the Comanches." Jesús nodded. Santa Anna continued, "And now your father is very proud of you, too."

Jesús almost said nothing, but the anger coursed through his veins too quickly and violently. As calmly as possible, Jesús said, "He is dead. He was hanged."

Santa Anna shook his head sadly. "Ah, murdered by the gringos . . ." He pointed toward the Alamo. "I promise, you will have your revenge."

"He was hanged by you," Jesús said, looking directly into Santa Anna's eyes. "At Orizaba. When you were fighting for the Spanish."

Everyone tensed. Jesús waited for Santa Anna to order his arrest and execution. He wondered if he would be tortured first. He wondered if his grandfather would ever find out what had happened to him.

To his astonishment, Santa Anna began to smile.

"We are Mexicans now, my friend," he said to Jesús in a calculatedly benevolent voice. "That is an honor for which we all will risk our lives many times."

Santa Anna turned, suddenly angry, fixating on the cannons. "Why is this battery so far back?" he demanded.

The battery sergeant looked to the others, then stepped forward. He said, "Your Excellency, with respect, and for your safety . . . It is said that the Davy Crockett is in the Alamo." He pointed to the Alamo. "I have heard many stories of this great man. From my cousin."

Santa Anna said to the battery sergeant, "You are afraid of this Crockett?"

He dismounted and took a few steps toward the Alamo. The sergeant moved forward, trying to make his point to Santa Anna, who paused.

"It is said he can leap rivers — from there to here," the battery sergeant said. "And his rifle is accurate. He can shoot a fly off a burro's swishing tail at yards."

Santa Anna looked at the battery sergeant and shook his head, as if he had never seen a bigger coward in his life. He strode toward the Alamo, swaggering, hands on hips.

At the palisade, Seguin watched as Crockett smiled, slowly loaded his rifle and took the ramrod from the muzzle. He carefully lifted the gun and peered down the sight. Autry whispered to Seguin, "I have seen him shoot an ant off an antelope at six hundred feet."

A few other men gathered around, sensing something important. Everyone had heard about his otherworldly prowess with a rifle. Now they were about to see it in action.

Crockett's finger tensed on the trigger.

"That's it, Generalissimo," Crockett said, squinting one eye as he aimed. "Twenty more feet and I will give ya a little peck on the cheek."

Santa Anna strutted in front of the cannon placement. He dug his heels in the dirt, making a mark. "Move them to here!" he ordered.

At the palisade, Crockett took a deep breath and held it. Every man watching did the same. Crockett's finger squeezed the trigger. . . . Santa Anna looked in the direction of the Alamo. On the wall, six hundred feet away, there was a tiny puff of smoke. . . . The uniform on Santa Anna's shoulder tore open. He stumbled backward with a look of shock on his face. Batres and the battery sergeant rushed to his aid. Santa Anna quickly regained his composure and waved them away impatiently. Stepping back a step or two, the president glared at the Alamo. No one said a word.

The men surrounding Crockett were cheering and slapping him on the back. Crockett relaxed from his sniper position and smiled. "Wind kicked up," he said and tossed a handful of dust in the air.

Santa Anna continued to step backward. Now safely behind the cannon, he shouted, "Answer the pirates!"

Under the direction of the battery sergeant, the cannon crew loaded the gun, lit the fuse and a ball soared through the air toward the old mission. It landed in the middle of the Alamo's courtyard. As it rolled across the dirt, men scattered in every direction, seeking quick shelter. Travis ducked into his headquarters and braced himself for the blast.

The cannonball rolled to a stop . . . but it did not explode. It sat there on the ground like a time bomb, the wick still sparking. Travis emerged from his headquarters and pointed to Ward. "Get that shell and take it to Captain Dickinson," Travis said.

Ward and the other men hesitated, looking to Bowie and Crockett for orders that did not seem quite so insane.

Travis said impatiently, "We can reuse it."

Ward still did not move. Sparks continued to come off the ball.

Ward finally shook his head. "You get it yourself," he said.

Bowie and the men watched this direct disobedience, waiting for Travis to demand Ward's arrest, wondering what they would do if he did. Instead, with a look of contempt on his face, Travis stared down Ward as he walked to the shell, pulled out the burning wooden fuse, dropped it on the ground and stepped on it. Around the compound, every man stopped what he was doing in order to watch as Travis carried the shell to the eighteen pounder. There, he handed it to Almeron Dickinson and said, "Give it back to them."

Dickinson nodded and smiled. "Yes, sir."

When the Mexican ball was loaded in the Alamo's largest cannon, Travis shouted, "Fire the cannon!"

Dickinson touched a light to the cannon and sent the ball hurling back toward the Mexican cannon emplacement. Nobody said a word, but Bowie was clearly impressed with Travis. Bowic's men, seeing him impressed, were impressed themselves. Travis turned to the men below him. "Fire once from each cannon!" he said.

There was a moment's hesitation among

the men. They had all voted for Bowie to command them, and now they were not sure what to do. Bowie said to them, "You heard the colonel."

Travis turned to him. "Lieutenant Colonel . . . Colonel."

Bowie almost smiled. "You heard the man," he said. "Let us give 'em a taste."

Men cheered, racing to their artillery posts, loading and firing cannon — one, two, three shots in a row. The response from the Mexicans was immediate — and deafening. Over the constant roar of the cannon, the Texians could hear the disconcerting sound of the Deguello. The men of the Alamo could only crouch, in as much safety as they could find, and wait it out.

In his headquarters, Travis put the finishing touches on another letter:

. . . I have every reason to apprehend an attack from Santa Anna's whole force very soon; but I shall hold out to the last extremity, hoping to secure reinforcements in a day or two. Do hasten on aid to me as rapidly as possible, as from the superior number of the enemy, it will be impossible for us to keep them out much longer. If they overpower us, we will fall sacrifice at the shrine of

our country, and we hope posterity and our country will do our memory justice. Give me help, oh my country! Victory or death!

As Travis wrote furiously, Joe made coffee. Seguin stood at the door. "You called for me, Colonel?" he said.

Travis completed the letter, signed it, then folded the paper. He looked up at Seguin and said, "We have no idea if any of our couriers made it out. You know the land and the language." He held the letter out to Seguin.

Seguin shook his head and said, "Colonel, you are asking me to leave my men behind."

Travis said, "I am asking you to deliver a message to Houston and return with a response. I am counting on it." Seguin stared at him, about to say something else. Travis broke in before he could utter a word. "I am ordering it," he said.

Travis continued to hold the letter out. He hesitated for a long moment, but finally Seguin took the letter and walked away.

Joe brought a cup of coffee to Travis's desk and carefully set it down. He said, "He comin' any day now ain't he, Mister William? Colonel Fannin?"

Travis turned to Joe, wishing he could lie. He decided to give it a try. He smiled heartily and said, "Any day now, Joe."

Joe, accustomed to white men who said one thing and meant another, sighed and went back to his cot.

Out in the Alamo courtyard, near the main gate, Seguin finished saddling a horse. Bowie's horse. Bowie leaned against the doorway of his quarters alongside the main gate. "Do not give her too much water," he said to Seguin. "She's just like me — drink too much and she's not worth a damn."

"I will bring her back to you, Santiago," Seguin said.

Bowie coughed. "Bring yourself back safe," he said. "Her, I do not think I will be needing anymore."

Seguin mounted. As he prepared to ride out, he spotted Travis walking over to him. Travis said, "Tell Houston I will fire a cannon at dawn, noon and dusk each day our flag still flies."

Seguin nodded.

Travis shook his hand. "Go with God."

Seguin whistled distinctively to his men on the west wall; it was a private signal they had developed for themselves. They might be fighting side by side with the gringos, but it was always best to stick together. Seguin called out, "I will see you soon, my friends!" He waved. When he did, men on the north wall started firing their rifles and one cannon as a diversion. Bowie slapped the horse's crup and Seguin raced out the gate.

Crockett stood at the palisade, watching Seguin thread away into the night. Bowie walked over to him. "Makes a man ponder the possibilities, do it not?" he said. Bowie slumped in the shadows at the end of the low barracks. "Even the great Davy Crockett."

Crockett said, "You are kind of famous, too, Mr. Bowie."

Bowie said, "Not famous, notorious. There's a difference." He peered at Crockett. "Lose your fur cap?"

Crockett smiled a little sheepishly. "I just put it on when it is extra cold." Bowie still stared at him, not convinced. "Truth is," Crockett said, "I only started wearing that thing because of that feller in that play they did about me." He looked off into the darkness beyond the fort. "People expect things," he said softly.

Bowie nodded. "Ain't it so." They sat silently for a moment, then Bowie said, "Can I ask you something?"

Crockett said, "All right."

Bowie asked, with a look of studied seriousness on his face, "Which was tougher:

jumping the Mississippi or riding a light-ning bolt?"

Crockett grinned. "Stories are like tad-poles. Turn your back on one and it's grown arms and legs and gone hoppin' all over cre-ation." His smile faded a little and he looked Bowie in the eye. "And I tell you, I did not make one cent off that book that feller wrote. If anyone ever tells you they wanna write you up, Jim, you make 'em pay you first."

A cannon shot boomed from the Mexican lines and hit the north wall opposite them. It brought their attention back to their situa-tion.

"Can you catch a cannonball?" Bowie said. Neither man smiled this time.

Crockett sighed. "If it was just simple old me, David, from Tennessee, I might drop over the wall some night and take my chances," Crockett said. "But this Davy Crockett feller, they are all watching him. He's been fightin' on this wall every day of his life."

Bowie nodded. He understood what Crockett was saying. Perhaps, he under-stood it better than any other man in the fort could have. "Sam Houston sent me down here to blow this fort up," Bowie said. He paused for a long moment while both he and Crockett considered the idea. Bowie said, "I wish I had listened to him."

Crockett said, "I wish I had not."

Bowie tried to rise but collapsed. Crockett and Autry helped him to his feet and walked him the few steps to the bed in his quarters. Standing that close, Crockett could feel the heat of the fever radiating from Bowie. They gently laid him on his cot and Juana came over to him with a damp cloth to soothe his face. Travis walked into the room as Autry left to return to the palisade. Sam sat opposite, ready to help if ordered, but unwilling to volunteer.

"He is burning with fever," Juana said.

Travis said, "Draw him a tub of cool water. If the fever breaks, try to get him to drink something." He paused. "Something not whiskey."

At the top of the hill to the south of the Alamo, Seguin, now safe, stopped his horse. He turned and looked back on the lights of Béxar and the mission. Down below were his hometown, his friends. He would return. He swore it to himself, and to them.

Chapter Twenty-two

Colonel Frank Johnson sat by the window of his quarters and watched the cold rain hammer down on the streets of San Patricio. When his aide, Private Todish, brought him a cup of fresh coffee, Johnson thanked him, took a cautious sip, and chuckled to himself. It was a good night to be snug and warm inside. He listened to the howling wind and driving rain and smiled when he thought of Grant and his company, out in the wilderness trying to round up wild horses. They must be miserable right now. But Johnson was perfectly content. There was nothing he enjoyed more than a warm bed on a cold, stormy night, especially if that bed contained a willing lady. But there was no such good fortune tonight. The citizens of San Patricio were not altogether thrilled to have them there. That meant the local señoritas had not been nearly as friendly and accommodating as in other towns — especially Béxar.

Todish turned down Johnson's bed and withdrew. Johnson picked up a favorite novel, *Quentin Durward*, and pulled the candle on the table a little closer.

Grant had worried about splitting their command. His wild-horse expedition left Johnson holding San Patricio with only thirty-four men. "The horses are crucial," Johnson had told him. "We are in no danger here for the moment. The sooner we are fully equipped, the sooner we can move on to meet Fannin at Goliad and then move on to capture Matamoros." Grant had reluctantly agreed, and rode out the next day with twenty-six men, including Placido Benavides and Reuben R. Brown. Both of them were excellent horsemen and Benavides, especially, knew the area like the back of his hand.

They could be expected to return in the next day or so with a herd of wild horses. If Grant and his men were unsuccessful, then they would simply have to move on, farther south, and hope that they would have better luck closer to Matamoros.

Johnson read the thrilling prose of Sir Walter Scott for nearly an hour until he found his eyes drooping with fatigue. He stood up, stretched and yawned. As he took the first step toward his bed, he felt a violent explosion. It rocked the house so brutally that Johnson was almost thrown to his knees.

At first he thought it was a particularly hellish thunder. But when it happened five times in quick succession, he knew what was causing the uproar: cannon fire.

On the hill above San Patricio, General José Urrea smiled benignly at the scene. The Texians had been so oblivious of danger that he found his task almost too easy. When his intelligence reported that a small party of Texians had ridden out of San Patricio two days earlier, Urrea sent other scouting parties to report on the defenses of the town. The foolish Texians had divided their few men into five separate parties. Two were guarding horses. One stood paltry sentinel at the main road leading into town, and two others guarded the outer edges.

Urrea knew that these five parties constituted nearly the entire Texian force. There could not be more than five or six other men in town. He had pulled his army into position earlier in the day, without alerting the Texians down in San Patricio. When the hard rain began to fall at dusk, Urrea knew that the time was right to act. No one would ever expect an attack during such weather. He lined up three cannon and aimed them at the town. Then he dispatched troops to cover each of the five parties of Texians. The result would not even be an attack, in the strictest sense of the word; it would be more like target practice.

Urrea waited until nearly three o'clock in the morning, to make sure that the Texians would be caught totally off guard. His riflemen took every precaution to keep their powder and muskets dry, and raced silently to their positions, two hundred yards from San Patricio. The cannon fire would be their signal to rain volleys of musket balls on the rebels.

Because of the driving rain, Johnson barely heard the musket fire in the distance, but the relentless cannon fire convinced him that the battle was already lost. He thought that placing his men around the town would make it certain that the Mexicans could not approach on any side without being spotted. Johnson had not counted on an attack like this, not in the middle of the night; not in a driving rainstorm. Now his men were hopelessly separated and there was no way to get them together again, or even to get orders to them.

The Texians at their posts were startled out of wet blankets and uncomfortable sleep by volley after volley of gunfire. They jumped to their positions and began firing into the darkness. The small, separated parties fought bravely, but they were beaten before they started. In moments ten Texians lay dead or dying on the ground. As over a hundred Mexicans began to descend into the town, the remaining eighteen Texians stood up with their hands over their heads.

Johnson knew that a few of his officers were in town, but he did not know where. Even Todish, his aide, had vanished without a trace, no doubt scurrying into the darkness to save his own skin. Johnson thought about it for a moment, as the house continued to shudder with the cannon blasts, and decided that Todish's plan was a good one. Discretion must be the better part of valor on this rainy night. Dressing quickly, Johnson slipped out of the house, ran down the street and scurried out to the nearby woods. Once there he would keep running until he couldn't run anymore.

Dr. Grant sniffed the air and said, "It smells like rain."

Plácido Benavides stretched out comfortably on his bedroll and pointed toward the horizon, over the trees. "Look how dark the sky is over San Patricio," he said. "I wager that they are getting soaked." He was still for a moment. "Listen," he said. "Do you hear thunder?"

Reuben R. Brown smiled and sipped from his coffee cup. "Well, better them than us. At least they got roofs."

Benavides laughed, but Grant did not. Grant almost never laughed. Just one more reason why Benavides would rather have been with Johnson than with Grant. He had fought alongside Johnson during the siege of Béxar and had spent several perilous hours with him under fire at the Veramendi House. He admired Johnson's bravery, but he also appreciated his sense of humor. Grant, Benavides believed, was completely lacking in humor. But he had to admit that the Scotsman was brave, the kind of man who always rode to the sound of the guns, no matter how desperate the situation.

Brown had arrived in Béxar the very day that General Cós and his troops were filing out of the Alamo in defeat. Feeling that he had missed all the action, Brown had enthusiastically joined up with the Matamoros Expedition. He volunteered for this wild-horse roundup in much the same way — he far preferred to be doing something, even something dangerous, than to spend idle hours in tedious safety.

Benavides pulled his blanket up around his neck. "Perhaps we had better get some sleep while we can, before we get soaked with whatever is raining down on San Patricio right now."

The next morning dawned bright and clear, with no sign of rain in the sky. Grant, Benavides and Brown broke camp and began riding at an easy gallop back toward town. About a half mile behind them, the other twenty-three men of their party were riding herd on over four hundred wild horses. Brown was delighted at their good luck. It had taken only three days — three arduous days — to round up the horses and now, with them, the last obstacle to moving on Matamoros was hurdled. Now they were in for some real action.

Up ahead in the woods, about sixty mounted dragoons waited. General Urrea had questioned some of the Texian prisoners during the night. One Texian, a former New Yorker named Groneman, had cracked under the threat of torture and revealed where Grant and his party were. Urrea was not certain that they would return today, but he knew they would come back soon. The dragoons settled in for a long wait, but it was less than an hour after they arrived that they heard the thundering of hundreds of approaching hooves. Like the attack on San Patricio the night before, this was almost too easy.

The dragoons allowed Grant, Benavides and Brown to ride past, then the sixty horsemen emerged from the wood and raced forward, cutting off the main force, lances leveled. The startled Texians reached for their guns, but many of them were impaled before they could make a move. Others had pistols at the ready. They fired several shots, knocking two of the dragoons out of their saddles.

At the sound of the gunfire, Benavides whirled around. "Grant! Brown!" he yelled. "Behind us!"

Grant and Brown turned their horses around and galloped back. When they reached Benavides he had already loaded two pistols. Impatiently, he waved them on, "Let's go!" he said. "We have to help them!"

He started to ride toward the fight, but Grant quickly grabbed his reins. "Not you," he said. "If the Mexicans are here, then they have already come through San Patricio. That probably means that the town has fallen. You need to ride on to Goliad and warn Fannin about this."

Benavides shook his head furiously. "No!" he shouted. "This is my fight, as well as yours."

Brown said, "Grant's right, Plácido. You grew up here. You know every crack and crevice in the ground. You can make it. Maybe we couldn't."

Benavides looked at the two men. He knew they were right. Without another word, he nodded firmly, turned his horse and galloped away.

Brown and Grant looked back at the battle raging two hundred yards away. They saw that the ground was already littered with Texian dead. There seemed to be almost no Mexican casualties. The dragoons were encountering far more trouble from the wild horses, which were stampeding, breaking through the Mexican ranks and disappearing into the woods.

Grant said, "What do you think?"

Brown smiled a rueful smile. "Never did want to grow old, anyway. I believe we had better ride in and die with our boys."

Grant held his hand out and Brown shook it. "Let us go amongst 'em," Grant said. "God bless you."

The two men rode directly for the Mexicans, firing their pistols from the saddle. They brought down two more Mexicans with four bullets. One dragoon wheeled around and rammed a lance through the breast of Brown's horse. The horse pitched forward and Brown flew from the saddle, landing unhurt in a pile of brush by the road. As the dragoon came for him, Brown leaped to his feet and sprinted toward a riderless horse. He jumped into the saddle, narrowly avoiding the tip of the dragoon's lance.

Grant, his pistols empty and with no time to reload, pulled his sword from its sheath and slashed away at the attacking Mexicans. He sliced a deep cut into one Mexican's arm and managed to stab another in the throat. Brown reloaded one pistol and shot a Mexican as he rode up behind Grant. Brown shouted, "They are all dead, Grant! We'd best get out of here!"

Grant was not the kind of man who shrank from a fight, but he was also not suicidal. He nodded at Brown and turned his horse around. The two Texians raced down the road with fifteen dragoons in close pursuit. Brown managed once again to load his pistol. He heard Grant call, "Look out!" and turned to see the lance of a dragoon just a few inches from his back. Stretching his arm behind him, he fired the pistol point-blank into the Mexican's face. Dead, the rider continued to sit upright in the saddle of the galloping horse for several dozen yards before slipping off and rolling into the woods.

Grant and Brown were able to maintain their lead, mile after mile, but the Mexicans showed no sign of slowing. They heard men calling from behind them, "Surrender!" "Do not force us to kill you! Surrender!"

Grant shouted, "They want us to give up, Reuben."

"I think we had better not," Brown replied. "We know what they do to men who surrender."

After a gallop of nearly seven miles, all of the horses showed signs of exhaustion. Somehow, Grant and Brown managed to stay out front. Suddenly, Brown felt a blinding pain in his arm and felt himself being pulled from his horse. A dragoon had thrown his lance. Its point had embedded itself just above Brown's elbow. The weight of the lance threw off Brown's balance and he fell to the ground. The Mexican who brought him down rode up to Brown with a rope. Brown raised his pistol and fired. Blood spurted from the man's temple and he fell to the ground, jerking spasmodically for a few seconds before going still.

He had no time to reload. Other dragoons were dismounting and walking toward him.

Behind them, he heard Grant scream. A dragoon had pulled him off his horse and the Scotsman's body was immediately pierced by several lances.

With effort, Brown got up and attempted to run. A Mexican looped a lasso over his head and dragged him to the ground. Unable to move, Brown looked at the Mexicans with curiosity. He was too exhausted and in too much pain to be frightened. Just before he passed out he thought, *I wonder why they are not killing me.*

Brown woke up in a cold brown room with stone walls. He had been covered by a thin blanket. His arm had been bandaged and a plate of bread and a cup of coffee had been placed on a small table beside his cot. The door to the room was open, but two Mexican soldiers stood guard there. When they heard him stirring, one turned around and said in perfect English, "Good morning."

Brown took a sip of coffee. It was cold but felt wonderful coursing down his parched throat. When he felt that he could speak again he said, "Where am I?"

The soldier said, "Matamoros." He laughed. "Is that not where you wanted to go?" The soldier repeated his sentence in Spanish and the man beside him burst into laughter. The first soldier said, "Texian, come here." He pointed down the hallway. "There is something that you should see." Brown cautiously stood up. Every muscle in his body screamed with pain. He limped over to the door and looked toward where the Mexican was pointing.

In a room down the hall, Grant's bloody corpse had been placed on a table. It was surrounded by a group of laughing Mexican officers who plunged their swords into it over and over, as if enjoying a particularly grisly party game.

Brown felt the bile rise in his throat. "My God!" he said. "Why are they doing that?"

"That is James Grant," the soldier said, as if that were explanation enough. "Many of the officers knew him."

Brown was aware that Grant had been involved in some shady business dealings in Mexico. He could only guess that some of those dealings involved some of the men who were currently having such a gleeful time mutilating his corpse. He watched in horror for a few seconds, wondering if this was some sort of macabre preview of what the Mexicans had in store for him.

Brown limped back to his cot and sat down. He leaned his head against the cold stone wall and closed his eyes, waiting for them to come and kill him, too.

In the Public Building at San Felipe, the faces that glared at each other in the smoky, dimly lit hall of politics had not changed much. Burnet, Baker, Rusk and Smith still opposed one another. Behind them and at all points around the room were the same men with the same self-righteous expressions, the same polarization.

Governor Smith, now looking exhausted after weeks of debate, stood up before the hostile War Party and indicated a man seated to his left. The man had a broad, friendly face framed by tightly curled hair and prodigious muttonchops. He smiled amiably at the men facing him. No one smiled in return.

Smith said, "We have Mr. Harold Thatcher-Rhyme of the country of England." There were some low boos at the mention of England. "He represents interests willing to invest five million pounds in the new country of Texas."

Smith expected this news to be greeted by hearty cheers. Instead, the applause from the Peace Party was nearly drowned out by the jeers from the War Party. Burnet stood at the podium in the middle of the room, his wild shock of black hair aiming at the ceiling like marsh weeds, his face tight and angry. Glaring at Thatcher-Rhyme, Burnet boomed, "Need I remind anyone, for this soldier, the War of 1812 is very fresh in my mind."

Thompson, the ill-tempered and corrupt South Carolinian, growled, "For me, too!" Others shouted in support. Thatcher-Rhyme stared at them in shock. He could not believe that these hooligans were in charge of creating the republic of Texas.

Smith kept on. "We must have resources to support our army and navy. . . ."

"Resources!" Burnet bellowed. "Sir, at this very moment our soldiers are held in the Alamo against a force of thousands. They have put their hopes in Colonel Fannin, who despite his pedigree, has found himself ill equipped to lead, much less march an army. In his letters he begs to be replaced." He handed one of Fannin's letters to Smith, who sat down and began to read. With each line, Smith's face dropped more and more.

In a quieter voice, Burnet said, "And there are other letters. . . ." He pulled a letter from his vest pocket and held it aloft. "This from Colonel Travis," he said. A pall came over the room. Even the blustering aggressors of the War Party knew the gravity of Travis's situation.

Burnet read the letter aloud. ". . . and so I call upon you in the name of liberty, of patriotism and everything dear to the American character . . ." At the word "American," Burnet glared at Thatcher-Rhyme, who rolled his eyes and sighed deeply. Burnet continued, ". . . to come to our aid with all dispatch. . . . If this call is neglected, I am determined to sustain myself as long as possible and die like a soldier who never forgets what is due to his own honor and that of his country — victory or death!"

The room was uncharacteristically silent. "Can we allow these brave men to perish while we talk?" Burnet said. Around the rooms there were murmurs of "No."

"That is right!" Burnet shouted. "We must fight! We must go to the Alamo!"

Now the room roared back to its usual volume. The men cheered and shouted, "Hear! Hear!" Even the Peace Party realized that this was an action that must be taken.

Burnet noticed him first. Sam Houston stood in the doorway, watching the proceedings with an expression of distaste.

"Houston!" Sherman said in surprise. Mosley Baker glared at him and demanded,

"Why are you here?" The head of every man in the room turned toward Houston. He stood there for a long moment, taking it all in.

"I came to stop you people from killing yourselves," Houston said, stepping into the room, "a service for which I feel certain I will never be properly thanked."

He began walking among the crowd. "We can afford amateur military operations no longer," he said.

Burnet called out from the podium, "Are you slewed, Houston?"

Houston ignored him, looking around accusingly at the self-righteous politicians surrounding him. "We can afford amateur government no longer," he said.

Burnet shouted, "Houston, you are raving drunk!"

Houston continued to speak calmly, addressing neither Burnet's insults nor the angry mood of the room. He said, "You stripped me of my men to pillage a town of no military value three hundred miles away." He grasped the seated Sherman by the shoulders and put his face close to his ear. "How did that work out for you?" Sherman winced and wriggled out of Houston's grasp. The faces of the War Party were grim. They knew exactly how the

Matamoros Expedition had worked out.

Houston indicated an empty chair at the table. "Where is the illustrious catamite, Dr. Grant?" he said. "What has become of his conquering Matamoros party?"

No one spoke.

"Dead," Houston said. "Gone. We must not repeat the same mistake." He sat down in what had been Grant's chair and gazed from face to face. "I will raise an army," he said quietly but firmly. "We will relieve the Alamo." The men listened closely. Was he actually saying things that they agreed with?

He picked up a page of the unfinished declaration of independence and brandished it in Sherman's face. "But," he said, "we will do this only when we have declared independence and created a government that can be legally recognized by the nations of the world." His voice grew even quieter. Some of the men had to strain to hear what he was saying. "For that," Houston said, "is what every besieged man in the Alamo is fighting for."

Still, no one said a word. But they all knew he was right. Thatcher-Rhyme stood up. He could not help himself. "Finally!" he said, gesturing toward Houston. "Good God. Listen to the man!"

Chapter Twenty-three

The San Antonio River swirled and eddied happily, a ribbon of tranquility winding and curving through a countryside anticipating spring. It flowed without interruption. The presence of an army in Béxar had no effect on it, just as it made little impact on the day-to-day lives of the Béxarenos who had stayed behind. War threatened and cannon fire shook the timbers of their homes. Nevertheless, through it all, meals had to be cooked, floors swept, animals fed, babies bathed. About fifty yards upstream from the footbridge, near the south wall of the Alamo, a woman knelt beside the river, washing her clothes, just as she did every week at the same spot. Armies would come and go, men would live and die, but life somehow always managed to go on, in all its mundane splendor.

As she scrubbed hard lye soap onto one of her husband's two shirts, the woman's thoughts were only of the myriad of chores that faced her. When she heard a sudden noise behind her, she nearly shrieked at being shocked out of her reverie. A *cazadore*, or light infantryman, knelt behind her, holding a finger to his lips. "Shh . . ." he cautioned. Behind him, moving like silent death through the woods were the Matamoros Permanentes, one hundred strong. They marched in formation, double time, heading for the jacales that had been built near the southwest corner of the Alamo.

Daniel Cloud once again found himself in the position of sounding the alarm. He saw them first and shouted, "Here they come, here they come!"

The woman hurriedly gathered her laundry and rushed back to her home in Béxar, praying that she could get out of range before the shooting started.

In the courtyard of the Alamo, men ran past the earthwork redoubt whose twin cannon were aimed directly at the fort's main gate. Then each climbed ladders to the top of the low barracks and hustled up the ramp to the eighteen pounder or took an empty slot at the palisade.

Crockett and the others at the palisade

checked to make sure that their rifles were loaded. "You fellers keep a sharp lookout," Crockett said to Autry. "I will go see what Travis makes of this." Crockett ran up the ramp at the southwest corner and stood at Travis's side.

The Mexicans were just out of range. For a long, silent moment the men of the Alamo simply stared at them, and they stared back — two sides sizing each other up. Then a Mexican officer barked a command and the soldiers double-timed into a new formation closer to the Alamo. When they were in position, they lined up to fire.

Travis held his arm out. "Hold your fire," he said. "They are measuring our strength."

The officer shouted "Fire!" and the Mexicans sent a volley into the Alamo. Musket balls hit around Travis. Men all around him — including Crockett — ducked for cover, but Travis stood firm. The men on the wall stared at him as if he had gone insane.

Calmly, Travis said, "You may fire at will, gentlemen."

A volley from the Texians blasted the Mexican ranks. Autry had a stack of loaded rifles next to him. He aimed the first one and fired. A Mexican fell, a musket ball in his forehead. Autry nodded to himself with satisfaction, then picked up the next rifle. He fired again and, once more, a soldado fell dead. "At this rate," he said, "I am going to give Crockett a run for his money."

All along the south wall, men were firing as rapidly as they could reload. Crockett paced around near the eighteen pounder, a big grin on his face. "Make 'em count, boys," he called out. "Do not waste your powder!"

A bullet hit the wall a few inches from Crockett's foot. He jumped back in surprise. "Pert near blew my bunions off," he said. Crockett aimed at the man he believed shot at him. A single shot to the chest and the man was down.

Travis leaped to the eighteen pounder and a musket ball pinged off the barrel. All around him, the men noticed his bravery and were mightily impressed. Without realizing that they had had a change of heart, many of the men in the Alamo had begun to think of Travis as their commander, no matter which way they had voted that night in the cantina.

Almeron Dickinson loaded the big gun. Travis nodded at him. "Mr. Dickinson . . ." he said. Almeron touched the cannon with his torch and, in the distance, one of the jacales splintered apart. This was too much for the Mexicans; they fled back to their lines.

Autry whooped and shouted, "Lookit 'em go! Run, you rabbits!" The other men cheered. Crockett turned to Travis and said, "Them little shacks offer pretty good cover."

"I agree," Travis said, "but we cannot waste more cannon shot."

Crockett smiled. "I wouldn't mind stretchin' my legs."

An hour later, sharpshooters fell into position, taking aim. The main gate opened and Crockett and four of his men scrambled out holding torches. Crockett headed toward the jacales, his men fanning out behind him. The men approached the little timber shacks cautiously. Crockett, in the lead, circled to the back of the first hut. Using his torch, he lit the straw roof. Immediately, he heard a noise within and before he could shout a warning, two Mexican soldiers burst through the flaming door, firing their weapons. One musket misfired, exploding in the hands of the soldier, splitting his face open from chin to eyebrow. The other soldier shot and missed, then jumped at Crockett, pulling a large knife from his belt. Crockett fumbled to reload but the man was only inches away. Suddenly, and soundlessly, a hole opened in the Mexican's chest and a crimson spray hit Crockett full in the face. Surprised, the soldier fell to his knees, then crumpled to the ground, dead.

Crockett heard cheering from the walls of the Alamo. Looking in that direction, he saw Travis lowering a rifle and handing it back to its owner. Crockett gave a little salute of gratitude, but Travis did not respond.

In a few more moments, the jacales were blazing furiously. With the dry wood of their walls and the straw on their roofs, they only lasted a few seconds before collapsing into several heaps of ashes. Cheering, the Texians congratulated each other and began to return to the Alamo. Crockett brought up the rear. A strange sound made him stop in his tracks. Behind him, a wounded cazadore, still alive in the grass, his leg mangled, was trying to load powder into his Baker rifle. Crockett turned and saw him, quickly unsheathing his knife. When he did, the cazadore crossed himself, dropped the gun and began slowly and painfully dragging himself backward through the grass. Crockett followed along, watching him curiously, as if the soldado were a fly who had lost a wing and was staggering in a futile circle. The Mexican began muttering prayers. He stopped and curled himself into a ball, his eyes shut tightly, waiting for the gringo to finish him off.

Crockett sheathed his knife and grabbed the cazadore's rifle, which was lying on the ground. He admired the weapon for a moment, and then shouldered it. "Muchas gracias," he said. Crockett turned and followed the others through the high grass. The cazadore, in shock, watched him disappear, back toward the old mission.

Rather than walk back through the gate, Crockett headed straight for the low wall at the southwest corner. Travis and Autry leaned over the wall and extended their arms to help Crockett climb back into the fort. Around them, the men cheered, whooped and slapped Crockett on the back.

But the cheering was interrupted by the terrible sound of a scream. In Bowie's quarters, Juana tried her best to comfort her brother-in-law as he shouted and moaned in delirium. Travis and Crockett rushed to Bowie's room, to see him thrashing around on his bed. He foamed at the mouth, his eyes open but seeing nothing. Travis and Juana tried to hold him, but he was almost too much for them.

"Oh, no, please God," Bowie screamed. "My baby . . . our baby!! Ursula!"

After an agonizing eternity, Bowie finally

relaxed. He seemed almost lucid for a moment, looking around the room as if wondering why these people were staring at him. Then he fainted dead away. Soon, his soft snoring told them that he was asleep.

Juana sat down on a stool, exhausted. "He cries for my sister," she explained to Travis and Crockett. "His wife and the baby she carried. Dead from cholera."

The two men looked at each other, both knowing what this meant. Any hope that Bowie's illness would pass was now gone. He was clearly deteriorating, growing more and more ill with each passing day. Travis no longer felt a surge of elation at the thought that he was the supreme commander at the Alamo. Now he felt only pity for Bowie, and the heavy weight of responsibility on his own shoulders.

When Travis and Crockett emerged from Bowie's quarters there were fifty or sixty volunteers standing around in ragtag formation. Travis was instantly alert for trouble, half expecting a mutiny. William Ward stood in front of them and said to Travis, "Is he going to get better?"

Travis shook his head. "I do not know," he said.

Travis tried to walk back to his quarters, but Ward blocked his way. "Up there on that wall," Ward said, "we killed six Mexicans and lost nary a man."

Ward and Travis stared at each other. Crockett gripped his rifle, on guard in case the volunteers were about to start something.

"We can take 'em," Ward said. He looked back at the other men. A movement rippled through the crowd as they came to a sort of attention. Even Ward straightened up as he faced Travis again. He said, "We can take 'em . . . sir."

Travis looked around the group of men. He could see that they wanted to believe what Ward had said, and wanted Travis to reinforce that belief. Travis stared back at them, saying nothing. But the look on his face said that perhaps for the first time he understood what leadership was all about.

Chapter Twenty-four

The men of the Alamo heard a faint bugle call, one that they had never heard before. They rushed to the west wall and looked toward Béxar. Esparza and Dickinson stood together near the eighteen pounder.

"What is that?" Dickinson said.

Esparza looked uneasy. He said, "The bugles signal the arrival of reinforcements." He sighed. "I had better go see Colonel Travis," he said.

But Travis was already heading his way, trotting up the ramp from his quarters. When he got to the nest of the eighteen pounder, he raised a field glass to his eye and peered toward town. He saw more Mexican troops pouring into Béxar — hundreds more. Esparza stepped over to Travis's side. Travis was intently listening to the trumpets.

Travis said to Esparza, "How many?"

Esparza hesitated. He did not really want to tell Travis.

"Three more battalions," he said. "A thousand more soldados."

Travis looked grimly at the flurry of activity in Béxar. "At least now we know what they were waiting for," he said.

Esparza pointed to the north end of town. "Over there," he said. "What are they working at?"

Travis put the field glass to his eye and looked in the direction indicated by Esparza. Dozens of Mexican soldiers were on their hands and knees hammering away, building something. Only when they stood up and lifted their handiwork could Travis make out what they had constructed: ladders.

Travis lowered the glass and sighed. All along the wall, the men of the Alamo also stared at the ladders, all thinking the same thing. Scurlock made a mark on the top of the wall with his knife — that made ten marks. They had been inside this hellhole for ten days. He stared at the mark and looked over to where the ladders were being built and carried. He shook his head. "We are all going to die," he said.

In the courtyard, a few men piled trunks

near the church, constructing makeshift breastworks around the entrance. Green Jameson moved frantically from place to place around the fort, looking for weak spots, instructing his crews how to shore up walls and make repairs.

At the well, Sam and Joe had dug deep enough that they were well below ground and could converse in private. Sam said, "When they come over these walls, you just throw up your hands and holler 'Soy Negro, no disparo!' "

"What does that mean?" Joe said.

Sam said, "Mexican law say there ain't no slaves, right? An' contrack or no, that is what you is. Mexicans see your color, you tell 'em not to shoot, and they will pass you by."

Joe looked at Sam with a glint of pride in his eyes. He said, "Mister William, he gon' give me a gun."

Sam shook his head in disgust. He thought, *What am I going to do with this one?* Sam said, "You clean up they shit, take care of they horses, wash 'em, feed 'em. Damn if you ain't going to die for 'em, too."

Joe looked down at his hands, which were cracked and blistered. He started digging again. The shovel bit the earth, hit a rock and stopped.

Without looking at Sam, Joe said, "How

do you say them words again?"

Inside the long barracks the uniformed members of the New Orleans Greys were digging, too, still working on the trench in the barracks' dirt floor. One Grey stopped for a moment and wiped his brow. "How good an idea is this? Once we get in here, can we get back out?"

Another kept digging. "Always good to have a fall-back position," he said.

The first Grey solemnly surveyed what they had done. He said, "About the size of a grave, ain't it, Captain?"

In the southwest battery, Travis called Esparza and Dickinson to him. "Captain Dickinson," he said, "I am re-assigning you and Private Esparza to the battery in the rear of the church so you can be near your families." Dickinson looked at Travis, wondering what this meant. Travis looked out toward the town, avoiding Dickinson's gaze. He said, "And I have arranged for a replacement for your midnight watch." Dickinson and Esparza glanced at each other and went to get their things to relocate to the church. They passed James Butler Bonham on the ramp. "Colonel?" Bonham said. Travis's look acknowledged him but he said nothing.

"I want to talk to you," Bonham said.

Travis nodded. "Go ahead."

Bonham said, "Well, some of the men are uncertain about the loyalty of the Tejano you sent for help."

Travis glared at Bonham. "Colonel Bowie has absolute faith in Captain Seguin," he said.

Bonham shrugged. "Perhaps, then, he just did not make it." He stood up a little straighter and plunged ahead. "I would like to give it a shot," he said.

Travis gave Bonham a biting smile, then walked away.

Bonham called out, "Billy!" Travis stopped and turned around. Bonham said, "That look you just gave me is exactly why people did not like you growing up. If you think I just want out of here, you are wrong."

Travis looked down, thinking about it. "I cannot afford to lose another man." He glanced at Bonham and said, "Particularly another good man."

Bonham said, "But . . ."

"I have sent fourteen messengers out since we retreated to this fort," Travis said. "Not one of them has come back."

Bonham saw the desperation in Travis's eyes. He smiled and said, "But you haven't sent me."

Travis stared at Bonham, then nodded. "All right," he said. "But come back to us, Jim. We need you."

Bonham went to prepare his horse and Travis sprinted back to his quarters to write another, angrier, letter, begging for help.

> . . . *Let the Convention go on and make a declaration of independence, and we will then understand, and the world will understand, what we are fighting for. If independence is not declared, I shall lay down my arms, and so will the men under my command. But under the flag of independence, we are ready to peril our lives a hundred times a day, and to drive away the monster who is fighting us under a blood-red flag, threatening to murder all prisoners and make Texas a waste desert. I shall have to fight the enemy on his own terms, yet I am ready to do it, and if my countrymen do not rally to my relief, I am determined to perish in the defense of this place, and my bones shall reproach my country for her neglect . . .*

An hour later, they walked toward the gate. Bonham was leading his horse. Travis had given him a small packet of letters with instructions on where to take them.

"You ever think about Red Bank, Billy?"

Bonham said. "South Carolina was a lot different than this."

Travis shook his head. "I try not to dwell on the past," he said. "I would rather look to the future."

Bonham mounted his horse. "Comes a time," he said, "when the past is all you have. When all your future is . . . used up."

Travis and Bonham looked at each other solemnly. It seemed to Bonham that Travis's eyes were always sad these days. Not hopeless, just grief-stricken. They shook hands.

"I will be back, Billy," Bonham said. "Or die in the attempt."

Travis lightly patted Bonham's horse. "I know you will, Jim." He thought of something, reached into his jacket and pulled out a white handkerchief. "When you ride back in," Travis said, "tie this around your hat. We have some pretty good shots in the fort. See a horseman coming toward us, they might just blow you to kingdom come. We will all be able to see this from a distance."

Bonham nodded and put the handkerchief in his coat pocket. At a signal from Travis, the gates opened. He mounted his horse, touched his hat and rode out.

Travis said quietly, "Go with God."

The Yturri house, already one of the most

splendid homes in Béxar, now shone with extra brilliance. Long, beautifully tapered candles glowed in every room. The polished mahogany table was laden with delicacies surrounding a large crystal punchbowl filled with a special elixir fashioned by Santa Anna's personal chef.

All of Santa Anna's officers were resplendent in their dress uniforms. Béxar's leading citizens — those who had not fled in terror upon the advance of the Mexican army — were dressed in their absolute finest. A current of excitement ran through the room. It was not every day, after all, when the president of Mexico and the general of all her armies was to be married in one's own town. And the fact that his intended was a lovely local girl, the daughter of a prominent family, just made the occasion all the more glittering.

The guests gathered in formation behind the happy groom and his trembling bride. Santa Anna and his fiancée, Juanita Maria Diaz, stood before a large gold cross, reverently waiting to recite their vows. Santa Anna beamed with pleasure. Juanita simply looked frightened. Her mother — indeed, everyone she talked to — had kept insisting to the sixteen-year-old that she was being complimented by a great and rare honor, that the marriage would make her one of the most important women in Mexico. Yes, her husband may be a little older than she might have wished, but he was still a handsome and virile man . . . and wealthy . . . and powerful — indeed, the most powerful man in the country. And, as she stood before the altar in her exquisite lace wedding gown, being gazed upon with envy by the cream of Béxar society, Juanita knew she should feel lucky. But she did not. She felt a little sick. She did not want to leave her friends, her family and her home in Béxar when she moved with her new husband to Mexico City. No matter what splendor awaited her there, it could not make up for a lifetime of memories here.

Juanita was also frightened about the wedding night. Her friends, pretending to know more about the subject than they actually did, had already warned her that the act could be painful in the extreme, that it was something that men wanted but that women merely endured. But Juanita, to her shame, knew that she wanted it, too. She had felt the stirrings of adulthood, when dancing with handsome officer Martín de Soldana or while watching some of her father's workmen bathing, shirtless, in the river. She dreamed of the act, longed for it.

But not this way. Not with this old man, no matter how wealthy and powerful. Everyone acted as if Juanita were being given a rare gift. To her, it felt as if she were being sold into slavery.

Her mother stood behind Juanita. A small smile played upon her lips, but there was no happiness in her eyes. She hoped that she had made the right choice for her daughter — and for herself. Soon, they would be ensconced in a palace in Mexico City and their brilliant future would make all this worthwhile. Yes, she had done the right thing, she was sure of it. It was a very great honor. Indeed, it was her way of serving her country.

General Castrillón looked intently at Juanita's mother, then whispered to General Cós, who stood beside him, "What do you think your sister will say when she hears that her husband is getting married . . . again?"

Cós, whose sister was already married to Santa Anna, gave Castrillón an innocent look. "And who will she hear it from?" he said. His expression clearly added, *Not me!*

The more devout Catholics in the room thought that the Latin vows being intoned by the priest did not sound quite right. Most of them shrugged it off — he was undoubtedly new to the order and was still struggling to learn all of the ceremonies of the church. Anyway, he had obviously been found worthy by His Excellency Santa Anna, so who were they to question him?

No one recognized the priest as Santa Anna's aide-de-camp Batres. As he struggled melodramatically to remember lines he had heard in church, the rest of the congregation nodded pleasantly, moved by the beautiful ceremony.

Bowie's eyes were open, but it was not clear to anyone that he could actually see anything. His entire body was drenched in sweat. With no other way to comfort him, Juana arranged an altar of candles and plaster saints on tables around the room. On his bedside table, at the center, she placed a cameo of Ursula.

Ana Esparza passed a chicken egg in circles over Bowie's forehead, heart, and intestines. Sam watched from outside the doorway. He had seen such ceremonies in New Orleans. They unnerved him, seeming uncomfortably close to devil worship.

Juana said, "He has been stabbed three times, once through the lungs, shot two or three times, cholera, and malaria, every two years. . . ."

Ana cracked the egg into a glass and looked closely at it. The yolk had a red spot in the center. "He is already dead," Ana said. "And this is the place he's been sent."

Ana crossed herself and left the close, dank room. After several hours with Bowie, she was desperate for fresh air, for sky — eager to immerse herself in the youthful promise of her children and the steadfast love of her husband.

Behind her, Bowie shifted and groaned and called out for his dead wife. He called to Ursula and . . . she came to him. As Bowie stared in astonishment, Ursula sat before him, in her wedding gown. Bowie reached for Ursula, tears streaming down his face.

Juana took his hand. There were tears on her face as well. She leaned down and kissed him on the lips, quieting him, soothing him.

At the palisade, Crockett turned to Autry and said, "I have had about as much of this wood fence as I can take today. Let us go a-wanderin'."

Autry pointed over to the north wall. Joe was walking among the men with a pot and a ladle. "Looks like supper's gettin' to them first," Autry said. "I propose we head in that direction."

Crockett smiled. "You are a practical man, Micajah."

The men on the north wall were exhausted and dirty, but their faces brightened when they saw Crockett approach. Many of them called out to him in greeting.

"Thought we'd come set a spell with you fellers," Crockett said. He peered at their faces in mock seriousness. "I don't owe none of you men money, do I?"

They laughed and made a place for Crockett and Autry to sit. Joe passed them each a plate of stew and some corn tortillas to dip into it. Crockett nodded his thanks.

Daniel Cloud said to Crockett, "You must have been in many a scrape like this."

"Oh, sure," Crockett said. "First time I stood up to speak before Congress, my mouth was dryer than a Quaker in a cracker barrel."

The men laughed delightedly.

"Yes, sir," Crockett said, grinning, "saw so many politicians run for the door I thought the buildin' was on fire!"

Cloud said, "But Mr. Crockett . . ."

"Please," Crockett said modestly, "call me David. Mr. Crockett was my father."

Cloud smiled and said, "David. All right, but David, in all your Indian fightin', you must have —"

Crockett shook his head. "I was not ever

in but one real scrape in my life, fellers."

Cloud looked at him in disbelief. Joe walked around the group carrying his clay pot filled with stew, looking for plates to re-fill. "You was in the Red Stick War," Cloud said, as if challenging Crockett to own up to his heroism.

Crockett nodded, "Yes, sir, that is true. I was in that. I reckon I was just about your age when it broke out. The Creeks boxed up four, five hundred people at Fort Nims and massacred every one of 'em. This was big news around those parts, so I up and joined the volunteers."

Other men moved in close to hear Crockett's tale.

Crockett said, "I did a little scoutin', but mostly I fetched in venison for the cook fire. You know, I am a tolerable good hunter."

The men laughed.

"Well sir," Crockett said, "we caught up with them redskins at a place called Tallusahatchee. We surrounded the whole village and come in from all directions. It was not much of a fight, really. We shot them down like dogs. . . ."

Sentries on the wall peered down as they listened, not watching their posts. Crockett, as always, had the men in the palm of his hand.

Crockett continued, "Finally, what was left of them Injuns crowded into this little cabin. They wanted to surrender, but this squaw loosed an arrow and killed one of our fellers, so we shot her and then . . . then, well, we set fire to the cabin." Crockett paused for a moment to let the image sink in. The men were nearly hypnotized, hanging on his every word.

Crockett frowned. "We could hear 'em screaming to their gods in there," he said. "We could smell 'em. Anybody who run out was cut down right quick. But mostly they just burnt up in there."

Crockett put down his plate of stew. He had not eaten a bite.

"We had had nary to eat but parched corn since October, and that was near gone," he said. "The next day when we dug through the ashes we found these potaters from the cellar. They'd been cooked by the grease that run off them Indians. We ate till we near burst."

The rapt faces of the men were trained on Crockett. They barely dared to breathe.

Crockett smiled a little. "Since then, you pass me the taters, I will pass 'em right back."

The message settled in on the faces of the men. They had begun to relax a little, when the sharp snap of a gunshot broke the moment.

Scurlock turned into the fort from his post on the south wall and shouted, "I think I hit one of 'em!"

All over the Alamo, men scrambled to their positions. But instead of the Deguello or "Charge!" they heard a furious stream of cussing — in plain English. From the bottom of the wall, the muffled voice of Colorado Smith muttered, "Son of a goddamned shit-arse bitch! What do I look like, you blind turd?"

Grimes raised his eyebrows in astonishment. "I think they are talkin' American."

Colorado Smith's voice was still muffled but louder, and angrier. "Open the gate! God damn you! It's us!"

Several men rushed to open the main gate and several men on horseback, led by Colorado Smith, rode in. There was a whoop from the defenders. Men from all over the Alamo came running toward the gate to greet the newcomers.

Micajah Autry pounded Crockett on the back. "They are here! Reinforcements! They are here!"

In the courtyard, Colorado Smith dismounted and saluted Travis. He said proudly, "I figure this is every able-bodied man in Gonzales."

Most of the men gathered around, shaking hands and slapping backs as the Gonzales men dismounted. Almeron and Susanna Dickinson spotted George Kimball among them and rushed to him. "George!" Dickinson cried, furiously pumping his hand, "who is minding the shop?"

Kimball smiled. "Kimball and Dickinson's is temporarily out of business," he said. "As soon as this ruckus is cleared up, we will get back to it, make it bigger and better than ever!"

Galba Fuqua stood by shyly. Susanna embraced him. "Galba, what in the world . . . ?" she said. "You are too young to be here."

Galba looked as dignified and adult as possible. "All the other men were a-comin'," he said. "Figgered it was my duty." He shook Almeron's hand. "I was with 'em when the Mexicans tried to steal our cannon. I am gon' be with 'em when they lick the Mexicans here!"

Travis said, "How did you get all these men through?"

Colorado Smith said, "Those soldados think they got it all sewn up tight, but you avoid the roads, there's this little sliver you can ease on through. Didn't nobody bother us till some peckerwood here in the fort started in ta shootin'." He looked around accusingly, then turned to one of the Gonzales men who was wrapping a cloth around his foot. "How's the foot, Eli?"

"How the hell do you think it is?" Eli said angrily. "Son of a bitch shot me. And me comin' to help."

Many of the men laughed in spite of themselves. Eli sputtered furiously.

Travis smiled broadly. He said, "And Colonel Fannin is behind you?"

Smith looked puzzled. "He ain't here?" He threw his saddlebag to the ground. "I shoulda known. When I talked to the prissy coward I shoulda known he was not going to do nothin'."

Travis looked around with a sinking feeling. The newcomers did not look as plentiful now as they had a few moments ago. He said, "How many rode in with you?"

Smith said, "I brung thirty-two men, Colonel. Counting me."

Travis turned away to conceal his disappointment. Crockett saw the dejected faces of his comrades. He said in a loud and lively voice, "And if they ain't the purtiest lookin' bunch of Texians I ever seen! Let's hear it for Gonzales, fellers!"

The Tennesseans raised a cheer, and the

others joined in. Almeron Dickinson looked at George Kimball, then to his wife. He tried to smile and cheer along with the others, but he could not. His disappointment was too deep. Putting his arm around Susanna's shoulder, he walked her back to the baptistery. She lay down on the palette she had made of blankets and straw on the floor and held Angelina in her arms.

Susanna smiled up at her husband. "I know what you are thinking," she said. "But if those men got through, others will get through."

Almeron nodded. "I should never have left you in Gonzales in the first place," he said. "I should have stayed with you."

Susanna said, "And then you would have come here with this bunch — you know you would have. And Angelina and I would be home alone, with no one to cook our lunch for us."

Almeron laughed a little. He bent down and kissed his wife on the forehead. She grasped the back of his neck and pulled him to her, kissing him fiercely on the lips. They embraced and she whispered, "No matter what happens, no matter how bad it gets, I would always rather be with you. We are together. It's the only thing that matters."

Almeron stroked her face. "You're right,"

he said. "That's the only thing that matters."

Within moments, both Susanna and Angelina were asleep. Almeron looked down on his wife and baby and sighed. Then he lay down beside them, and held them close to him, all night long.

A small army of workers swarmed about the Yturri house, clearing up the remains of Santa Anna's wedding party. All the guests had gone home, declaring it the social event of the season. Santa Anna, Castrillón and Almonte stood at the window facing the Alamo, sipping small glasses of port. Santa Anna heard faint cheering drifting from the fort.

"Reinforcements?" he asked.

"No, Excellency," Almonte said. "A few men on horseback, that is all."

Santa Anna shook his head in puzzlement. "I leave a corridor wide open for Houston. Here, come here, come to us, bring your army. This is your opportunity to be a great gringo hero. . . . Still, he doesn't come. What can I do?"

Neither Castrillón nor Almonte had an answer for him. Santa Anna walked toward his bedroom and his waiting bride, eager to get to the most pleasurable event of the evening. He had a thought, stopped and turned. "Send a message that we grant safe quarter to any Tejano choosing to leave the Alamo," he said.

Castrillón was surprised by Santa Anna's merciful gesture. "You will pardon them, Excellency?" he said. "The men who have made war on you?"

Santa Anna smiled. "They will take their freedom," he said, "and the men left behind will think about escape . . . about life . . . and they will not fight like men resigned to death."

Castrillón nodded. Now he understood. It was not mercy at all — just strategy.

"Good night, General," Castrillón said. Santa Anna gave Castrillón and Almonte a small wave of the hand and the two officers stepped out into the night. The other workers had finished their tasks and were leaving out the back entrance.

Santa Anna walked to his bedroom door and opened it. Inside, Juanita sat on the bed. Her mother had dressed her in an elaborate and expensive nightgown, and then had kissed her on the forehead and walked quickly out of the room. Now, Juanita waited, alone, terrified. When she saw Santa Anna standing in the doorway, smiling lasciviously, she gasped. He ran his eyes up and down her body. So fresh, so innocent — like a beautiful country ripe for invasion. No matter how many times he did this, Santa Anna thought, it never lost its thrill. The new husband stepped into his bridal chamber and closed the door.

Chapter Twenty-five

Hermann Ehrenberg was cussing up a blue streak in German. His friend, Petrussewicz, agreed in Polish. They were standing in a long, stalled column of Texians that stretched all the way back toward the walls of Fort Defiance.

"You do not vote in the army," Ehrenberg said furiously. "There is a commander. He decides what you are supposed to do and you follow his orders, right or wrong!"

Petrussewicz looked up the line toward Fannin. "In Poland," he said, "this man would be dead. A mutiny . . ."

His words were drowned out by the clattering hooves of James Butler Bonham's horse as Bonham raced past them toward the head of the column. James Fannin was supervising a crew of Texians as they tried to jack up an overladen wagon with a broken axle. The unhitched team of oxen grazed placidly nearby as the Texians cursed and strained to lift the wagon, with no success.

Fannin considered the situation from all angles. "We may have to unload it first," he said, to general groans from the men. At their protest he quickly stammered, "Unless you think otherwise . . ."

Bonham rode up and dismounted, barely able to disguise his fury. "You haven't left yet?" he demanded of Fannin.

Fannin gestured toward the problem. "We have had a misfortune with our supply wagon," he said.

"You had the message from Travis three days ago!" Bonham said. "The situation in the Alamo is desperate!"

Fannin explained patiently, as if to a child with below-average intelligence, "Dr. Grant and Mr. Johnson took all the decent wagons and livestock. I cannot expose my men in the open without —"

Bonham felt like screaming. "You are exposing them now!" he shouted.

Fannin nodded reasonably, as if that point had only now dawned upon him. "You are quite right, Lieutenant," he said. "Quite right." Fannin looked up at the sky and called to his second in command. "Have the men pull those cannon back to the fort," he instructed. "It has gotten too late to leave today."

Several of the men scowled at the turn-around, but grudgingly headed back toward the fort. Bonham was desperate. "Let me take a hundred of your men," he said, "and whatever they can carry. We could reach the Alamo by . . ."

Fannin pointed firmly to the fort.

"Goliad is my key position," he said. "I will abandon it empty of powder and provision or I will defend it to the last man. But I will not divide my command! Colonel Travis has his situation to deal with and I have mine. My troops will not move until they are properly rested and equipped for the campaign."

Bonham looked at Fannin with disgust. "And you will equivocate until it is too late to save either garrison."

The two men stared at each other for an uncomfortably long moment. In South Carolina and Georgia, where Bonham and Fannin had grown up, duels were fought for less than this. Fannin broke the staring contest first. He looked away, watching his men march back into Fort Defiance. "We can only guess which is the proper course of action," he said softly. "That, sir, is the agony of command."

In San Felipe's Public Building, everyone was working together for the first time. Women were sewing the Texas flag while, across the room, Rusk and others were immersed in drafting a declaration of independence.

Houston walked to a map on a wall. He traced from Copano to Refugio, Goliad to Victoria, and, finally, Gonzales. He said, "I have ordered Colonel Fannin to retreat from Goliad to Gonzales. John Forbes is mustering more men throughout South Texas and bringing them to Gonzales. I expect fifteen hundred men to be there when I arrive. We will ford Olmos Creek upstream from Béxar, relieve the Alamo from the west then withdraw to Gonzales and fortify in a line southeast to Columbus and Brazoria."

The room buzzed in favor of Houston. Even the men who had been booing him and calling him a drunk and a coward only days earlier were now offering their full support.

Rusk said, "You will have command of the regular army, Houston. The militias will have their own command."

Houston said firmly, "No." He faced

down Rusk and the men around him, challenging the room. He said, "I will have command of all or none."

Houston strode over to the table where the constitution was still being worked on. He glanced at it, picked up a quill and scribbled "Sam Houston" on the bottom. Then he looked up and faced the men again. "Finish this government," he said. "Do your calling and I shall do mine. I will lead an army. You will birth a nation." The room was silent. Houston raised his arm into the air and shouted, "Gentlemen, again, to Texas!"

The room erupted into cheers. Thatcher-Rhyme seemed pleased. Everyone was. Except Burnet. As Houston headed for the door, Burnet caught his arm and said, "Houston, if I hear of you drunk, it is over. You will never have an official role in Texas again."

Outside, Houston finished packing his saddlebag. He held a bottle of whiskey in his hand, considering it carefully. He debated whether to pack it. There was a long trail ahead, many lonely nights, many times when this bottle would provide some very good company. Houston was just about to shove the bottle into his saddlebag when he realized that Mathew Ingram was watching him. The boy regarded him with the absurdly hopeful expression of a puppy dog.

Houston ignored him for as long as he could, but when Mathew refused to break his stare, Houston turned to face him and said, "You have a horse?"

Mathew nodded his head. "Yep."

"How about a gun?"

"I can find one," Mathew said.

Houston looked the boy up and down. He gave a last longing glance at the bottle and, with a sigh, smashed it on a rock. Mathew watched with Houston as the precious liquid seeped gradually into the earth.

"Well, boy," Houston said, "go get 'em."

Mathew whirled around and ran toward his father's store. He knew that his father was away making a delivery to a ranch outside of town. He would not be back in San Felipe for another two hours. By then, Mathew knew, he would be long gone. Off fighting a revolution with Sam Houston. As he rummaged through Ingram's storeroom looking for ammunition for the rifle he was taking, he nearly whooped with giddy glee. Adventure, at last!

Houston and Mathew left San Felipe a half hour later and rode at a moderate pace along the road to Gonzales. The boy was eager for conversation, for insight, for some kind of prediction about the adventures that lay ahead. Houston was thinking mostly about the bottle he had smashed. That was a bad idea, he thought. A really bad idea.

"When do you think we will see action?" Mathew asked, his horse loping just behind Saracen.

Houston continued to look straight ahead. "Don't know," he said.

They rode for a few more minutes in silence. Mathew said, "Do you think we will fight Indians, too?"

"Don't know," Houston repeated.

This time, they rode for a solid hour, Houston looking at nothing but the road ahead, wishing there were someone he could kill for a single sip of whiskey.

Mathew tried again. "What were you doing when you were my age?"

Houston grimaced, thinking only of the bottle. "Can't remember," he said.

Mathew nodded. "You were probably in school," he said. "Probably doing what you were supposed to be doing."

Houston said, "Probably."

"Really?" Mathew said.

Houston looked over at Mathew. "My two brothers were teachers, the apostles. I loved to learn but if anyone could remove the joy from something, it was the apostles. I ran

354

away and lived with the Cherokee."

Mathew smiled. "I am running away right now, but maybe I will kill Santa Anna."

Houston looked at him as if he had gone crazy. Mathew said, "My pa says I am idle and lazy. Well, maybe I was, but I am not anymore. I am reformed."

This pious statement caused Houston to snort out a laugh. "You and me, boy," he said. "You and me."

They rounded a bend and down below spotted the first signs of the Gonzales army — a handful of tents and a few men. Houston thought it was the most pitiful and unpromising display he had ever seen. Mathew was awestruck.

"Did you ever see so many people in all your life?" the boy said.

Houston just stared, wondering how he was supposed to win a war with no more of an army than this.

As they rode into camp, Houston spotted Mosley Baker, J. C. Neill and a few others arguing outside a tent. Houston dismounted, handed Saracen's reins to Mathew and walked toward them. "Where is everybody?" he demanded.

Neill said, "Thirty men from here in Gonzales already left for the Alamo." Off to the side, a young man with a fife in his shirt pocket said, "General, my brother and four real good men are on their way from Brazoria."

Houston looked around. Four real good men. It was, it seemed to him, a sorry state of affairs. And here he was without a bottle.

"Assemble the men," Houston said.

Elbowing her way through the crowd was a woman of about thirty-five, tall and straight, her dark brown hair carefully arranged in ringlets which framed her handsome face. She was being led toward Houston but seemed to be looking at some distant point beyond him. "I need to talk to him," she said. "I need to talk to General Sam Houston!"

Houston walked over to her. "I am Houston," he said. Taking a closer look, he could see the reason that she seemed to be gazing beyond him. She was blind. She reached out both hands as if feeling for something. Her hands brushed his face. Houston took them gently into his own hands. "How can I aid you, ma'am?" he said.

"God bless you, sir," she said. "You are already helping me. My husband's there. At the Alamo. His name is Millsaps. Isaac Millsaps."

Houston looked around the crowd helplessly. Mrs. Millsaps grasped his hands tighter. "He said it was his duty," she said. "To go, to try and save those poor men. And I understand that, I do. We have six children and they cry for their daddy. But today I told them that you had come and that you were going there. To bring him back. To bring them all back. And I just wanted to meet you, to thank you. God bless you, sir."

Houston was too dumbstruck to say a word. He watched silently as she was led away. At that moment, behind him, Houston heard a distinctive whistle. He turned to see Juan Seguin riding down the road. When he reached Houston, he pulled his horse to a halt and jumped down from the saddle. Houston shook Seguin's hand warmly and they began to walk together through the camp. "How many?" Houston asked. "How many in the Alamo?"

Seguin followed Houston for a few moments as he looked over the assembled troops, Mathew included. The general stared into the face of each man as they passed. The men were dusty, buck-skinned. Some wore sombreros, others wore top hats.

"Well?" Houston said.

Seguin looked away. "About a hundred and fifty," he said. "Not counting women and children."

Houston stopped, taken aback. "Women and children?" he asked.

Seguin nodded. Houston sighed and started walking again, continuing to inspect his troops. He said, "If Bowie had just done what I asked . . ."

"Santiago is not well, general," Seguin said. Houston shot him a hard look. That was not news he wanted to hear. "But morale is good," Seguin continued. "Travis has lost some of his rough edges and Crockett keeps the men amused. . . ."

Houston stopped cold. He had been stunned more than once today, but this was too much. With a thick voice he said, "Crockett? Crockett's there?"

Seguin nodded. "With a group of your fellow Tennesseans," he said.

The news made Houston feel a bit lost, as though he had suddenly wandered into a fog or stepped into a weird dream. Without another word, he walked away from the troops, leaving Seguin staring after him. Mosley Baker and J. C. Neill also watched as Houston walked out into the field, alone. When he had gone about a hundred yards from the camp, Houston bent down to his knees and put his ear to the ground. He could feel a subtle vibration. Accompanying it, he thought he could hear the distant sounds of cannon fire.

He was startled by Mosley Baker's voice directly behind him. "When we moving out?"

Houston stood up. Baker and Neill were standing behind him. He looked past them to the assembled men. "We need more men," he said. "Stronger men, younger men. If they arrive every day, soon we will have enough, but for now, we wait."

Baker and Neill could not believe their ears. Baker said, "If we cannot run, we walk. If we cannot walk, we crawl, but we must go to the aid of those boys in the Alamo! It is only right!"

"No," Houston said in a low voice.

"General," Neill said pleadingly, "I am the man who left Travis there!"

Houston snapped angrily, "And I am the man who sent him!" He slapped his thigh, trying to think of some way to let his anger manifest itself. God, how he wanted a drink. "Gentlemen," he said, "I do not enjoy waiting any more than the next man, but I will not sacrifice Texas!" He closed his eyes and gave the anger — and the craving — a moment to pass. When he opened his eyes, he had softened a bit. He looked beyond Baker and Neill and eyed the troops. "What do you have here," he said, "a hundred men?"

Baker said, "A hundred and twenty-four."

Houston closed his eyes again and sighed deeply. He said, "These hundred and twenty-four men cannot pierce an army of thousands."

The officers looked at one another with the vague stirrings of despair. If this was the kind of mathematics that Houston was calculating with, it meant that they were never going.

Houston said, "Colonel Fannin is en route from Goliad with men. We will wait." He turned and walked away. Seguin trotted up to him. "What should I tell Travis?" Seguin said.

"Nothing," Houston said. "You are staying here."

Seguin was flustered. "General . . . Sam . . . I gave my word," he said.

Houston stopped and looked at Seguin. He knew that for this man, his word was his bond. He knew that he was issuing an order that went against everything he believed. He put his hand on Seguin's shoulder and said, "I am sorry, Juan."

Seguin said, "I have to go back . . . please . . ."

Houston shook his head. "No," he said.

"You will stay with me. You will be of more service to Texas alive than dead."

Houston walked away. Seguin stared after him disbelievingly. Baker whipped off his hat and threw it to the ground in disgust.

Chapter Twenty-six

Gregorio Esparza stood at the bottom of the
cannon ramp just inside the front door of the
Alamo church. Out in the courtyard, a group
of civilian Tejanos was packed to leave, saying
good-bye to their friends and loved ones.
Gregorio had decided to stay, even though he
had pled with Ana to take the children and
flee to safety. She had refused, as he knew she
would. Little Enrique stood by Gregorio's
side and the father ruffled his boy's hair absently as he watched the others — men he
had grown up with, men he had loved and
trusted — desert their posts. He knew that
the matter was a complicated one, that blood
and patriotism sometimes made for contra-
dictory emotions and loyalties. But the other
Tejanos were against Santa Anna and, as far
as Gregorio was concerned, they should de-

fend their beliefs. With their lives, if necessary.

Up on the west wall, the rest of Seguin's cavalry company also watched silently. If they were angry at the departing Tejanos, they did not allow it to show on their faces. They would not betray such emotions before the Anglos. They would always stick together — even if they were splitting apart.

Bowie could see the scene from his bedroom door, which looked directly out onto the courtyard. He had had a bad night, wracked by coughing and delirium, but now he was lucid. He could not quite manage to sit up, but Juana had placed an extra pillow under his head so that it inclined forward. She sat beside him with a cool, damp cloth, periodically soothing his brow with it. Sam stood nearby, watching.

Earlier in the day, two of the Tejanos, Menchaca and Garza, had come to Bowie to ask his advice. "If Colonel Travis says you can leave . . ." Bowie had said.

"I have a family," Menchaca said. There was a slightly defensive tone in his voice, as if already prepared for a challenge.

"Like a lot of these gringos do," Garza said. "Like I do."

Bowie could barely speak. He felt weaker every day. "You should go if you can," he said to the two men. "The war will not end here. Don't die needlessly."

They both nodded and left without another word. Now, Bowie could see Menchaca with the group about to leave. Garza was up on the wall, staring at the departing Tejanos without expression.

"You look better," Juana said to Bowie brightly. "Your fever broke."

Bowie said in a low, hoarse voice, "Thank you for tending to me, Juana. And now I want you to leave." He looked over at Sam. "You, too, Sam," he said.

Sam straightened, with an amazed look on his face. "You giving me my freedom, Mister James?" he said incredulously.

Bowie coughed. "No, I am not," he said. "You are my property till I die. I get out of this bed, I'm huntin' you down." Bowie looked hard at Sam, and Sam understood what his master was saying. He nodded, feeling a surge of elation but showing nothing on his face.

Bowie said, "Now go, both of you. Santa Anna will not make the same offer twice."

Sam turned and walked away without saying anything further. He paused for a moment at the door, waiting for Bowie to say something more. "Thank you," maybe. Or even a simple "Good-bye." Years of service, of suffering, of loyalty. Did they mean nothing? Sam glanced back at Bowie, giving him one more chance. Bowie's face was turned to the wall. Sam picked up his pace, almost trotting over to join those about to evacuate the Alamo.

Juana watched Sam hurry to leave, but she stayed seated beside Bowie's bed. "We are all that is left," she said, stroking his brow with the damp cloth. "We are family."

Bowie said, "A couple of years doesn't make us blood, Juana."

Juana smiled and said, "You loved her. Her blood was yours. Your blood is mine."

Bowie turned away. Tears stung at his eyes, as they did almost every time he summoned up the face of his beautiful Ursula, as they did every time he remembered his loss.

He said, "They thought I married her for your father's money."

Juana said, "Gossip," and dipped the cloth, now warm, into the basin of water.

Bowie gasped for breath. ". . . The only thing in my life . . ." He shook his head, frustrated by his inability to speak for very long. "I was off chasing silver mines," he said. "All my life, whatever I had in my hand, I'd drop it and run after the next fortune, the next adventure. . . ."

Juana busied herself so that Bowie would not see that her own eyes were filled with tears. "My sister truly loved you," she said. "It was in her eye. And she never doubted your love for her. She never doubted it for an instant."

With considerable effort, Bowie turned over on his side. He placed an arm over his eyes and sobbed.

The Texians watched impassively as the group of Tejanos passed through the open main gate, pulling their horses and carrying their belongings. Sam had been told that the Mexicans did not make war against Negroes, but he was taking no chances. He had borrowed a sombrero and serape and insinuated himself into the middle of the group, becoming as inconspicuous as possible. He kept his head down, staring resolutely at the ground as he walked. In that sense, he was just like the others. None of the Tejanos made eye contact with any of the Texians as they left. Ana, Juana, Gregorio and the other Tejanos watched them go with sadness on their faces. No one waved good-bye. Finally, the last of the group was outside the fort. The gate closed behind them, sealing in those who remained.

A lone horseman galloped up to the crest of Powder House Hill and then paused.

James Butler Bonham had already tied a white bandanna around his hat, as a signal to Travis and the men of the Alamo. But he was not quite ready to ride down that hill. He started forward, then back, forward, then back — getting up his nerve. Below, between Bonham and the Alamo, were several hundred Mexican soldiers and a cannon emplacement. In order to gain entrance to the Alamo, he would have to ride directly through them. He muttered encouragingly to his horse, then said a little prayer.

Finally, Bonham took a deep breath, grimaced, and spurred his horse down the hill, toward the impenetrable cordon.

He kept his eye on the gate of the Alamo, neither looking left or right. He blasted past soldiers sitting by cook fires, leaped over hedges, lowered his body as far as possible, so that he was hugging the neck of the horse, just holding on.

The ride was so sudden that it took a moment for the soldiers to figure out what was going on. Flustered, they ran toward him, kneeling, aiming, firing . . . and missing. Dozens of musket balls whistled past Bonham's head.

Autry at the palisade first noticed the flurry of activity. "Rider!" he shouted. "Rider comin' in!" The men of the Alamo gathered along the wall, craning to see, loading their rifles. In the distance, they saw Bonham galloping straight toward them. A dozen mounted lancers were hard on his heels. If only one caught him with the tip of his lance, if Bonham's horse stumbled in the uneven terrain, he would be overtaken and destroyed in the space of a few seconds.

Crockett shouted, "Better give him some help, boys!" He fired and the lead lancer dropped from his saddle. The horse just behind him trampled the body, and horse and rider went tumbling head over hooves down the hill. Someone passed Crockett another rifle. He fired again. Autry and two or three others followed suit. Two more horses fell, bringing their riders hard to the ground. One of them got up again and started to run. He was shot in the back by a Texian musket. The lancers gave up the chase and began retreating back up the hill. The men opened the gate and Bonham galloped in.

As Bonham dismounted, the men gathered around, watching him nervously.

Ward called out, "You don't have two thousand more just like you stashed away somewheres, do you?"

"When they comin'?" Scurlock called out. "When the hell they comin'?"

Bonham looked at the men briefly, then

concentrated on unhooking his saddlebag. He said, "Where is Colonel Travis?"

Scurlock pointed toward Travis's quarters and Bonham walked away. The men watched him for a moment, then looked at each other. Ward said, "Well, that sure don't sound like good news."

Travis stood up excitedly when he saw Bonham. He held out his hand, but Bonham shook it limply. He had a grim look in his eyes. "What is it, Jim?" Travis said.

Bonham reached into his saddlebag and pulled out a small packet of letters. Travis sat at his desk and read them. Joe and Bonham watched Travis read the last letter, then toss it down onto his desk. He stood up angrily.

"Where did you get these?" Travis said.

Bonham replied, "I crossed two of our couriers on the way back."

Travis looked at Bonham, beginning to understand. "Afraid to return," Travis said. "Who can blame them?" Bonham stared at him and Travis looked away. "And where is your letter?" Travis said. "What says Colonel Fannin?"

Bonham continued to say nothing. Travis sat down wearily. He felt too overcome to speak. After a moment he said in a quiet voice, "Captain Bonham, you rode through the possibility of death to deliver a message that promises it. Why?"

Bonham said, "I believe you have earned the pleasure of a reply . . . sir."

Travis slowly nodded a thank-you. Bonham returned the nod and walked out.

In the courtyard, the men had gathered in a large group. As usual, Scurlock and Ward were in the middle of it. "I say we run for it," Scurlock said. "That is our best hope." Several voices in the crowd shouted in the affirmative. "Yeah! That's right!"

Ward said, "Our horses are starving and weak. Their lancers would skewer us like sausages."

"Our relief could be over that hill . . ." said Grimes.

One of the New Orleans Greys suggested, "We could go out at night. In formation, some would make it."

The crowd was silent for a moment, considering their options. Grimes said quietly, "We could try surrendering."

A few in the crowd hissed at the sentiment, but many of them were at least willing to consider it. "Surrender?" Scurlock said. "Check if that red flag is still flying."

Crockett stood at the back of the group, listening, saying nothing. After paying close attention to the debate for a few moments, he walked over to Travis's headquarters.

Inside, Travis had handed a flintlock rifle to Joe and was showing him how to work it. He did not notice for a moment that Crockett was standing in the doorway. Then he glanced up and nodded.

"Colonel Crockett," he said.

Crockett's eyes were dark and grave. Travis could not remember ever having seen those eyes without a twinkle, without the sense that a witticism was brewing behind them. Now they were filled with something like sadness.

Crockett said, "The men need a word from you."

Travis shook his head. "I . . . I do not know what to tell them."

Crockett walked into the room, smiled a little in greeting to Joe, then stood at the window, looking out at the compound, which was milling with frightened, disgruntled men. He spoke as though to himself. "My time in Washington — the fellers in Congress made a good deal of sport of me." He looked at Travis and shrugged a little. "I learned a hell of a lot from them — learned how to dress, what fork to use in polite company — but I never learned to lie."

Travis followed Crockett's gaze. He was used to seeing the men as a garrison, a group over which he had command. But now he did not see a group — only individuals. Tom Waters sat near the palisade, holding a long leather strap. His dog gripped the other end with his teeth and was growling with mock anger, shaking his head wildly. Near the door of the church, Almeron Dickinson held his baby daughter Angelina, rocking her silently as young Susanna walked toward them with a bucket of water from the well. The Esparza family sat in a group; Gregorio had an arm around his wife's shoulders, saying nothing. The children had cornered a huge insect and were laughing delightedly at its quick movements. There was Micajah Autry puffing contemplatively on a pipe. Daniel Cloud, Isaac Millsaps, Green Jameson, Jim Bonham. Travis had known Bonham when they were both boys in South Carolina but he could not in truth say that any of them were his friends. They had their duty, just as he had his. But at this moment, the responsibility for their predicament felt terribly personal.

Crockett said softly but firmly, "These people in here been through an awful lot. I would allow these men have earned the right to hear the truth."

Travis sat for a moment. With a vague

feeling of shame, he had the fleeting feeling that he was about to break down. Dreams, plans, regrets; it all came to this; a meaningless death in a far-off country. He gathered the letters from his desk and stood up.

As soon as Travis stepped into the courtyard, everyone in the Alamo turned toward him expectantly. They had not known he was going to talk to them — he had not known it himself — but the moment they saw him, they knew it was time to listen. Travis raised the hand holding the pieces of paper and stepped into the center of the crowd. He did not speak in a loud voice, but the hush that enveloped the place made his words plain to everyone.

"I have here pieces of paper, letters from politicians and generals," Travis said, "but no indication of when or if help will arrive. Letters not worth the ink committed to them." He scanned the faces that were looking at him, searching for a reason to hope. With a wrench of his heart, Travis knew he had no hope to offer.

"I fear that . . . no one is coming."

He slowly crumpled the letters and dropped them to the earth. He looked at the useless letters for a moment, then met the eyes of his men. It struck him what an eclectic company it was — Irish, German,

French, Tejano. Men from nearly every state in the Union. Young, old, educated, ignorant. Seasoned fighters, scared kids. Patriots. Scoundrels. Preachers. Lawyers. Poets. Men of every description. But to Travis, right now, they all looked like heroes.

"Texas has been a second chance for me," Travis said. "I expect that might be true for many of you men. It has been a chance not only for land and riches, but also to be a different man. I hope, a better man. There have been many ideas brought forth in the last few months of what Texas is, of what it should become." He looked at the group of Tejanos from Seguin's company. They stared back at him without expression. Travis continued. "We are not all in agreement."

Travis looked from man to man, trying to form the words to say what he now knew that he had to say.

"The Mexican army hopes to lure us into attempting escape," he said. "Almost anything seems better than remaining in this place, penned up." He glanced at Crockett, standing by Travis's door. "But what about our wounded? What about the sick? In the open, without our cannon, they will cut us to pieces. We will have deserted our injured and died in vain. If, however, we force the enemy to attack, I believe every one of you will prove himself worth ten in return. We will not only show the world what patriots are made of, but we will also deal a crippling blow to the army of Santa Anna."

He took a few steps and glanced toward Bowie's room, wondering if he could hear. "If anyone wishes to depart, under the white flag of surrender, you may do so now. You have that right. But if you wish to stay with me, here, in the Alamo, we will sell our lives dearly." Briefly, he considered asking them to decide then and there whether they would stay or go. But he knew that this was a decision that each man had to make in his own heart. Travis nodded curtly at them and said in a hoarse voice, "God bless you."

Nobody spoke.

Nobody moved.

Joe had stepped out of their quarters and, standing slightly behind Crockett, looked at his master with a pride that slightly surprised him. Travis no longer had the heart to look the men in the eye. He knew what decision they would all make, and their lives suddenly became an almost unbearable weight on his shoulders. He touched his hat in something like a salute, then walked back to his quarters. The men silently parted to let him through. At the doorway, he locked eyes with Crockett, but neither man said anything. Then he stepped inside, followed by Joe.

The compound was still quiet. Travis stood at his desk and looked out at his men. With a sigh, he closed the window and sat down.

Crockett walked back over to the palisade and sat down beside Autry. "Still got time to go," he said quietly.

Autry smiled faintly. "I will tell you what, David. When you get ready to go, you just tell me and I will be right behind you."

Crockett said, "I just hope you can keep up. I am liable to streak out of this place so fast I will just leave my shadow behind."

Autry nodded. "I am sure you will. But until you start running for your life, why don't you give us a tune?"

Bowie was nearly sitting up on his cot when the cheery sound of Crockett's fiddle started up just outside his door. Tired of the darkness, he had asked Juana to light all the candles in his quarters. Perhaps if all the shadows in the room were dispelled, so would be the bleak visions which taunted him night and day.

There was a soft knock on the door. As it opened, Bowie looked up to see Travis standing respectfully in the doorway.

Bowie coughed and said, "What troubles you, Buck?"

Travis removed his hat and stepped inside. With Bowie, he always felt a little like a student in trouble, brought before the schoolmaster. "I spoke to the men earlier," Travis said. "About our situation. You deserve to hear as well."

Bowie said, "I heard. Through the door. Every word."

"My words," Travis said. "How painful for you."

Bowie shook his head. "Good words."

"We could try to get you out," Travis said. "With an escort. If you are captured, perhaps, given your condition, mercy would be extended."

Bowie coughed again. "I do not deserve mercy." He almost smiled. "But I do deserve a drink. You have anything stronger than water?"

Travis said, "I don't drink, Jim. You know that." He sat down on a stool at the foot of Bowie's bed. "I gamble. Go to whores. Run off on wives, but drinking . . . that's where I draw the line."

Crockett's merry fiddle tune had turned into a melancholy Irish air. It seemed appropriate to the general sadness in the air. "You

know, Buck," Bowie said, "if you live another five years, you might be a great man."

Five years. What would he give for another five years? Travis patted Bowie's boot
and said, "I think I will probably have to
settle for what I am now." Almost reluctantly, he stood up. "I will see about fetching
you a bottle."

When Travis left the room, Bowie dis-
solved in another fit of coughing. He
reached for the cameo on the bedside table
and gazed at Ursula's silhouette, beautiful
but frozen, so unlike the warm, animated,
loving face of his wife. Soon, Bowie thought.
Soon.

Chapter Twenty-seven

At the palisade, Crockett was just putting the finishing notes on his Irish air when, over in Béxar, the Mexican army band struck up the strident notes of the Deguello. Autry sighed and began preparing for the barrage that he knew was about to commence. "God," Autry said, "I despise that tune."

Crockett listened for a moment. Slowly, a smile crept across his face.

"Just figgered it out," he said.

Autry looked at him. "Figured out what?"

His fiddle in his hand, Crockett stood up and scurried to a nearby ladder. He climbed to the top of the main gate building and ran to the westernmost end, looking down on the nest of the eighteen-pounder cannon. With a grin, he raised his fiddle to his chin and began to play. His lively melody made no attempt to drown out the Deguello. Instead, he wove a new melody around its harsh call of no quarter. The men in the Alamo listened with astonishment as he turned the Mexicans' promise of death and destruction into a lively, somehow haunting, tune of hope, of defiance, of something like happiness.

The Mexican soldados heard it, too, and were as delighted by the sounds as the Texians. Jesús was standing at attention in formation and smiled at the wonderful music coming toward them. His sergeant saw Jesús's smile, and grinned himself. He said, "Croque . . ." and every man in the line knew who he was talking about.

For both sides, for these brief moments, there was no siege, no battle, no war — just music floating through the air. The men of the Alamo had known fear that day; they had experienced anger and desperation. But now, if only for an instant, they felt peace. Some even dared to feel encouraged. If one lone Texian fiddle could beat the massed Mexican bugles at their own game, then maybe a small band of soldiers really did stand a chance against those overwhelming odds. Nobody much believed that, but those who considered it were comforted by the thought, even if that comfort was destined to stop as soon as the music did.

Up on top of the main gate, Crockett lowered his fiddle, his improvised concert ended. He looked down at the men of the Alamo, washed in the soft reds and golds of the sunset, and grinned happily. "Amazing what a little harmony will do, ain't it?" he said. He hurriedly climbed back down the ladder and back to his post, to prepare for the barrage that was about to start.

But strangely . . . it did not.

It began to sink in to the garrison that no cannon were being fired and for some reason they knew that no cannon were going to be fired. The defenders slowly pulled their fingers from their ears, came out from their cover and stared at each other.

"Well," Scurlock said, "if that ain't the damnedest thing."

From the west wall, near Travis's headquarters, came a shout from young James Allen. "Rider going out! If you want to write letters, now's the time!"

Across the compound, men scrambled for any kind of paper they could find. Some found scraps of brown wrapping paper. Others tore the blank endpapers from books they carried in their packs. Isaac Millsaps thought of his blind wife, left behind in Gonzales. A lot of people thought she was a mighty strong woman, to raise six children without being able to see a thing. Millsaps knew her true strength was greater than anyone could suspect. He had never been much of a provider. He even thought of himself as a ne'er-do-well. Would never have been worth a damn, he thought, except for Mary. She was the spirit of their household, the heart. But, Isaac was ashamed to admit, even to himself, that she was the muscle, as well. She raised the children and, to a great extent, she raised him. If he never came home, she would get along just fine without him. Without her, though, Isaac did not think he could last for a month. He laughed to himself. He had been in this damned fort for less than a week and now he was about to go and get himself killed. He said to himself, "I guess that is a pretty fair indication of how well I can do without her." He squatted in a corner and began to scrawl:

Dearest Mary, I hope someone with a kind voice is reading this to you. If you could see, you would know how beautiful is this land, our home. I pray to the Almighty that we will be together again soon. Kiss the children for me. . . .

Jim Bonham wished that he had a proper quill to write with, instead of this tiny stump of a pencil. Always proud of his penmanship, he wanted his last message to have an elegance that his family, back on the plantation in South Carolina, would appreciate — and expect. He wished that he could gather all his warm memories of that place into these hastily scribbled words — the lush green forests where he and his father and cousins used to hunt for deer and boar; the languid creek where he had scampered after tadpoles as a boy, and beside which red-haired Essie Burke had introduced him to a very different kind of scampering when he was fifteen; the melancholy call of the whip-poor-will, and the even sadder songs that drifted up to the Bonham house from the slaves' quarters; the parades, the cotillions, the picnics — family. It was too much to express. Bonham had to settle for a few cursory, heartfelt words.

Know that my heart is with you all until the day, by God's will, we are reunited. Please remember me to my father and tell him to think of nothing but of coming here to this fair country when it is free . . .

William Ward, on the north wall, stared

into the night and thought of Ireland. Although he and his fellow Irishmen delighted in singing tearfully of their green homeland, the truth was, Ward did not miss it much. Life was hard on his father's farm, where hope was in as short supply as money. If rocks and regrets were potatoes and beef, they all would have been fat and happy. But Ward had been desperate to leave. And when he arrived in Texas — was it only eight months ago? — he knew that he had found the garden spot that he had always dreamed of.

> *My dearest Da,*
> *When this fight is over and we can set about the task of settling our land, I will have money enough to bring you to this blessed Texas, where the land is fertile and the future filled with promise. That day will come only after a struggle but we know what awaits us, and we are prepared to meet it. . . .*

Micajah Autry glanced over at Crockett, who was writing his own letter. Friends for only a few months, they had already forged a bond that both knew would last a lifetime. Autry softly barked out a bitter laugh at the thought. A lifetime . . . It was too late for regrets, but Autry thought of his wife, Nora, and felt a stab of pain. Never one to wax poetically romantic in his letters — he struggled to even remember his last missive to her — Autry decided to take this time to reassure her, and himself, about exactly what he was doing here.

I go whole hog in the cause of Texas. I expect to help them gain their independence and also to form their civil government, for it is worth risking many lives for.

He considered adding a postscript declaring his undying love, revealing to her that his own life was one of those at risk, that he never expected to write another letter to her. But he wrote none of those things. He simply signed the letter, folded it and wrote her address on the outside.

Crockett was writing to his daughter. It would not do at this late date to make her worry. If worse came to worst, she would learn of it soon enough. No, this letter would be a lighthearted, optimistic one. He liked it best when everybody was happy.

I am now blessed with excellent health and am in high spirits although I have been received by everybody with open ceremony of friendship. I must say that what I have seen of Texas it is the garden spot of the world. The best land and the best prospects for health I ever saw.

A dark thought flitted across his mind, wondering how his own health would be at this time tomorrow. But those kinds of thoughts were for his own rumination, not for a cheery letter to the folks back home. He continued writing.

I am in hopes of making a fortune for myself and my family, bad as my prospect has been. I hope you will all do the best you can and I will do the same. Do not be uneasy about me. I am among my friends.

Daniel Cloud's thoughts were not of a beloved daughter or a distant wife as he leaned against a cannon in the apse of the church, but of a sweetheart who was tantalizingly, torturously close by. Isabella was only a mile away, in her home in Béxar, but she may as well have flown away to a distant star. Her father, a loyal Mexican citizen and proud supporter of Santa Anna, had been incensed that one of these upstart gringo rebels had the nerve to pay court to his youngest daughter. Isabella's mother was more understanding, and even smiled at Cloud when her husband looked the other way, but she made it clear that nothing further could come of any of it. Cloud knew that there were nearly insurmountable obstacles to their happiness, but he had convinced Isabella — and himself — that once he made his fortune, her father would have to look at him in a different light. He would prove himself and they would be happy, blissfully happy, in this vast Eden. As it was, he was ordered into the Alamo so quickly that they never even had a chance to say good-bye.

My dearest Darling,
In my mind's eye, I see you as you were at the fandango, with your white lace dress and that accursed long fan. Remember how I teased you to stop hiding your face behind it, and how you smiled at me. There was no other woman in that room but you. There is no other woman in my heart but you . . .

Travis was writing, too. As Joe watched impassively, Travis stared at the page on his desk, halfway through a letter and unable to complete it. James Allen knocked on the door.
"Sir?"
Allen stood in the doorway, a satchel around his neck, a handful of letters in his

hand. "I have gathered most of the men's letters," he said.

Travis looked at Allen, then back down at his own letter. "Spare me a moment more?" he said.

Allen nodded, and said, "Yes, sir," and walked away.

With a sigh, Travis once again put his pen to paper and wrote, "Take care of my little boy . . ."

Reading the words on the page made Travis stop again. Tears welled up in his eyes and he quickly wiped them away, lest they fall on the letter and smear the ink. The letter read:

Take care of my little boy. If the country should be saved, I may make for him a splendid fortune; but if the country be lost and I should perish, he will have nothing but the proud recollection that he is the son of a man who died for his country.

Travis read the letter again and hesitated, as if putting off signing and sending it would hold off the inevitable. Then he dipped his quill in the small copper inkwell and signed his name for the last time in his life.

Crockett passed his letter to Autry with instructions to give it to Allen when he came back. He looked around the walls of the Alamo and saw men praying, thinking, remembering. There were no sounds from the Mexican fortifications to indicate that an attack was imminent but the men knew. Somehow, they just knew.

Crockett stepped into Bowie's quarters. Bowie smiled slightly when Crockett entered the room. Crockett smiled back, but he was dismayed at the way Bowie looked. Even if Santa Anna did not come in to finish the job pretty soon, it was clear that Bowie had only days to live.

"Have a seat, Congressman," Bowie said, nodding toward the stool at the foot of the bed.

"Now Jim," Crockett said, grinning, "you ought not go about saying that word too loud. I pride myself that I have made friends in this place, but if you go around reminding them of my sordid past, they might think less of me."

Bowie laughed and the laugh turned into a cough, and the single cough led to a spasm that lasted nearly a minute. When at last it ended he sank against his pillow, exhausted. "I would not worry about it. I doubt if many of the men could think less of you than they do now."

Crockett laughed, "Well, thank you for

your kind sentiments. A man always likes to know that he's well thought of."

"How are the men doing?" Bowie asked.

Crockett glanced out the ornate cross-shaped window. Through it, he could see part of the solemn façade of the Alamo church and the outside of the palisade. It was a cold night and there was no moon. "I believe that morale is pretty high, all things considered. The men have had a chance to write letters. Young Allen's riding out with them in a while. Did you want to write one? I could help. My spelling is gradually improving, day by day."

Bowie coughed again and shook his head. "Nobody to write to. Anything I got to say, I will be able to say to Ursula pretty soon, I expect."

Crockett looked at the floor. His head was beginning to ache.

Bowie saw the pained look on his face. "You scared, Davy?"

Crockett glanced up and grinned. "Skeered? I have been skeered a time or two in my life. But I often found that something that frightened me at first usually turned out to be something different by and by. On my wedding night with Polly — well, I was all a-tremble. You see, being a God-fearing country boy, I did not know much about the ways of love, and I could not help but feel that something mighty big was about to happen to me and I was not altogether sure that it was going to be a good something. Skeered? Yes, sir, I was skeered as a rabbit. But by the time nature had taken its course, I found it was a fear that I wanted to experience again as soon and as often as possible."

Bowie laughed.

"This here . . ." Crockett waved his hand toward the compound outside Bowie's door. ". . . This here might be something like that, I reckon. Seems awful fearsome from this side of things, but it might turn out to be all right, by and by."

The two men were silent for a moment. Crockett could never let melancholy overtake a room for very long and he suddenly brightened.

"I remember another time," he said with a smile. "I must-a been no more'n six years old and we were at a barn raising back in Tennessee. Well, we all lived so scattered that anything like this come to be kind of a cross between a circus and a tent meeting. The womenfolk would fill the tables with fine vittles and as soon as the sun started going down and the barn was built, there'd be fiddle music and dancing and all kinds of shenanigans. When I got a little older, I found there was some real fine shenanigans to partake in."

"Now hold on just a minute," Bowie said. "You just got through telling me that you approached your wedding night with fear and trepidation."

Crockett waved his hand dismissively, "I do not recall using the word 'trepidation,' and besides I'd prefer it if you did not cut the starch out of one of my tales with something as lowly as the facts."

Bowie smiled a little and said, "Sorry."

"Now," Crockett continued, "there was a feller at this barn raising who had the most fascinating talent. Had a voice that come out of his pocket. Yessir, believe me, the voice come right out of his pocket! And then, to add wonder to a marvel, he put that goldurned voice into my pocket. Well, sir."

Crockett looked down at his pocket and worked the flaps like a little mouth. He spoke in a falsetto voice: " 'Hello . . . Hello . . . I am trapped in your pocket.' Well, Jim, I liked to jump right out of my socks."

Bowie laughed.

"And that was not all, not by a long shot," Crockett said. "He also had him a moon-faced doll, mean as ten hornets, wearing a tricorn hat. She was real as you or me." He looked at his hand. " 'Hello. Hello. You are that young Davy, ain't ye?' Like to skeered me half to death, but at the same time I just could not get enough of it."

Both men laughed. Then Crockett's smile dropped and he picked up Bowie's pistols, checking their powder. When he was satisfied that both guns were loaded and in good working order, he placed them back on the table beside Bowie's bed.

Crockett looked at Bowie and said, "I rode on a steam train. I rode on a steamboat. I killed many a bear and got elected to Congress. Had two fine wives and some loving children. Not a bad life, I reckon. But sometimes I think I'd trade all them memories for five more minutes of that doll in the tricorn hat."

The two men, now friends, shared a knowing smile. Bowie removed his knife from its scabbard and stuck it into his bedside table, beside the pistols. He said, "They will come from all sides to keep you occupied but the real attack will be focused on one wall. Hold your wits and always keep one eye behind you."

Crockett looked up at Bowie. His eyes glinted with uncertainty, but Bowie shook his head ever so slightly.

"You do not need me any more than you need that fur cap," Bowie said. "You been on these walls every day of your life."

Crockett patted Bowie's leg and stood up. "I will see you later, Jim."

Bowie nodded and closed his eyes.

As Crockett emerged from Bowie's room, he saw James Allen riding out of the south wall gate. Somebody called out, "Godspeed, Jim." The sound of Allen's galloping horse gradually receded into the night. The Mexicans did not even try to stop him. It was as if they did not even care.

Crockett settled in at the palisade beside Autry. Many of the men had drifted off to sleep, but Autry was peering off into the distance.

"Better get some sleep, Micajah," Crockett said.

Autry smiled a little. "Something tells me I will be getting sleep enough, soon enough."

Crockett said, "Well, Jim Allen just rode out. Maybe he will bring back some help and we will get out of this thing all right."

Autry smiled wider. "You are an optimist, are you not, David?"

But Crockett was not smiling. He said, "Well, yes and no."

Chapter Twenty-eight

A cheery fire warmed the main room of the Yturri house. Candelabra were set on the table and on nearby floor stands; the entire room flickered with soft, golden light. The massive mahogany table was meant for large, luxurious dinners and festive social occasions. But tonight, the only one enjoying dinner and basking in the loveliness of the room was Santa Anna. His generals sat or stood uncomfortably while the president delicately placed a chicken bone on the fine china plate before him. There were no plates before the others. A large map took up most of the table. Santa Anna's aide, Batres, stood to the side with a long stick in his hand, to be used as a pointer.

In the next room, Santa Anna's bride, Juanita, waited. He was always at his most ardent after a show of force. Gathering all his generals before him and issuing commands to them would feed his sense of power. He merely had to speak, and they would act. Juanita had learned that as well. It did not pay to resist her husband. That only made things worse. Sometimes, when he barked orders at her in bed, telling her to do the most distasteful and immoral things, she thought about saluting him and saying, "Yes, Your Excellency!" But she knew that her moment of whimsy would result in a caning. And once he started caning her, his thoughts seemed to drift naturally toward other ways to hurt her, disgusting ways. No, it was best simply to do what he said, and pray for it to be over.

In the dining room, some of the generals looked at the map, studying its details. It had been drawn by cartographer Colonel Ygnacio de Labastida, who was not among those present. The map showed an overview of the entire area: all the buildings in Béxar, the jacales of La Villita, across the river, the winding river, the farmlands and wooded areas. Near the top of the map was a drawing of the Alamo compound, and it was upon this section that most of the generals' attention was focused.

Santa Anna, having completed his dinner,

nodded at his manservant Ben, who immediately set a small plate of apple slices before the president. Then he refilled Santa Anna's coffee cup and discreetly stepped back.

"General Cós," Santa Anna said, "you will be given opportunity to redeem yourself."

Cós nodded nervously. "Thank you, Your Excellency."

"You will lead the first charge," Santa Anna said, "Here, at the weak north wall."

As he spoke, Batres pointed at the spot with the stick.

Cós said nothing, but his face made clear that this was not exactly the assignment he would have chosen for himself.

If Santa Anna noticed the look, he ignored it.

"Colonel Duque will follow — from the northeast," Santa Anna said, as Batres pointed. "Romero, from the east. Morales from the south. General Ramirez y Sesma, your cavalry will patrol the perimeter of the compound in order to insure that no one escapes or retreats."

Each of the generals nodded as his name was mentioned, and continued to study the map. Castrillón had not glanced at the map once. He had been listening, biting his tongue, trying to talk himself out of saying what had to be said — but that which could only turn out badly for him. Finally, he took a deep breath and said, "Excellency, our twelve-pounder cannon arrives tomorrow. Why risk the lives of so many of our own who will die trying to take a wall that can easily be demolished by cannonade? In one day, the wall could be knocked down, forcing the Texians to surrender."

Santa Anna looked at his dinner plate, and nodded toward the bones. "What are the lives of soldiers," he said, "but so many chickens?"

"And if they surrender?" Castrillón asked.

Santa Anna dismissed the idea with a wave of his hand. "They are pirates, not soldiers. No prisoners."

Castrillón said, his voice growing in urgency, "Your Excellency, there are rules governing —"

Santa Anna pounded the table with his fist. Every man in the room jumped at the sound and braced himself for the onslaught. "I am governing!" Santa Anna shouted. "And you, sir, have no understanding of the difficulties that entails!"

The president stood up and paced the room for a moment, calming himself. No one else moved; they barely breathed. Santa

Anna leaned across the table toward Castrillón. His voice was lower now, more reasonable, as though he truly needed his generals to understand his point of view.

"I am committed to giving our country a national identity," he said. "Did we gain independence only to let our land be stolen from us? It stops here. It must. For if it doesn't, our grandchildren and their grandchildren will suffer the disgrace of one day begging for crumbs from the gringo."

He peered at every face around the table, and each general tried hard to meet his gaze. "Without blood, without tears," Santa Anna said, his voice nearly a whisper, "there is no glory."

Castrillón sighed and looked down at the table. He knew that the die was cast.

Santa Anna sat down again at the head of the table. He slowly ate another apple slice, smiling as he savored it. His demeanor was so completely different from the raving madman of a moment before that they might have been two different people. "And now," he said, "for the details."

He nodded at Batres, who passed out papers to each general — the orders of attack. Santa Anna said, "You will find all of your orders here. We will attack before dawn, so have your men ready and in place by two in the morning. That means you will have to awaken them by midnight and make them get ready."

The generals — most of them — nodded in assent.

Santa Anna continued, "Each column must be equipped with ladders, crowbars and axes to help them gain entry to the fort."

Almonte peered at the orders, then looked up.

"Excellency," he said, "it is very cold. It is written here that the men cannot carry blankets or wear their topcoats. Surely you —"

Santa Anna snapped, "I will have them carry nothing that may impede the rapidity of their motions. If they are cold, they will be warmed soon enough, in the heat of battle. Oh, and make sure that every man is wearing shoes."

Castrillón said softly, "Many of our men do not have shoes."

"Well then," Santa Anna said impatiently, "at least make sure they have sandals. I will not have this battle lost over bare feet."

Silence hung over the room for a long moment. No one else seemed as confident of victory as Santa Anna.

He nodded curtly, "That is all." The men stood and prepared to leave. "Oh," Santa

Anna said, "one more thing. Make sure that your men remain silent. If we surprise the rebels in their sleep, our task will be that much simpler." His voice softened. "Gentlemen, the honor of our nation is at stake. Tell your men that I expect each one to do his duty, to exert himself, and to give his country a day of glory and satisfaction. Tell them that their supreme commander knows well how to reward brave men."

The generals saluted and stepped from the warmth of the Yturri house into the bitter cold of the Béxar evening.

Chapter Twenty-nine

Silence enveloped the Alamo. When the expected barrage did not take place, the Texians were surprised and curious, but most of them were too exhausted to be suspicious. Almost none of the Texians had been able to sleep through the night for the past two weeks, and now the blessed quiet seductively enticed them to close their eyes. Some had the presence of mind to make sure their guns were loaded and nearby; others just drifted off at their places on the walls. Some even slept standing up.

Albert Grimes, the eighteen-year-old Georgia boy, was almost asleep when Captain Martin roughly shook his shoulder. Grimes jolted awake, instantly alert — and peeved.

"What the hell . . . Oh, sorry, Captain."

Martin nodded. "Sentry duty, son. We all have to take a turn."

Grimes glanced over the north wall to the little dugout about twenty yards outside the Alamo's walls and groaned. "Tonight? Captain, I swear I do not know if I can stay awake."

"You had better, Grimes," Martin said. "If you do not, either the Mexicans will slaughter you or I will."

Grimes smiled, but Martin was not joking. With a sigh, Grimes stood up, checked his flintlock, powder and shot and slipped over the wall. He ran, crouched low to the ground, to the dugout. There were no signs that he had been spotted by the Mexicans. He settled in and peered through the darkness toward the northern cannon positions. He wished that he had managed to bring a cup of coffee with him. It was damn cold and it would help him stay awake. But he had jumped without thinking — always a failing of his, he thought. Now here he was sitting in a hole in the ground, while behind him, the lucky men in the Alamo were sleeping like the dead.

In the Mexican camp just across the river, Jesús also was sleeping peacefully. His sunny dreams of home were rudely interrupted by the sergeant, who awakened him as quietly as possible. It took a moment for Jesús to get his bearings. Looking to his left and right, he saw his fellow soldados preparing for battle: tightening belts, loading weapons, kneeling for last prayers, all without uttering a word. Not for the first time, Jesús wished that there were a priest to give his confession to. His officers had told the men that the Alamo would fall easily, that it would be a grand and glorious victory for Mexico. But, Jesús wondered, do men not die, even in easy battles? The Texians were outnumbered, but they were still behind walls, they still had cannon. It seemed to Jesús that the odds were not nearly as much in the Mexicans' favor as everyone kept insisting.

When all of the soldados were ready, they formed columns. The sergeants and other officers walked along the rows of nervous men, quietly repeating orders over and over: "Be very quiet. Do not do anything to betray our position. Load your rifles and fix your bayonets — and do it silently."

The officers gave the order to move forward, depending primarily on hand signals and whispered commands. They crouched low and walked toward the Alamo on cat's paws. Jesús fell into step with hundreds of men, led by General Cós, quietly approaching the fort from the north. They stopped about two hundred yards away, in a small forest. Jesús's hands were freezing and his feet felt numb. He was trembling, as was nearly everyone else he could see. He hoped that his fellow soldados could not tell that he wasn't trembling entircly from the cold.

At the palisade, all the Tennesseans were sleeping — all but Crockett. His loaded rifles were propped up beside him, but he held his fiddle in his lap, staring straight ahead. He had the strong urge to play a tune, but he knew that it would only wake up the men. Still, he thought, music can be a tolerable comfort at a time like this — take your mind off the fear. With one finger he plucked a string, then stopped. Had he heard a noise outside? Standing up, he peered over the palisade and into the black of the night. Nothing.

Four hundred men under Colonel Duque peeled off from the main force and headed for the center of the north wall. Many of the men carried the ladders that they had spent the previous day building.

The three hundred riflemen under Colonel Romero also carried ladders. They headed toward the low walls of the cattle pen on the east side of the Alamo.

To the south, a hundred riflemen under Morales moved toward the palisade. Only two of them lugged ladders. The palisade was low but tricky. If anyone got over it, it would not be because of ladders.

In Béxar, the cavalry mounted their horses and began riding, as quietly as possible, to their predetermined place on the east side, behind Romero. They were not part of the attack — they were just there to skewer with their lances any gringo who tried to make a run for it.

Jesús heard the arrival of more men on the north side. He looked back and was a little shocked to see that it was the band, their brass instruments out of their cases and ready to play. Jesús wondered, is the battle going to be set to music?

The Mexican army was nearly in place, on all four sides of the Alamo. At a motion from the officers, the men lay down on the ground to wait for the order to attack.

At the north wall, neither William Ward not Dolphin Floyd had been able to join the others in sleep. They sat silently, wrapped in their own thoughts, for a long time. Then Floyd chuckled.

"What?" Ward asked.

Floyd said, "What time you reckon it is?"

Ward looked into the sky. "Hard to say, lad. Hasn't the moon been behind a cloud all night?"

"Would you say it is after midnight?" Floyd said.

"If I were to guess, I'd say well past midnight. Two, maybe three in the morning."

"Well then, sir," Floyd said smiling, "you can wish me a happy birthday."

Ward smiled back. "You do not tell me so?"

"Yes, sir, March sixth," Floyd said. "I am twenty-one years old today."

Ward patted Floyd on the back. "Happy birthday, me boy-o. And many, many more."

Travis also found it difficult to sleep, but he knew that he had to. He was as exhausted as any of the men, and they relied on him to keep a clear mind — now, more than ever. He returned to his quarters and saw that Joe was already asleep. Travis lay down on his bed and covered himself with a thick woolen blanket. Thoughts of Charlie, of Rebecca, of Rosanna, filled his mind. He also thought of the girl in Béxar . . . Was that only two weeks ago? Such tenderness. He had purchased her body, but she had given him more: solace, warmth, comfort, kindness.

He left a tall candle lit but fought the temptation to read himself to sleep with the volume of poetry that he carried with him always. He said softly to himself, "Tyger! Tyger! burning bright . . . In the forests of the night . . . What immortal hand or eye . . . Could frame thy fearful symmetry?" He had loved that one since childhood. And the thrilling, chivalrous works of Sir Walter Scott. And, of course, Shakespeare. So much to read, to know; so many wonderful and important ideas. Travis wondered if all those ideas had paved the road that led him directly to this terrible place.

Grimes scanned the darkness from his dugout position as long as he could. Several times he felt his eyes closing. With great effort he forced himself awake. He considered pinching or slapping himself — anything to remain sharp. He certainly did not want to have to face the wrath of Captain Martin. But soon, even his sternest resolve could not keep him awake. Grimes's head drooped onto his chest and he slipped to almost a sitting position, his rifle propped on the edge of the shallow pit. He hoped, as he drifted off, that he would not have to wake up for a long, long time. But he did wake up when a hand roughly covered his mouth, and two more held his arms. Grimes's eyes popped open as a bayonet was rammed into his chest. Before he had time to react, another bayonet stuck deep into him, just below the ribs. Earlier, he had had so much trouble keeping his eyes open. Now, they would never close again.

The army was moving forward silently, on every side of the Alamo. Jesús was filled with terror, and all around him, his fellow soldados were quaking with fear and anticipation. To his left, he saw the eyes of José Torres dart back and forth, as though something inside him were about to explode. And so it was:

"Viva Santa Anna!" Torres shouted.

Across the way, a voice called out from Duque's column: *"Viva la Republica!"*

There had been no order to charge, but suddenly, the Mexicans were running toward the walls of the Alamo, screaming like demons. Jesús wished desperately that he could run in the opposite direction, but he was swept along in this wave of horror, and nearly wept with fear as he saw the fort grow closer and closer.

Adjutant John Baugh, the officer of the day, was the first man to see the charge, from a parapet on the west wall. He turned into the compound and shouted, "They are on us! The Mexicans!"

Travis, not yet asleep, was on his feet in an instant. He shook Joe by the shoulder, grabbed his sword and shotgun and raced toward the north wall. As he ran, he called out as loudly as he could, "Come on, boys! The Mexicans are upon us!"

In the Alamo church, Bonham, Dickinson, Esparza and the rest of the cannon crew woke up and sprang to their places at the guns. Already primed, it was the work of a moment to load them and fire both cannon into the wave of men approaching from the east.

Crockett flung his fiddle aside and grabbed the nearest rifle. His men rose up at the palisade. Autry got off the first shot, but it was too dark to see if it hit its mark. His only comfort was they were massed so thickly out there, he was almost certain to hit something.

Texians came sprinting out of the long barracks, rifles in hand, spreading out in four directions for their stations. Men who had been sleeping at their places on the walls were now firing into the night. There was no time to reload. After each shot, the men threw those rifles to the ground, then picked up the next. Only when every flint-lock was empty could they risk a moment to kneel behind the wall and ram in more powder and shot.

Jesús had not yet fired a shot. He gripped his rifle in his hands and just kept running toward the wall, closer, closer. The combined rifle and cannon fire from the north wall ripped through the tightly packed militiamen. The air was filled with screams of agony. Jesús was screaming, too. He had not been hit but he was wet with the blood of the men who were dying around him. They seemed to be dropping by the dozens. He tried to remember the words of the Rosary, or any prayer he had ever heard. But his mind was blank, filled only with the sickening dread of impending death.

At the next massed rifle blast from the north wall, more men fell. Others turned and began to run back to the protection of the woods. Jesús was swept along with them again, being pulled this way and that way, like a goat on a leash. The retreating men ran directly into their own officers, who threatened them with saber and broadsword, pistol and lance, to turn around again and head back to the Alamo.

"Charge!" a sergeant shouted. "Charge!"

On the platform at the rear of the church,

the two cannon fired almost continually into Romero's column, knocking the first line of attackers off their feet. Dickinson and Bonham had trained their crew well. After each blast, the men loaded both cannon in seconds and fired again. Romero's disoriented men scattered frantically toward the cattle pen to the north, but the little cannon there met them and drove them back. Texian gunmen fired volley after volley into their ranks and the Mexicans kept heading north, hoping to find cover somewhere.

At the palisade, Crockett and his men kept up a withering fire into Morales's advancing column. Mexican soldiers fell left and right. The single cannon of the Tennesseans fired from its embrasure at the center of the palisade. The men of Morales's regiment who were still standing after the blast turned west, toward the lunette that protected the Alamo's main gate. When the cannon fired, the concussion awoke Bowie; the noise of the rifle fire had not disturbed his fevered sleep. Through his cross-shaped window, he could see Morales's men running past. He looked frantically around the room for Juana, then remembered that he had told her to spend the night in the baptistery with the other women. It was hard for

Bowie to catch his breath, but he inched his way toward a sitting position on the bed and once again checked his pistols. They were primed and loaded.

Jesús sprinted toward the north wall, screaming without knowing it. Another cannon blast shook the ground under his feet and several men to his left were shredded by canister shot. He slammed against the base of the wall with a dozen other survivors. Above him, the Texians, including Travis, continued to fire, but Jesús noticed that they could not manage to fire straight down, where he was. For a Texian to do that, he would have to climb onto the top of the wall, leaving himself open. Within moments, the ground against the north wall was crowded with soldados, amazed to find themselves, for the moment, in relative safety.

Colonel Duque's men, losing momentum, slowed down fifty yards from the north wall. "Halt!" Duque called out. "Ready . . . aim . . . fire!"

His men could barely see through the smoke and the darkness. The front row of his ragged column unleashed a volley at the north wall. Almost none of their bullets reached the Texians for whom they were intended. But several of the men with Jesús were hit by the volley from their own side. Jesús dove for the ground as balls ricocheted off the wall by his head.

At the palisade, Crockett and his men kept up a steady stream of fire at the Morales column as the Mexicans continued their frenzied retreat toward the west. The soldiers, trying to avoid the Texians' bullets as they moved in panic to the right, ran directly into their own officers, who angrily drove them on, cursing and striking the men.

On the west wall, the gunnade fired out through its hole in the wall. Here, however, the Mexicans managed to jump aside before the blast. As soon as the gunnade fired, a half dozen soldados, knowing the Texians would have to reload, wheeled and fired their muskets into the hole. The two Texians operating the gun were blown back. One of the Mexicans began to chop at the hole with an ax.

As more Mexicans massed directly under the walls at north and west, the Texians were forced to expose themselves in order to fire down on them. For the soldados, this was a little like target practice: Each time a Texian came into sight, he was brought down by three, four, five Mexican musket balls. When a Texian fell, there was no one to take his place, so each Texian death left larger and larger gaps along the wall.

To the north, ladders were being pushed up against the wall, but the Texians knocked them down as soon as they were set up. General Juan Amador, impatient with this deadly game, began to climb up the wall itself. As Jameson had feared, the ragged wall with its chinks and holes provided perfect hand- and footholds, and soon dozens of soldados were swarming up it.

Travis fired his shotgun directly into the approaching mass of men. He blasted the face off a Mexican soldier, and his falling body swept three more soldados along with him to the ground. "Depress the cannon!" Travis shouted. "Keep them off the walls!"

Joe handed a loaded rifle to Travis and took the shotgun. As Joe reloaded it for his master, Travis moved to the edge of the wall, leaned over and fired directly into the right ear of the man standing directly next to Jesús, causing a thick red spray to explode out the left side of his head. In terror, Jesús fired blindly upward, without aiming, without even looking in the direction of the shot.

Jesús's musket ball slammed into Travis's forehead, knocking him back, head-over-heels down the ramp. His body rolled to a stop at Joe's feet. Joe stared at the lifeless Travis, whose eyes were wide open as if caught by surprise. In other circumstances, he might have felt a certain sadness, or perhaps relief. But shock and terror had shut off his other emotions. As the Mexicans began swarming over the position, hacking and stabbing the Texians, Joe gently lay the shotgun down beside Travis's body and walked, as if in a trance, back toward Travis's quarters.

As Joe walked through the courtyard, he was surrounded by explosions, screams of fear and pain, the acrid smell of gunpowder. Texians were beginning to abandon their places on the walls and were searching, panicked, for places to hide, or for better defensive positions. Joe was oblivious to all the mayhem. It seemed to him like a dream, filled with strange shapes, weird sounds, inexplicable images. Behind him, the Mexicans started to top the walls in twos and threes. They were running toward the buildings around the courtyard where they had seen the Texians retreat. But just as Joe could not be completely sure that he was seeing them, they did not seem to be aware of him at all. When he reached Travis's quarters — where only minutes before he had been sleeping, snug and warm — Joe stopped and looked around. He could not think of anything to do, so he walked to the back wall and sat down. Beside him was Travis's leather saddlebag, ornately monogrammed WBT. Joe picked it up and held it tight against his chest. He began to repeat over and over, *"Me naygro, yo soy naygro . . ."*

The north wall was now almost undefended. Dolphin Floyd fell across the cannon, a bullet wound in his temple. Young Galba Fuqua was hit point-blank in the face, the musket ball shattering his jaw. He staggered backward but did not fall. His bottom jaw dropped unnaturally and the pain was unbearable. Holding his jaw together with both hands, Galba rushed down the ramp, running toward the church.

A few other Texians pushed ladders away from the edge with their rifle butts or fired down at the climbing Mexicans, but each time, another ladder and another soldier took its place. William Ward looked past the struggle just in front of him to a wave of charging reserves. He had almost no men left. "Fall back!" Ward shouted. "Spike the cannon!" Just as he turned to do so, Ward was hit in the back of the head by a musket ball. He stood there for a moment, wavering like a scarecrow in a hard wind. Then, his body went limp and dropped to the ground.

To the north and the west, Mexican artillerymen began firing Congreve rockets at the Alamo. As the missiles hit, the thatched roofs of the buildings along the west wall began to burst into flames. Overhead, flares were flying in the air. Attached to parachutes, they sparked red and white. This fireworks display would have seemed beautiful and thrilling on another day. But this morning it served only to illuminate the horror inside the walls of the Alamo.

The cannon crew on the ramp in the rear of the church was keeping up a steady fire, but at this point, there were almost no Mexican soldiers in sight. Nearly every Mexican survivor who had at first attacked from the rear of the compound on the east side had moved around to the north or south, searching both for protection and for an easier entrance to the fort. Dickinson could see across the compound that the Mexicans were now swarming over the north wall. He turned to Bonham and shouted, "I will be back." He raced down the ramp to the baptistery, where Susanna and the baby, along with other women and children, were hiding in the shadows.

"Susanna!" Dickinson cried.

She stood up, panic in her eyes. Little Angelina was screaming, backed by a chorus of weeping and moaning from the others in the room. Susanna embraced her husband, burying her face in his chest. He wanted to say something, wanted to craft a farewell that would sum up his love for her and the child, and his deepest regret for getting them all involved in this hopeless situation. But there were no words for any of this. Smelling her hair brought a barrage of fleeting images of happiness, images he hoped he could retain for the next little while. Perhaps if he held on to them long enough, when the time came, he could step directly from this dark reality into that warm and welcoming dream world forever.

Dickinson held Susanna almost at arm's length as they looked desperately into each other's eyes. After a long moment, Dickinson kissed Angelina on the head, then quickly turned and ran back up the ramp to his post.

Green Jameson was loading the eighteen pounder in the southwest corner when he saw a mob of blue uniformed enemy rushing across the compound from the north. He called out, "They are over the wall! Turn it, turn it!" The crew struggled to wheel the big cannon around.

Crockett, at the palisade, heard Jameson's cry and turned around. His Tennesseans had kept anyone from coming over their fragile wood fence, but the Mexicans had just kept running around the outside to the opposite side of the fort. Now Crockett stared in horror as hundreds of Mexican soldiers came streaming over the north wall, rushing down the ramps in wave after wave.

Crockett turned to Autry and shouted, "Behind us!"

"Give 'em hell," Autry replied. Crockett and the other men began firing almost without aiming into the throng of invaders, reloading frantically.

A rifle was stuck through a loophole in a wall of the long barracks. A white cloth hung from the barrel. It was waved back and forth as a gesture of surrender. Several Mexicans approached cautiously to apprehend the ones who were giving up. When they opened the door, a barrage of gunfire cut most of them down.

Other Mexicans, seeing the act, seethed at the deceit by the Texians and with an infuriated roar swarmed into the room, viciously hacking and slicing the defenders with bayonets.

Elsewhere in the long barracks, the New Orleans Greys raced into their fallback trenches, slamming the doors shut, and waited for their very literal last-ditch effort.

The Mexicans followed them inside almost immediately. The soldados flooded into the smoke-filled rooms, shooting, stabbing, screaming with blood lust as the Texians fought back with knives, rifle butts, fists, teeth. The darkness of the rooms made the struggle even more horrible. No one could be completely sure that he was not hacking away at one of his comrades instead of one of the enemy.

Jameson had the eighteen pounder completely turned around now, and fired it directly into the wave of Mexicans inside the compound. The blast scattered bodies and severed limbs; it cut a bloody swath not only through the throng of soldados but through individual soldados as well.

"Reload!" Jameson shouted. Before anyone could prime the big gun again, a musket ball exploded through Jameson's chest and he fell face-forward. A volley of gunfire from the ground just outside the southwest corner cut down the rest of the Texian crew from behind. Immediately, ladders began to appear on the wall and soldados climbed over. A sergeant barked an order and several Mexicans began pushing the dead bodies of the Texians off the cannon and swinging it toward the church.

Twenty sick and wounded men lay on cots in the infirmary on the second floor of the long barracks. Those who could hold knives or pistols braced themselves for the inevitable attack. Others simply lay there, cringing in fear. Some of the more seriously wounded, mercifully, were unconscious or in a daze. Amos Pollard, the main surgeon of the Alamo garrison, stood at the doorway of the infirmary, unarmed. When the Mexicans finally rushed up the stairs he shouted, "These are wounded men! They are noncombatants." Before he could say more, he was run through with two bayonets. Soldados swarmed through the infirmary, quickly dispatching the rest of the patients.

Now there was more of the attacking Mexican force inside the walls of the Alamo than outside. Like a ship rapidly taking on water, the Alamo's walls were covered by a steady flow of Mexicans. They streamed in over the north wall, over and through the west wall, up and over the lunette at the main gate, into the cattle pen.

But not over the palisade. There, Crockett and his men crouched with their backs to the wooden emplacement and fired into the compound. They continued to move sideways, trying to make it into the fortified front entry of the church. Tom Waters set down his dog. "Go on now, Jake, get outta here," he urged. But the dog refused to leave his side. He was licking Waters's hand when Waters was hit by a blast from several Mexican muskets. He fell into the shallow ditch by the palisade and lay faceup. The dog, not knowing where else to go, burrowed in next to his master's body and watched the Mexicans stream by.

Several Texians, watching in panic as the enemy swept toward them like a multidirectional tide, leaped over the palisade and started to run into the darkness. "Try to get to the Alameda!" called out one of the Texians. The others, desperate for any idea that might mean escape, took his call to heart and headed south, for the road out of town.

They scattered, but this was precisely the moment that the lancers had been waiting for. The horsemen easily caught the fleeing men and impaled each one on a lance. It was almost like sport. But one Texian, armed with a double-barrel shotgun and a single-barrel pistol, stopped abruptly in the middle of the plain. He raised his shotgun and pulled the trigger. A lancer, half of his neck blown away, dropped off his horse. Another lancer cried out, "Eugenio!" and bore down on the Texian, who raised his pistol at the charging Mexican. He pulled the trigger — and it misfired. A second later, the Texian was run through by the lance. Foamy blood poured from his lips as he fell to his knees. The lance protruding from his chest propped him up and he died kneeling, as if in prayer.

One of the running men was overtaken by two horsemen, who simply trampled over him, the horses' hooves cracking his spine and caving in his skull. Another was mowed down by a lance that was flung like a javelin from horseback.

Two men were able to reach a thicket, trying to evade the trio of lancers who rode rings around them. Yelling with excitement, the lancers herded them like stray calves, their horses' hooves splashing in the swampy ground. One man dove into the tangle of spiny underbrush, but was immediately pinioned by a pair of lances. He screamed as he was pierced again and again.

The other man vanished. The lancers carefully rode around the thicket, looking at the underbrush, knowing he could not have gone far. Suddenly, a shot rang out from under a bush. Too angry to be cautious, the lancers rode toward the bush. The Texian had fired only a single shot because he had only a single gun and one bullet. Then he bundled himself on the ground with his arms wrapped around his head. "Don't kill me," he cried. "Don't kill me...."

The lancers did not understand English. Even if they had, they were in no mood to grant this gringo's wish. He was trampled by their horses first, then perforated repeatedly by their lances.

In the baptistery, Susanna Dickinson held her baby tight, hiding in the darkness of a corner with Juana and the Esparzas. To see Almeron, all she would have to do was step out of the room and look up the ramp, but she could not bear to do it. If he were still alive, she would not be able to resist running to him. If not, she did not think that she could stand seeing him. So she sat and held her child and wept.

Suddenly, Galba Fuqua burst into the baptistery. He ran straight for Susanna.

"Galba!" she screamed, quickly standing up.

He was holding his shattered jaw in place with both hands, while blood gushed from his mouth and the wounds in both sides of his face. He tried desperately to say something to Susanna.

She ran to him and tried to tie a bandage under his jaw but he shook his head angrily. Once again, he tried to speak, but could make nothing but grunting, moaning noises.

"What can I do, Galba?" Susanna said.

Tears filled his eyes. He gave her a hopeless look, shook his head once again and ran back out into the thick of the battle.

Crockett, Autry and other Tennesseans were just outside the door of the church, at the barricade made up of trunks, desks, barrels and whatever scraps of wood they could find. They were as far as Galba got. Running blindly, he was immediately riddled with bullets and fell back against the façade of the church. He died directly under the statue of St. Francis.

While Crockett and the rest savagely defended the entrance to the church, several Mexican soldiers climbed to the top of the long barracks and began firing into the roofless building from there. Bonham was struck with a bullet from above and staggered backward. A second later, he was cut to ribbons by gunfire from above. Almeron Dickinson looked around wildly for the source of the gunfire but he never saw the riflemen on the long barracks roof before they riddled him with bullets. Bonham rolled down the ramp and came to rest directly in front of the baptistery. Susanna saw him and instinctively ran to his side, screaming. Ana

Esparza darted from the baptistery and grabbed Susanna by the arm to drag her back to safety. Gregorio, already hit twice, saw his wife exposing herself to danger and shouted, "Ana!"

Ana and Susanna looked up the cannon ramp. Almeron was slumped over one of the cannon, blood pouring from bullet holes in his chest, back and legs. Gregorio, bleeding from his arm and his side, started toward Ana but was cut down by a blast of withering fire from the roof. The two women shrieked in horror. Susanna fell to the ground, screaming. Ana pulled her to her feet and dragged her back inside, where Juana and the other women and children huddled. When they were in the baptistcry again, Ana and Susanna collapsed into each other's arms, wailing with grief.

With a bone-rattling crash, the eighteen pounder in the southwest corner was fired down at the chapel entrance, blowing apart the thrown-together breastworks. Autry was shredded in the blast and fell backward, gasping. The other men crouched behind what was left of the barricade and tried to keep up a steady fire. They knew that one more such blast would finish them all.

Crockett knelt by Autry's side and lifted his head. His own arm was bleeding.

"Micajah," Crockett said in an anguished voice.

"They've killed me," Autry said hoarsely.

Crockett's eyes filled with tears. "I am real sorry about all this."

Autry stared directly into Crockett's eyes. He looked startled. The expression on Autry's face did not change at all when he died a second later.

With a deafening concussion, another blast hit the remnants of the barricade. Three men were blown apart. Crockett and the few surviving Tennesseans were thrown to the ground by the blast. Although dazed, they were able to get up and retreat into the church.

Lying in his bed, Bowie had been listening to the progress of the battle. He could tell that the Alamo's cannon were now firing into the compound instead of out, and could hear the enraged cries of the approaching Mexicans. He aimed both of his pistols directly at the door and waited. One last fit of coughing left Bowie breathing hard, gasping. Suddenly, his door slammed open and Bowie tensed, glaring at the Mexicans with watery eyes. A half-dozen soldados rushed into the room, bayonets gleaming. The first two in the door were brought down by twin blasts from Bowie's pistols. But the others followed so quickly that he had no chance to reload. His legendary knife was stuck in the bedside table. A second before the Mexicans plunged their bayonets into his chest, he reached for the table . . . past the knife . . . to Ursula's cameo. He was dead before he was able to reach it. Bowie's eyes were open in horror as the soldiers stabbed and hacked him with their bayonets. One officer placed the barrel of his musket to Bowie's temple and pulled the trigger.

Crockett's men were gathered by the cannon ramp inside the church. They were holding rifles, knives and chunks of stone, dug in for one last stand. There was no more ammunition. They would have to meet whatever was about to happen with little more than scraps. They stared at the doorway, which was draped in smoke, and waited for the inevitable.

Crockett turned toward the sacristy and saw little Enrique Esparza huddling with a few other children and their weeping mothers. The boy seemed so out of place in all this that Crockett felt disoriented for an instant. In fact, Crockett himself seemed desperately out of place. He had come to Texas looking and hoping for many things — none of which was a brutal death in a ragged ruin of a church. He nodded a small greeting to Enrique as, suddenly, fifty screaming Mexicans charged through the smoke, firing their rifles, thrusting their bayonets. Crockett grabbed his rifle by the muzzle and held it over his head, ready to use it as a club. He swung hard. The gun thudded against the skull of a soldado, and then he and his men were overwhelmed by a sea of bayonets. All was frenzy, chaos, and pain — horrible pain. And then, it was over.

Chapter Thirty

Miles away, Sam Houston knelt low, his ear to the ground. Travis had promised to fire the Alamo's cannon on a regular schedule as long as the fort still stood. But Houston heard nothing, neither the Alamo's cannon nor Santa Anna's bombardment. With a sigh, he slowly rose, bearing the weight of all that was tragic about the situation.

Deaf Smith stood nearby. Seeing Houston's troubled face he said, "Sam?"

Houston shook his head. Then he looked up, straight at the sun, bright and hot in the sky.

A flock of buzzards made lazy figure eights. There were enough of them to soften the pain of staring at the sun, but their presence just made things all the clearer. Finally, his eyes could not take it any longer, and he lowered them, peering around the courtyard of the Alamo.

David Crockett was on his knees, hands tied behind him. All around were the bodies of his friends. Several of them also had their hands tied. They had been forced into kneeling positions after they were captured, and summarily shot. One of the Mexican generals had pled for their lives. At least, that is how it seemed to Crockett. But the obvious leader — could this be the infamous Santa Anna? — would have none of it. The gaudily dressed general watched men die all around Crockett with a look that indicated only casual interest, as he might watch baby ducklings frolic in a pond.

Beyond the circle of his friends, Crockett was surrounded by most of the Mexican army. Those directly in Santa Anna's line of sight were standing at attention, in sharp formation. There were cavalrymen on horseback. Pioneers with thick leather aprons and huge, bloody axes in their hands. Regular foot soldiers. An execution squad stood slightly to Crockett's right. One of them was the battery sergeant, who seemed nervous about pointing his bayonet at the legendary "Croque." They were all waiting for orders, to see what would happen next.

Beyond these men in formation, hundreds of other soldiers lined the walls, sitting informally, watching the show. Jesús stood with a crowd near the long barracks.

Crockett did not know why his comrades had been slaughtered or why he had been spared, but he soon got an idea.

"Crockett!" Santa Anna said, with amused satisfaction. "Davy Crockett!"

Crockett stared at him, without expression.

Santa Anna said in Spanish, "If you wish to beg for your life, this would be the appropriate time." He turned to Almonte and commanded, "Explain this to him."

Almonte stepped forward and said to Crockett in English, "Throw yourself on the mercy of His Excellency, Antonio López de Santa Anna!"

Crockett slowly looked around at the hundreds of troops surrounding him. A sharp frisson of dread jolted through his body and he wanted to close his eyes and make all this go away. Just when he began to feel that his body was about to start trembling with fear, he looked down at the ground and thought of something very peculiar indeed: *Lion of the West.* He almost laughed aloud. That silly Nimrod Wildfire. He had a lot to answer for as far as Crockett was concerned. That damned legend. Should have been a good thing, should have made him rich and powerful and the envy of all. But all it did was to get him killed. He spent a lot of time trying to convince people that he was David Crockett, the congressman, the man of substance and promise. But all they wanted to hear about was "Davy" Crockett, the backwoodsman, the bear hunter, the Indian fighter, the country buffoon. *Well, here it is,* Crockett thought. *Time to choose. Who are you really: David or Davy?*

Crockett looked up and stared at Santa Anna for another moment. He smiled a little. "You're Santanna?" he said in a hoarse voice.

Santa Anna understood him and nodded.

Crockett said softly, in a friendly, almost conversational tone, "Thought you would be taller."

Almonte looked confused. This gringo was not acting nearly obsequious enough.

Crockett said to Almonte, "Tell him I am willing to discuss terms of surrender."

Almonte was almost relieved. He turned to Santa Anna and said in Spanish, "He is willing to discuss terms of surrender."

Santa Anna smiled at Crockett pleasantly, enjoying this game of cat and mouse. He would listen to his terms, and then he would have the rebel killed. Today's victory would be complete.

Crockett said, "If the general here will have his men put down their weapons and peacefully assemble, I promise I will take you to General Houston and try my best to get him to spare most of your lives."

Almonte was stunned. Was this man totally insane?

"That said," Crockett continued, his smile growing a little wider, "Sam's a mite prickly . . . so no promises."

Almonte just stared at Crockett, wondering what kind of man would sign his own death sentence in this way. Were the stories about him true? Was he simply biding his time before performing some superhuman deed that would save his life and destroy his enemies?

"Tell him," Crockett said.

Almonte hesitated, glancing at the still smiling Santa Anna.

Angrily, Crockett barked, *"Tell him!"*

Almonte nodded and turned to Santa Anna. "He wants us to surrender, Excellency." The smile faded from Santa Anna's face. He bristled, raised his hand and nodded to the execution squad.

Castrillón stepped forward, a desperate

look on his face. "Excellency," he said, "please spare him!"

A sergeant who had not participated in the battle saw the moment as the perfect way to see blood and action and — perhaps more important — to please the president. He shouted to the execution squad, "Kill him!"

But Crockett did not hear any of it. What he heard was the voice of James Hackett . . . or was it his own voice? "I'm a screamer. I got the roughest racin' horse, the prettiest sister, the surest rifle and the ugliest dog in the district. I am half horse and half alligator with a whiff of harricane . . ."

"Kill him!"

Crockett grinned, staring directly into the eyes of the execution squad. He said, "I'm a screamer . . ."

The men moved forward swiftly and plunged a halfdozen bayonets into Crockett's chest.

Chapter Thirty-one

Joe was found in Travis's quarters, still sitting on the floor, still clutching the saddlebag. A Mexican officer cautiously entered and, when he saw Joe, quickly raised his rifle and aimed it straight at Joe's forehead. Joe held his hands in the air, praying he would not forget the words he had practiced for so long — *"Me naygro . . . me no disparo . . ."* The officer's face softened and he lowered his rifle. He spoke to Joe, but since he said none of the four Spanish words Joe understood, the frightened young man just looked at him, bewildered. The officer motioned for Joe to follow him. When Joe stood up, the officer took the saddlebag from his hands, then inclined his head toward the courtyard. Joe stepped out into the sunlight.

It was an abattoir. Joe impulsively

clamped his hand over his mouth, to keep from vomiting, to stop himself from screaming. The ground was carpeted with corpses, like statues stiffly carved in the horrible positions of their last seconds of life. Joe almost tiptoed through the carnage, trying not to look down. He tripped over a Texian's boot and fell face-first into the bloody dirt. He frantically scrambled to get up, willing himself not to succumb to the panic that threatened to overwhelm him.

Joe was led to an officer, splendidly dressed in a uniform of red, blue and gold. From his clothing and his attitude, Joe decided that this must be the commander — Santa Anna himself. Everything he had heard from the men in the Alamo made him believe that Santa Anna was the devil incarnate. Joe did not even want to try to imagine what horrors the president had in store for him. As soon as Santa Anna glanced his way, Joe said in a soft, pleading voice, *"Me naygro . . . me naygro.* Please don't kill me. I mean, *me no disparo . . ."*

Santa Anna smiled warmly and put his hand on Joe's shoulder. *"Tranquillo, mi amigo,"* he said. *"Te hemos libertado."*

Almonte, standing close by, translated for Joe. "Do not worry," he said. "We have made you free."

Santa Anna spoke to Almonte, who in turn spoke to Joe. "The general wishes to see the famous ones."

Santa Anna nodded. "Travis," he said, "*y el fanfurrón Buy.*"

"Travis," repeated Almonte, "and the great braggart Bowie."

Joe nodded. Maybe they really were not going to slaughter him. "Yes, sir, I can show you Colonel Travis and Colonel Bowie," he said. Joe walked to the north wall, followed by Santa Anna and several of his officers and aides. He carefully made his way up the ramp, slick with blood, until he found the body of Travis, exactly where he had fallen. Joe knelt beside him. Travis's eyes were open. The hole in his forehead was deceptively small. From the pool of blood which served as his pillow, Joe assumed that the hole in the back of his head was far larger and angrier. Curiously, looking at his master this way made Joe feel an unexpected sadness. The man had bought him and owned him like a horse or pig. And if Joe had ever displeased him, Travis would have sold him like any piece of property that had outlived its usefulness. But he had always been kind to Joe, after his fashion; and, for good or bad, the two men had shared their lives for a long time.

"This is Colonel Travis," he said to Santa Anna. "He was my master." Then he stood up and walked back down the ramp. The Mexican officers followed him all the way across the courtyard to view the corpse of James Bowie.

Toward the end of the day, Joe watched as the bodies of Travis, Bowie, Crockett and all the others were consumed by flames. The Mexicans had fed him and given him money and then set him free. They requested — not ordered — that he accompany Susanna Dickinson and her little baby to Gonzales. From there, he could keep going into Mexico where he could live as a free man forever.

In Gonzales, Houston watched with sinking spirits as his growing army drilled under the commands of Mosley Baker. They weren't bad shots, most of them, but they were not particularly military material, either.

Baker called out, "Fire by files. Ready . . . aim . . . fire!"

The soldiers aimed and "fired" with unloaded muskets. "Did not hit a gol-dang thing," called out one wit. Several others guffawed like idiots. Houston shook his head and started back to his tent. All around him were women and children who had sent their husbands and fathers to the Alamo. It seemed to Houston that their eyes reflected dimming hope. They stared at him as if accusing him, as if he were responsible for their despair. Except for the drilling army, Gonzales was a town of silence. All its citizens could do was wait, and hope, and dread.

On the way to Gonzales, Houston had sent an urgent message to Fannin, ordering him to bring his forces to meet Houston's. Once their two armies merged, they would be in much better shape to face the enemy. Houston knew that Fannin could be slow and indecisive, so he made sure that there was no ambiguity in the orders. *Come here,* they read, *now!*

A movement caught Houston's eye and his gaze drifted to the horizon. Two riders were approaching, hellbent.

"Béxar has fallen!" one of them shouted in Spanish as they rode into town. "All dead! All dead!"

Few of the Gonzales citizens understood the words, but they all felt the urgency and rushed toward the riders. Houston bellowed, "Juan! Find out what those men are about!"

Seguin ran over to the men, who had dismounted and were now rushing pell-mell through the streets, shouting, "The Alamo has fallen! Santa Anna killed them all!" Some of the women understood, and shrieked in terror. Seguin recognized the men as vaqueros who worked a ranchero just outside of Béxar. "Chato," he called. "Melendez! What is this all about?"

Melendez, a compact and sturdy man of about thirty, recognized Seguin and immediately took off his hat. "Don Juan," he said. "We have just come from Béxar. Santa Anna attacked the Alamo on Sunday morning." Chato's hat had blown off some miles down the road during their furious ride. His windblown hair made it look as though his head had been struck by lightning. "We watched from a distance. All dead . . . all gone. They burned the Texians' bodies."

The blood drained from Seguin's face. "All of them? Every man in the Alamo?"

"Yes," Melendez said. "We saw it all. They built three funeral pyres. There were no prisoners."

Houston had been listening with a furious look on his face. He stormed over to the vaqueros and jabbed his finger at Melendez's face. "I will not have you men ride in here, spreading your lies around this town!" he shouted.

Chato looked astonished. "Lies?" he said. "We have seen what we told you. Every word is true."

"Seguin," Houston said. "Arrest these scoundrels. They were obviously sent here as spies by Santa Anna himself."

"But General," Seguin said. "I know them. These are honest men."

"They are liars, sir!" Houston said. "Arrest them at once or I will have you arrested yourself!" Houston turned to the crowd. "Listen not to these men," he said. "They have come to sow dissension and fear so that we will lose our resolve. We must be steadfast."

Houston looked back at Seguin, who sighed and led the two men away. "I am sorry, my friends," he said. "Houston believes you. I can see it in his eyes. But he is trying to forestall panic. We will set you free tonight." Chato and Melendez looked at each other in bewilderment. They endured an arduous and dangerous ride for this?

Houston motioned to Deaf Smith. "Deef," he said, as quietly as he could. "I want you to ride to Béxar and look into what these men have said."

Smith nodded. "I fear it is true, Sam."

"So do I, Deef," Houston said. "But I do

not want the others to despair. At least not until we know for sure."

Smith gave Houston an informal salute and ran for his horse. Houston called out to his officers, "Keep drilling those men! We must be ready!"

Smith's Indian pony galloped with great speed down the road toward Béxar, but their journey was not as long as Smith expected. He had traveled less than two miles when he saw another horse and rider approaching him. This horse was not running. In fact, someone was walking in front of it, leading it along at a lazy saunter. When he got nearer, Smith recognized the rider as Susanna Dickinson. She was holding her baby. An intense sadness suffused her countenance. Joe was leading the horse. The scene looked to Smith like a pietà come to life.

Smith rode up to them and touched his hat. "Mrs. Dickinson, ain't it?" he said. She nodded but said nothing. Smith said hesitantly, "Have you news from the Alamo?" Susanna looked at him sharply but did not answer. Joe said, "We going to Gonzales, sir. We needs to see General Houston."

Smith nodded. "Well, he's there, all right. I will take you to him."

The appearance of these travelers in town

caused the crowds to gather again immediately. This time, the wailing of the Gonzales wives began even before Susanna or Joe had uttered a word. Houston heard the ruckus and emerged from his tent again. When he saw Mrs. Dickinson, he sighed heavily.

Joe kept his eyes on the ground as he led the horse into Gonzales. He recognized Houston and prayed that Houston did not recognize him. The Mexicans had freed him, but to these white men he was still, and always would be, a slave.

But even though Joe tried to avoid Houston's gaze, it did not work. Houston looked at him immediately. "You are Joe, are you not? Colonel Travis's man?"

Joe hesitated and said, "Yes, sir." He looked up at Susanna and said, "This here Missus Dickinson. Her husband dead in the Alamo." Joe shook his head sadly. "They all dead, General."

Houston said nothing. The air was filled with screams of grief and heartrending weeping. He had suspected it before today, felt it in his gut, knew it. But he had held out hope that his instincts had been wrong. Now they were confirmed, and there was no way to ignore the fact. The Alamo had fallen. Deep in Houston's mind was the nagging thought that the disaster was his fault. He sent Bowie there; he even, without meaning to, sent Crockett there. And then he did not manage to get help to them on time. While they were holding their ground for thirteen days, he should have been building an army. Instead, as far as he was concerned, he did little more than lollygag.

One thing was clear: If Béxar had fallen, the next points of danger would be Gonzales and Goliad. Today, Gonzales was a town of widows. He could not spare enough men to stay behind and guard the town, so he would just have to take the town with him.

"Sergeant Foster," he called out, "take a detail and sink those cannon in the river! We are moving out immediately!" Foster hesitated for a moment, shocked by the order. Then he gestured to a few men and they all dashed toward the cannon.

"Burn what you cannot carry," Houston shouted. "Rutledge, get the civilians together and put them in the baggage wagons! With haste, gentlemen!"

Three hours later, a line of wagons and horses started filing out of Gonzales. Some people rode; a great many more walked. All of them carried bundles of whatever few belongings they could manage to scrape together before abandoning their homes, and most of them were still crying and moaning with grief. Some were simply angry. A taciturn farm woman named Mrs. Headley packed up the few belongings she would take with her while her two little sons played heedlessly at her feet. She said to one of her distraught neighbors, "I am going to teach my boys about this. I am going to teach them never to let up on the Mexicans until we get full revenge for all this trouble."

Some of the women refused to leave. One officer suggested that they be dragged from their homes and bodily placed in the wagons. Houston shook his head. "I have little doubt that they will willingly join us," he said, "as soon as you men start putting the torch to every building in town." He was right.

One by one, the buildings began to blaze, as a dozen men with torches dashed from one wooden structure to the next. Houston was determined that they would leave nothing behind for Mexican plunder. The women in the wagons looked back at their burning homes, wailing and sobbing. Many called out their husbands' names, husbands who had gone to aid the Alamo and never came home again. Houston noticed Mrs. Millsaps in the back of a wagon, weeping plaintively, her six children, now fatherless, clinging to her skirts. Only a short time earlier, she had thanked him for going to help her husband in the Alamo — thanked him — and he had failed her, just as he had failed almost every woman in those wagons.

In the shadows, just beyond the edge of the firelight, Joe stood watching the sad exodus. He had done what he said he would do. He had brought the Dickinson woman and her baby to safety. Now it was time to think about himself. As the now mobile town of Gonzales — and the ragtag Texian army — retreated into the distance, Joe turned and started walking the other way, toward Mexico.

Chapter Thirty-two

Colonel James Walker Fannin paced around his headquarters. He knew what the men said about him, that he was weak and indecisive. That he considered everything from every angle and then still could barely bring himself to take action. But Fannin knew that the time for action was now.

The trouble was, which action should he take? Houston's orders had been quite explicit. Fannin was to abandon La Bahía and move his men out to meet Houston in Gonzales as soon as possible. He had tried to move the men out before, and it had not really worked out all that well. But he was willing to give it another try — if everything could be made to work out more advantageously.

As usual, however, there were complications. "I am not like these other simple-tons," Fannin thought to himself, "who are content to look at every situation in stark black and white. I see all the facets, all the layers. It takes time to develop the perfect course of action. I need more time!"

But he was running out of time. His men had urged him to go to the aid of Travis at the Alamo. But that was before they heard about Urrea's victory at San Patricio. Johnson, Grant, all those men, killed, wounded, missing. How could he leave after learning that? San Patricio was south of Goliad. That meant the Mexican army could be coming straight up the road toward Fort Defiance. Yes, he was right to turn his column around and bring it back into the fort. Right to do nothing but wait in readiness.

And then he learned the terrible news about the Alamo. All dead. If he had marched to Travis's aid, perhaps all of his men would be dead with them. Perhaps he would be dead himself. Then what good would they have done? Yes, he was right to wait.

And now this message from Houston, or-dering him to move out — not leaving it to Fannin's discretion but commanding it.

Fannin thought of himself as a good officer and he knew that he should obey Houston's order without further delay. But scouts had already informed him that Urrea was advancing on Goliad. The Mexican army, at this very moment, was probably no more than ten miles away. In response to this threat, Fannin had just sent out Amon King with over two hundred men to evacuate American settlers at Refugio. He could not make a move until they came back — his strength at La Bahía had been reduced by a third. Houston would just have to understand that.

Fannin paced and paced and tried to think it through. Houston would be furious if he didn't leave Fort Defiance immediately. But what if he left and then King came back to find La Bahía occupied by enemy forces? He would be slaughtered. No, Fannin could not let that happen. No matter what Houston would eventually say about it, he would just have to wait. Everyone would just have to wait.

So Fannin waited one day, constantly scanning the horizon for the return of King's men. The waiting extended to a second day, then a third.

"Rider coming in!" Fannin jumped up at the sound of the shout from the wall. He ran out into the courtyard, which was already filled with Texians, eager for news.

The rider, a former jockey from New Orleans, was named Nelson. He slid off his exhausted horse and said, "Which one is Fannin?"

Fannin stepped forward. "I am Colonel Fannin," he said.

Nelson took his hat off. "Anybody got any water?"

Fannin turned to a nearby private and said, "Fetch him some."

Nelson said, "I have news of King."

"What is it?" Fannin said.

"You want me to tell you out here, with everybody listening?" Nelson said. Fannin flushed with embarrassment and said quickly, "Come into my quarters."

Inside, Nelson was handed a tin cup of water. After draining it and wiping his mouth with the sleeve of his coat, he said, "King is dead. Him and his men was captured after a fight at Refugio. Them that wasn't killed in the battle was shot later on."

The blood drained from Fannin's face. He sat down behind his desk and held his head in his hands. King was not coming back. Now it was completely up to him. He got up, walked across the room, opened the door and stepped into the hallway. "Corporal Zaboly! Corporal Von Schmidt!" he called.

The two young officers hurried over to Fannin's quarters and stood at attention. "Sir!" Zaboly said.

"Men," Fannin said, "Houston has ordered us to move out. Zaboly, take a detail and bury all of the cannon. We cannot take them with us. They will only hinder our movements."

"Yes, sir," Zaboly said, and rushed away.

Fannin turned to the other man, a tall German immigrant who wore a monocle in his left eye. Fannin always assumed that he came from some aristocratic German family. "Von Schmidt," he said, "alert the men to prepare to move out at first light. Then dispatch a detail to burn all of the supplies. We don't want to leave anything behind for the enemy."

"Burn them now, sir?" Von Schmidt asked.

Fannin scowled impatiently. "No, not now. Just as we are leaving the fort!"

Von Schmidt nodded and went off to carry out his orders.

Fannin walked back into his quarters, feeling very much like a decisive commander. He still felt that way at daybreak, when all the men had assembled, ready to walk out of the fort. And he still felt that way as the day wore on and they had not been able to manage to actually leave. And, at sunset, he made another very decisive order. "Stand down," he shouted to the men. "We will move out the first thing tomorrow morning!"

The men groaned and grumbled. But no one was much surprised.

Fannin shouted, "Corporal Zaboly!"

The officer ran to his side. "Sir!"

"Corporal," Fannin said, "dig up those cannon. We are taking them with us."

Zaboly stared at his commander for a few stunned seconds.

"Snap to it!" Fannin said. "We have no time to waste!"

"Typical," said Young, a lieutenant from Illinois. "The man does not know which end is up." He muttered to a friend, a skinny kid named Winders, "We should move out under the cover of darkness. That is the only smart thing to do."

Winders looked to be about seventeen years old. He was laboring heroically to grow his first pair of muttonchops. He nodded solemnly. "I reckon the colonel knows what he is doing," he said.

Young looked at the boy as if he had grown a second head. Winders was the first soldier he had ever met in Fort Defiance who actually thought Fannin knew what he was doing.

The men were awakened before sunrise and stood in formation for another two hours. Young, and most of the other men, had the sinking feeling that they were going to be standing there all day again. For a while after the sun came up, a heavy fog blanketed the region. Most of the men realized that this was another good opportunity for them to move out with some natural cover.

But again Fannin waited, until the sun broke through the clouds.

When at last Fannin was ready to start the march, he called out, "Corporal Von Schmidt — fire the stores." Von Schmidt and five other Texians with torches ran over to the storerooms, carefully setting fire to all the wooden crates and burlap bags that were stacked against the walls inside. Within moments, the two rooms were blazing furiously, sending clouds of black smoke pouring into the sky. The men ran back to rejoin their ranks.

Fannin regarded the blaze with satisfaction. "Move out!" he called and rode out of Fort Defiance. Behind him, the column started moving slowly. The wagons, pulled by desiccated oxen, moved slower still.

Atop a nearby hill, a vaquero watched the rising smoke with a mounting sense of excitement. He knew what it meant. And he knew that General Urrea would want to know about it as soon as possible. He hopped onto his cow pony and rode furiously toward Urrea's camp.

While the vaquero moved with great speed, Fannin's column continued to creep along at a turtle's pace. Houston had ordered Fannin to bury all the cannon but because Fannin had changed his mind, the men were hauling every cannon in the place: nine altogether. They also were laboriously dragging along extra wagons laden with hundreds of muskets. They had only a few horses, and the oxen pulling their wagons were weak and starving, so hungry that they stopped every time they saw grass. Despite all efforts to get them moving, they stubbornly stood their ground, feeding themselves, since no one else had bothered to feed them.

Mile after agonizing mile, the column crept forward. Wagons broke down. A howitzer mired at a river crossing. One of the oxen dropped dead.

At midmorning, they were still only a few miles from the fort. Fannin decided that it was a good time to call a halt and feed the men. An hour passed while the men waited for the food to be served.

Captain Jack Shackelford approached Fannin. "Sir, is this really the best place in which to linger?" he said.

Fannin said, "We are only stopping long enough to eat, and then we will be on our way."

"But sir," Shackelford said, "Coleto Creek is just up ahead, not two miles from here. There we will at least have the protection of timber."

Fannin smiled. "Coleto Creek will make a good camping place tonight. We will start the march again soon. Thank you for your advice."

Shackelford was stunned. Fannin only planned to travel two more miles before making camp for the night?

The men were openly complaining about the delay in eating when Von Schmidt nervously approached Fannin at the head of the column.

"Colonel Fannin, sir?" he said, hat in hand.

"What is it?" Fannin snapped. He was hungry and in a bad mood.

"Uh, about the food, sir," the corporal said.

Fannin was growing more impatient. "Well?"

"Well, um, there ain't any," Von Schmidt said.

Fannin's eyes widened. "What do you mean, 'There ain't any'?" he said.

"Well sir," Von Schmidt said, "when you told us to burn the store, well . . . uh, I reckon we burned all the food, too."

Fannin was speechless. But a little farther back in the line, another Texian was not. "Mexicans!" he cried out.

Fannin whirled around and looked into the woods ahead. Mexican cavalry — hundreds of them. As Fannin watched in horror, the horsemen split into two groups and surrounded the Texians, making sure that the column could neither advance nor retreat.

Fannin shouted, "Unhitch two of the cannon! Get them loaded, for God's sake!"

The two cannon were aimed at the woods where the largest grouping of cavalry seemed to congregate. "Fire!" Fannin shouted. The two guns blasted six-pound balls toward the forest. They caused considerable damage to the trees they hit, but the Mexicans were unscathed. Most of the cavalry did not even bother to take cover from the blasts.

Suddenly, in the same woods from which

the cavalry had just emerged, a large group of Mexican infantry appeared. The garrison's physician, Dr. Barnard, ran over to Fannin.

"Sir," he said, pointing straight ahead, "if we move forward only a mile, we can take cover among those trees."

Fannin replied contemptuously, "And did they teach you military strategy along with your medical training, Doctor?"

Barnard said, "No sir, of course not. This is not military strategy — just common sense. We are right out in the open — easy targets for the Mexicans."

Shackelford said, "The doctor is right, sir."

"Perhaps he is," Fannin said, sternly. "But I am in command!" His expression softened a bit. "We were more thoroughly outnumbered at the battle of Concepción, Bowie and I," he said. "And we whipped the Mexicans without breaking a sweat. They just aren't fighting men."

"But at Concepción, at least there was cover," Shackelford said. "Here, we are but sitting ducks!"

Fannin glanced at Shackelford and the doctor, smiling as if he had a brilliant trick up his sleeve. "Form a square!" he yelled. "Place a cannon at each corner!" That would show them what a fine military mind he possessed. Fannin learned all about forming a square at West Point. "With this setup," he said, "we can hold off the army indefinitely." Barnard and Shackelford looked at each other, shook their heads and walked away.

"He has gone completely insane," Young muttered.

Winders replied, "Well, maybe it will all work out fine."

Young's voice was filled with bewildered fury. "Instead of seeking protection in the woods," he said, "here we are spread out on open ground!" He pointed at the Mexicans. "And that means that the superior force of Mexicans has full advantage of the forest. They can take cover and fire at us with ease. And all we can do is take it!"

Winders nodded. "I will bet you that Colonel Fannin has a plan."

Young sighed with dismay.

Only fifteen minutes after the Texians first spotted the Mexican cavalry, Urrea ordered his men to attack. Fannin had always had a keen interest in history. It was one of the courses he actually passed at West Point. Now, thinking back to Bunker Hill and the famous order, "Do not fire 'til you see the whites of their eyes," he decided to paraphrase. "Men," he called out, "hold your fire until the Mexicans are so close that no shot can miss." Several of the men stared at him in disbelief, and then went back to squinting down their gun barrels, waiting.

The Mexicans fired volley after volley, steadily closing the ground between them, but still the Texians did nothing but stand by. Feeling exposed and vulnerable, the men began to sit down or kneel, trying to make themselves a somewhat less tempting target. Several men fell. Still, they had not fired a shot.

It was not until the Mexicans were less than a hundred yards away that Fannin decided that the time was right, "Fire at will!" he cried. Eagerly, the Texians sent volley after volley into the enemy's ranks. The blasts drove the Mexicans back, but they immediately surged forward again.

Two miles away, a scouting party under Captain Albert C. Horton heard the gunfire and rode quickly to the crest of a hill to see what was going on. Hermann Ehrenberg knew that there were men down there who he had fought alongside since the siege of Béxar. He turned to Horton and said, "We had better go down and help them."

The other men in the scouting party looked away without saying a word. Captain

Horton said, "Son, that is clearly a losing battle down yonder. We must ride back to Victoria and find some reinforcements there."

Ehrenberg wheeled his horse around. "You can go to Victoria if you like, sir," he said, "but I am going to help my friends." Horton and the others watched as Ehrenberg rode down the hill, through the Mexican lines and toward Fannin's square. Then they turned and rode hellbent toward Victoria.

When Ehrenberg rode into the Fannin's troop formation, his Polish friend Francis Petrussewicz raised an arm in greeting. "Hermann, my friend!" he called out happily. Those were his last words. At the same instant, a Mexican musket ball struck him in the back of the head and he pitched forward, dead before he hit the ground. Ehrenberg rushed over to his friend and lifted his head, but it was too late.

Fannin stood behind a cannon, firing his pistol as often as he could reload. He felt a searing pain in his thigh and fell to the ground. Blood pumped from the bullet wound. He untied his cravat and frantically tried to bandage the wound. As he did so, Fannin saw the oxen falling, one by one. Mexican snipers were bringing them down.

That meant there was no way out. Fannin remembered the letter from Travis that he had read — "Victory or Death." Those were his choices now. And he had a sinking feeling that victory was not going to be the one that he achieved.

The Texians continued to fire, but their volleys had little effect on the Mexicans. The Mexicans, on the other hand, were in a fine position. Kneeling in high grass or behind trees, they could expose themselves long enough to get off a shot, then duck and reload at their leisure. Urrea watched the skirmish with satisfaction. It would last an hour or a day, but victory was certain.

The Mexican cavalry attacked, lances gleaming in the sunlight. The Texians aimed their cannon and their muskets at them and brought down dozens of them in a shattering volley. To Urrea this was a good indication that cavalry attacks were a bad idea in the present situation. He ordered his men to dismount and fight on foot — and, if possible, from a distance.

As the day wore on, the blazing sun beat down on the Texians unmercifully. They had little water to drink and none to spare with which to sponge down their cannon. When brilliant colors began streaking the sky in the west, many of the men offered up a prayer of thanks. It was over. At least for today.

Fannin called for a casualty report. Nine men dead; fifty-one wounded. Their oxen had been killed. They had no food or water and were rapidly running out of ammunition. To their relief, a light rain fell on them in the evening. The men lay on their backs with open mouths, trying to capture as much of the precious water as possible. Others tried to catch some in sheets of canvas, carefully pouring the few drops of water into their empty canteens. But even as the rain refreshed the men, it had a devastating effect on their remaining gunpowder. Worse, the coming of nightfall did not seem to have any effect on the Mexican snipers on all four sides of them; they kept up a series of random shots.

All of Fannin's men gradually accepted the harsh truth. They were completely surrounded. There was no way out. No hope for rescue.

Toward midnight, Fannin called the men together. "This is a tight squeeze," he said. "So we must strengthen our position. We are going to work through the night digging trenches and building breastworks behind which to fight." The men grumbled a little, but they knew that it was the only hope of protecting themselves. Without another word, they picked up shovels and any other digging utensil they could find. Those who could find nothing else dug with their bare hands.

As the rain continued to fall and the temperature continued to drop, the men of Fort Defiance dug and packed dirt. They bolstered their makeshift walls with their wagons. Some of the men ventured beyond the square formation and dragged the carcasses of the dead horses and oxen over to serve as additional cover.

And through it all, the Mexican buglers played. It was not Deguello but another discordant bugle call, *Sentinal Alerto*. They played it over and over, all night long, until the Texians thought they would go mad.

When dawn broke, Fannin and his men looked out at the Mexican army with a sinking feeling. The force was bigger than ever. Reinforcements had obviously arrived during the night. The manpower was disturbing. The fact that they had brought three cannon with them was even more so.

They could only watch in horror as all three field pieces began raining grape and canister shot upon them. Fannin's men crouched as low as possible behind their ragged breastworks, covering their heads with their arms, protecting themselves however they could.

They tried firing back, but their own cannon lacked the range of the Mexican guns. Urrea sat at a comfortable distance, able to blast the Texians to pieces if he so chose. The Texians could do nothing but crouch down behind their new barricades, praying that they would hold up against the bombardment.

But no sooner had the cannonade begun, than it stopped. An eerie silence hung over the field. Zaboly turned to Von Schmidt and said, "He is just sending us a message. They can kill us without breaking a sweat. They know it and we know it."

Fannin watched the deteriorating situation with mounting despair. He had vastly underestimated the military capabilities of the Mexican army, and had tragically overestimated his own. Reluctantly, he called his officers to him. He was grim-faced as they gathered around. Every few seconds he winced in pain from the wound in his thigh. "I fear we will have to surrender," he said, speaking loudly in order to be heard over the constant rifle fire and the unnerving blare of the bugles. "There is no other recourse."

Leon Watson, a Texian who had been a

newspaperman before joining the army, shook his head. "Colonel, you know how them Mexicans treat men who surrender." Others nodded in agreement.

Fannin said, "What choice do we have?"

Watson said, "Seems to me, if they will allow us to surrender under favorable terms, we would all be willing to do so."

"And if not?" Fannin said.

"Then we must be prepared to fight to the death," Watson said. "I would rather die fighting than be executed."

"Me, too!" Young said.

Zaboly agreed. "That's the way I feel about it."

Winders said, "Whatever you think is best, Colonel."

Fannin said, "I suppose I had better conduct the parley myself. Someone get me a piece of white cloth."

A few moments later, waving a white banner made from a linen shirt, and limping on his wounded leg, Fannin made his way toward the Mexican lines.

Shackelford called after him, "Remember, get good terms — or no deal."

General Urrea was standing at his cannon emplacement, like a host eagerly awaiting the arrival of his guest. He received Fannin politely and asked him to sit down. Fannin did so, with some difficulty.

"Sir," Fannin said, "I am willing to discuss terms of surrender."

Urrea offered Fannin a cup of tea, which he gratefully accepted. "If you gentlemen wish to surrender at discretion," Urrea said, "the matter is ended."

Fannin knew what "at discretion" meant. The Mexicans could do whatever they wanted. It might mean prison. Or execution. It might, on the other hand, mean that they would be treated well and exchanged for Mexican prisoners.

Urrea shrugged and smiled genially. "If you would rather not surrender," he said, "I shall return to my camp and renew the attack."

Fannin wanted to argue, to bargain for a better deal. But he knew he had nothing to offer Urrea. He had no choice but to accept the general's terms.

When he returned to his own breastworks, the men looked at him eagerly. Fannin shook his head. "They will accept our surrender at discretion," he said. "Otherwise, they continue to attack."

"I say we fight," said a rugged Texian named Huffines. "If we give up, they will just murder us anyway."

Other men murmured their agreement.

Fannin shook his head. "If we continue to fight, we will surely die. If we surrender, it is at least possible that we will live. I fear it is the only choice we have." He looked around at his men. "Shall we vote on it?"

Ehrenberg stood up angrily. "God damn it, man!" he said. "Enough of your votes! You are our commander. Command us!"

Fannin looked around. The men seemed to be in agreement with the young German. He sighed. "Then here is my command. We must surrender."

This time, Fannin did not walk back over to the Mexican ranks. He sent a messenger. Within the hour, his men were in a column again, making the long trek back to Fort Defiance. The wounded, including Fannin, were placed in the Fort's infirmary. The rest of the men were crammed into the church. And again, as before, they waited.

On Palm Sunday, after they had been sequestered for nearly a week, a Mexican officer stepped in and called for silence. When all the men were listening to him, he read from a piece of paper: "All Texian prisoners are to be returned to Matamoros this day. Gather what belongings you have, for we will begin a march for the ship within the hour."

A cheer of relief washed through the church. An Irishman named Feeley began singing a sea chantey from his days as a first mate. The other men began joining in. By the second chorus, everyone had learned the general tune and they all sang lustily as they marched out of the fort.

They were split into four groups. Some of the Mexicans explained that this was for their own safety, since they did not want the Texians to try and overwhelm them during the long march. The men of Fort Defiance bid exuberant farewells to one another as the groups marched away separately into the bright Sunday morning, singing cheerily.

When each group was out of sight of the others, the Mexicans ordered them to halt and turn their backs. Hermann Ehrenberg suspected at once that treachery was afoot. *"Mein Gott,"* he cried, "they are going to shoot us." The firing began immediately. Many Texians dropped dead where they stood. Others attempted to make a run for it. Most were cut down in flight. Ehrenberg's group was only yards from the river and he managed to make it into the brush. He dove in and swam furiously. Weissmann, a former doctor from New Jersey, dove in after him. He was immediately riddled with bullets and sank below the surface, leaving only a crimson cloud to mark the place where he had been. While musket balls pinged around him, Ehrenberg swam to the other side and disappeared into the woods.

Fannin, because of his leg injury, had stayed behind at La Bahía with the other sick and wounded. He was ushered out of the infirmary just before the other men were murdered in their beds. Fannin was placed in a chair directly in front of the church. A firing squad faced him.

Looking at the officer in charge in despair, Fannin said, "I have only these requests." He pulled out his gold watch. "Please see that this is returned to my wife. Also, I would ask that you give me a Christian burial." A tear was beginning to trickle down his cheek. "And please . . . please . . . do not shoot me in the face."

Hands trembling, Fannin tied a blindfold around his eyes and sat as straight in the chair as he could, determined to meet his end like a soldier. With a smile, the officer dropped the watch into his own pocket. He turned to the firing squad and said, "Aim for the face, boys. Fire!" Hours later, Fannin's body was tossed onto the fire that consumed the remains of the other four

hundred men who died in his command.
Twenty-eight men escaped.

Santa Anna drew a line in the sand with
his saber. "Sabine River," he said. "The
border with the United States."

He and his officers were standing in the
plaza of San Antonio de Béxar, in the
shadow of the San Fernando church. Like a
patient schoolmaster giving a lecture to
rather dim students, Santa Anna was map-
ping out his strategy in the dirt.

"Houston is running for help," he said.
"We must move quickly to cut him off." He
made a mark with his sword on one side of
the line and said, "Here we are in Béxar.
Fannin, here in Goliad" — he made another
mark — "must not be allowed to join
Houston. Colonel Morales, you will take a
thousand soldiers and sweep south." Another line. "General Gaona, you will take
troops and sweep north." Another line.
"General Ramirez y Sesma, you will march
straight through Texas."

Each of the officers nodded as his name
was called.

Santa Anna said, "I will attend to matters
here, then join you with men. We leave the
women here and we carry only bedrolls and
weapons." He looked at his generals with an

expression that said, *Any questions?*

Castrillón said, "Your Excellency, is it wise for you to be separated from the other forces?"

"It is time to finish our task," Santa Anna said. He looked around sternly. If the other officers had questions of their own, none of them had the nerve to ask them.

The Texian army continued to move eastward, accompanied by more and more settlers. Word of the disaster at the Alamo had spread quickly. Frightened farmers and townspeople were deciding that the dream of Texas was over, that it was time to get back to the safety of the United States. They were abandoning their farms and ranches, leaving small villages entirely deserted. Some of the settlers remembered painting G.T.T. — "Gone to Texas" — on the doors of their houses back home in the states before they had left everything behind for the "new Eden." Now, it seemed like the same situation in reverse. But what was there to return to?

Among themselves, the fleeing Texians were already starting to call this mass retreat "the Runaway Scrape." But not all of them wanted to flee. Some wanted to stand their ground and take back their Texas homes.

A settler rode up alongside Mosley Baker. "How far east we got to run to be safe?" the settler asked. "As long as you in the army keep retreating, we have to, too. Give me one good reason why you do not just dig in right here and fight."

Baker nodded toward Houston, who rode alongside the teamsters. "Ain't a good reason," he said, "but there he is, riding up front."

Houston had heard the talk. This eastward trek, it was rumored, was headed straight for Louisiana. Some believed that if they could draw the Mexican army over the United States border, then the American government would have to get involved. With the U.S. Army on their side, Texas was assured of victory. Others believed that Houston was simply running with his tail between his legs, desperately trying to put miles between himself and Santa Anna, lest the Napoleon of the West crush him the same way that he had crushed Travis and the others at the Alamo. And Houston knew that, no matter what the reason, the settlers blamed him for the loss of their homes, and everything for which they had worked and fought to build. It did not matter if his current action was retreat or strategy or blind panic. Either way, those people were all going to have to start over from scratch.

Seguin himself wondered what was in Houston's mind. He rode up to the general and they trotted along side by side for a while. "We had more deserters last night," Seguin said. Houston did not reply.

Seguin tried again. "Some of the men . . . they think we are headed for the border."

Houston still looked straight ahead. His face was without expression. "I hope Santa Anna shares their concerns," he said. Seguin did not know what to make of that response. Houston gestured toward a large clearing. "We camp here, wait for Fannin to join us." Then he galloped away, leaving Seguin no wiser about the situation than he was before.

The tents were pitched just in time. Just at nightfall, a relentless rain began to pour down on the camp. Except for the unfortunate sentries, everyone huddled in the tents, trying in vain to stay warm and dry. Out of the darkness, a rider appeared. Several Texians ran to greet him as he dismounted.

"They are all dead," the rider shouted. He was young but grizzled, an Indian scout named Singer. His voice was faint over the rain. "Goliad — all executed! Fannin and his men."

Houston strode out of his tent. "You

475

make your report to me, sir," he growled, "not to the public at large."

There was a look of panic on Singer's face. "I am sorry, sir."

They walked over to Houston's tent and stepped inside. "All right then," Houston said. "What happened?"

Singer said, "They was marching out of Fort Defiance. Got about as far as Coleto Creek. General Urrea caught up with 'em there."

Houston sat down in a field chair with a heavy sigh.

"Fannin surrendered, sir," Singer said. "Give up. They march 'em right back to La Bahía and shot 'em all in the back."

"All of them?" Houston asked.

"Yes, sir," said Singer. " 'Bout four hunnerd of 'em, I figger."

Houston said, "But if they were all killed, how did you find out about it?"

Singer wiped his forehead. "Well sir," he said, "they wasn't all killed. I met up with my friend Hermann Ehrenberg. He ran, got away. Said a few others did, too. Don't know how many." He shook his head. "Ehrenberg told me, I just couldn't believe it. Couldn't believe that Fannin would surrender to those Meskin bastards."

Houston could not believe it, either. The

Mexicans always insisted on surrender at discretion — and that always meant "no prisoners." Surely even an idiot like Fannin knew it.

Houston muttered, "God damn it." He looked at Singer and said, "Go get yourself something to eat and find a place to bed down." Singer nodded and left Houston's tent. But Houston himself did not emerge. The men outside stared at the closed tent with derision in their eyes. "Well, boys," one said with a sneer, "reckon we are about to start runnin' faster."

Within moments, the talkative Singer had spread word about Fannin's downfall all over the camp. The men talked of little else for the rest of the night. Some of them, in some perverse way, even found the news encouraging. Houston could not possibly ignore this, they reasoned. Now he would have to stand and fight. As the sun rose, the Texians emerged from their tents and began loading their weapons, checking their powder and shot, sharpening their knives.

Houston came out of his tent and surveyed the scene. "Break camp," he shouted. "We continue east!" The men stared at him, open-mouthed in disbelief.

"General Sesma and a good portion of the Mexican army is right across the river,"

Mosley Baker said. "And we are running? Alamo! Goliad! They have got to pay! If not now, when?"

Houston looked at Baker, then turned and went back to his tent. "We march in ten minutes!"

Seguin followed him in, dumbfounded. Houston began packing.

"They are ready to fight, General," Seguin said.

Houston ignored him.

"Sam!" Seguin shouted.

"No," Houston said calmly.

"Why not?"

"Damn it, Juan," Houston said, "because none of it means anything without Santa Anna."

"If you do not fight Ramirez y Sesma now," Seguin said, "I am afraid we will not have an army to fight Santa Anna."

Houston gestured out the door of the tent. "This army, this infamous army, has one battle in them. Maybe. I'd prefer it to count." He continued to pack.

Seguin stood there for a moment, then reluctantly nodded and turned to leave.

Houston stopped him. "Juan . . ." he said.

Seguin turned.

"Do not question me again."

Chapter Thirty-three

The Runaway Scrape was picking up speed. All along the road lay personal belongings — trunks, clothes, carts. There was even a piano dumped in the mud alongside the road as more and more settlers joined the exodus. Houston thought wistfully that if everyone riding with him were actually a soldier — instead of women, children and old men — he would have a formidable, and doubtless victorious, army.

Houston rode his white horse Saracen alongside a newcomer's wagon. The old-timer driving the wagon had a bottle on the seat beside him. Houston was transfixed by the sight.

"Where you coming from?" Houston called out.

"San Felipe," the old-timer said. He

raised the bottle and took a pull. It was hard not to notice how closely Houston was eyeing him, so the man held the bottle out, offering a swig to the general. Houston absently licked his lips. He thought that, at the moment, there was nothing on earth he wanted so much as a drink from that bottle. Then his eyes turned to the other people in the wagon — a little boy and a woman, older, but not nearly as old as the man.

Houston locked eyes with the little boy and the boy smiled back. "Your horse is the biggest," he said.

Houston nodded. "What's your name, son?" he asked.

"Charlie," the little boy said, transfixed by Saracen.

The woman seated by the child stared at Houston intently. He could not tell, but there seemed to be something behind her gaze — sadness, maybe. Or accusation.

She said, "Tell him your last name, Charlie."

The boy smiled and said, "Travis."

Houston made the connection and looked back at Mrs. Ayers, who was now openly glaring at him. Houston's horse slowed as the cart moved ahead, little Charlie staring back at a tortured Houston.

★ ★ ★

The rains that pummeled the Texian settlers and Houston's army the night before also created a sea of mud for Santa Anna's troops to slog through. Every step was an ordeal. The mud sucked shoes — even boots — off the feet of soldados and the wagon wheels could barely complete a single revolution without becoming stuck in the mire.

For Jesús, the hell of the Alamo campaign had led to a nightmare of a different kind. With every difficult step he thought, "What kind of place is this?"

Up ahead, another cannon was stuck in the mud. A sergeant summoned Jesús and four other men to try to free it with oxen.

Santa Anna gestured toward it dismissively. "Leave it!" he said. "Move!"

Castrillón said, "General, that is the fifth cannon we have discarded."

Santa Anna paid no attention to him. "We have a good moon tonight," he said. "We will make use of the light and keep moving."

The Mexican army continued its filthy march through the mud, as one more cannon was pushed to the edge of the road and abandoned.

Once again, the Texians were setting up

tents. Houston was pulling the saddle off Saracen when he saw a horseman coming toward him, riding slowly.

"Shite," he muttered, recognizing who it was.

It was T. J. Rusk. Nobody in the Texian army was getting enough to eat these days, but Rusk seemed as oversized and ebullient as always. His clothes were also neater and cleaner — and in better repair — than those of Houston's ragged soldiers.

"Sir," Rusk said, "the enemy are laughing you to scorn. You must fight them." He dismounted, pulled a letter from his coat pocket and began to read. "You must retreat no further. The country expects you to fight. The salvation of the country depends on your doing so. Signed David G. Burnet, President."

Rusk folded the letter and offered it to Houston. Houston ignored him.

"Where is the pig thief these days?" Houston said, tossing a pebble into the creek. "Harrisburg?"

Rusk said, "*President* Burnet — as well as the rest of the provisional government — have abandoned Harrisburg."

Houston walked away. "Seems they are retreating faster than I am," he said.

Rusk called after him. "Sir, I have been

given authority to replace you! General . . . ?"

Seguin approached Houston from the direction of the camp. He had overheard at least some of Houston's conversation with Rusk. "General," Seguin said. "Sam! Talk with him. Share your strategy."

Houston glared at him.

"Have you a strategy?" Seguin asked.

Houston said, "A general who has to cajole soldiers into following is no general. I am not fond of war councils." He peered into Seguin's eyes angrily. "Fannin was fond of war councils," he said.

"These men," said Seguin, gesturing to the men setting up camp, "they believe you are a coward."

Houston took this statement without a flinch. Even so, his face softened and he looked at Seguin.

"Did you know I told Crockett to come to Texas?" he said. "And the others . . . now they are dead at their posts — by my orders. . . ."

Seguin shook his head. "You warned them not to fort up."

"In these times it is very difficult to maintain your honor without losing your life," Houston said. "But can a man choose honor, and death, for another?"

Seguin did not know how to answer this.

Houston said, his voice deep with sadness, "They weren't good men, Juan . . . but *damn,* they were good men."

Houston turned to Rusk, still standing several yards away, and motioned for him to follow him. Houston, Seguin and Rusk walked to Houston's tent and entered.

"Have a seat, Rusk," Houston said, gesturing to a field chair.

"General . . ." Rusk said, as he sat.

Houston waited a long moment, then said quietly, "Twenty-odd years ago, Napoleon returns from exile in Elba, puts together an army and moves east. Swiftly — trying to gain power before an alliance between nations can occur. Wellington, with fewer men, fewer armaments, stays one step ahead of the French — teasing them with his presence — knowing that a large army will splinter in order to keep up."

Seguin and Rusk shared a look. Where was this going?

Houston continued, "He moves and he waits, moves and waits . . . for Napoleon to make a mistake — to fall into a scenario that condemns him to defeat. Wellington chooses the setting for victory before it exists for him, before he lays eyes on it. It has an open battleground, a sloping plane, cover for encampment and an opportunity to surprise the enemy flank."

Houston raised his eyes, fixing his gaze on Rusk.

"The Mexican army is splintered and though they do not know it, Santa Anna's troops subsist on gasps of air and sips of hope," Houston said. "I share Wellington's battleground vision, though I know not the name of the place I imagine. I, sir, do not consider myself Wellington. Santa Anna, however, does consider himself the Napoleon of the West. We shall move and wait until he makes a mistake and presents us with his Waterloo."

Rusk stared at the floor, considering what he had just heard. Then after a moment, he rose. "Thank you, General." He started to exit the tent, then stopped and turned. "General," he said, "might I enlist as a private in your army?"

A commotion outside brought all three men out of the tent. A Mexican soldier was being dragged into camp. He had already been beaten badly, and the Texians surrounding him looked like they were in the mood to beat him again. Seguin raced to his side. The look on his face was enough to make the Texians back away and give him room. Seguin propped the soldier by a tree, then knelt beside him and began asking questions in a low voice.

Houston called out, "Colonel Neill!"

Neill ran to his side. "Yes, sir."

"It is time for the noncombatants to move on, Colonel," Houston said. "Have them prepare their wagons and supplies and keep heading east."

Neill smiled. "Look, General, these have just arrived." He pointed toward two six-pounder cannon, brand new and shiny — at least in the spots that weren't covered in mud. "A gift from the citizens of Cincinnati," Neill said.

Houston looked at the guns and nodded with satisfaction. He said, "Start preparing shot and loads."

Seguin raced over with a saddlebag that he had taken from the captured soldado.

"Deaf Smith captured a Mexican courier," Seguin said. "His letters tell us Santa Anna is nearby . . . and separated from the rest of his army."

Seguin handed over the saddlebag. "The courier had this bag," he said. It was a fine leather bag with the monogram WBT imprinted upon it.

Chapter Thirty-four

The Mexican troops were dead tired when they were finally ordered to set up camp at the edge of the woods. Santa Anna, with Almonte, walked by the bedraggled men, inspecting and looking out onto the field in front of him. It was a half mile long, gently sloping up and away, with a stand of trees to one side. Castrillón strode to his side.

"General," he said, "we have reports of troop movement. Houston's army is less than three miles away."

Santa Anna's face broke into an excited smile. He said, "We will break camp and chase the coward."

Castrillón shook his head. "Sir, he's not moving. He is on his way here." Castrillón pointed to the far woods. "His scouts were spotted in those woods. Behind us. We are cut off from all our armies except Cós."

Santa Anna calmly considered this, idly scratching his neck. "How many men does Houston lead?" he demanded.

Castrillón replied, "Perhaps as many as seven hundred."

Santa Anna looked at Castrillón with contempt. He had that many with him now.

"Sir," Castrillón insisted, "we are at a disadvantage. Our backs are against a body of water with only a small bridge for retreat."

Santa Anna shrugged. "With General Cós's men we will dwarf Houston's army."

"But Cós will not be here until tomorrow," Castrillón said.

Almonte chimed in, "We should prepare breastworks and put the men on alert. We are only vulnerable tonight."

Santa Anna said patiently, "Houston has water at his back as well. Two cannon shots and he will run like a rabbit."

Only a few hundred yards away, the Texians dismounted and started unloading weapons, ammunition, tents and supplies. Houston walked past the men, strode through a copse of trees and stepped out into the open field. To his left was the San Jacinto River, which snaked all the way around to Buffalo Bayou, behind the

488

Texians' camp. To his right was the road to Harrisburg and Vince's Bridge, the only way in or out of the area. Straight ahead, about five hundred yards away, was the Mexican camp. The land between the Texians and the Mexicans was nearly flat, but there was a gentle rise in the ground. Houston looked at it with satisfaction. It just might be enough of a rise to allow his army to make it nearly all the way across the field before the Mexicans saw them. Just behind the Mexican camp was some marshy land that led to Peggy's Lake. With water on two sides, the Mexicans would have no place to run.

Down in the Mexican camp, hundreds of troops were busy preparing breastworks consisting of trunks, wagons — anything that could help serve as a makeshift wall.

Houston took a small black box from his pocket and extracted a pinch of snuff. He inhaled it and closed his eyes. He felt as if he were reliving a dream. He thought about what he had said to Rusk: "Wellington chooses the setting for victory before it exists for him, before he lays eyes on it. It has an open battleground, a sloping plain, cover for encampment and an opportunity to surprise the enemy flank." Each of those elements was there, exactly what Houston had been looking for. He opened his eyes and spoke to the field before him. "Do you have a name?" he whispered. "What do they call you?"

The Texians were fully aware of the proximity of the enemy. Every man was working hard, preparing to fight, eager to get to it after all this time. Houston walked back into camp and nodded at Seguin. He reached up and touched a leaf, gripping it between his thumb and forefinger. "Damp," Houston said. "We have to keep our powder dry."

Houston walked away, into his tent. Seguin just watched, saying nothing. Mosley Baker and Rusk walked over to Seguin and said in one voice, "Well . . . ?"

Seguin just shook his head.

Mosley Baker said, "He don't make up his mind soon, we will fight without him."

Seguin noticed a familiar face among his Tejanos. He walked over and said, "Menchaca, how did you get here? I thought you were in the Alamo."

Menchaca looked at Seguin with a slight expression of shame. "I left, Don Juan," he said.

Seguin's brow knitted. "Left," he said with quiet fury. "You deserted your post?"

"No, no, it was nothing like that," Menchaca said. "Santa Anna offered us amnesty. Even Santiago Bowie told me to leave."

"Bowie?" Seguin said.

"Yes," Menchaca said. "Bowie said that the fight would continue. I saw that the Alamo was done for. It made no sense to stay there and die. For what?"

Seguin looked off into the distance. For what, indeed? "Then why are you here?" he asked.

Menchaca sighed. "Just because I did not want to perish in the Alamo doesn't mean that I do not believe in our cause," he said. "I want to defeat Santa Anna. I knew I could not do it from there. I thought maybe I could do it from here."

Seguin patted him once on the shoulder and said nothing more.

All along the now completed breastworks, the Mexican soldiers were on their guard, waiting, watching for the attack they knew was imminent. Behind the men, Castrillón stood watching the woods in the distance, alert to any movement, any hint that the Texians were on their way. They stood at the ready. Their energy was nearly depleted from the rigorous march from Béxar, but they were prepared to fight — indeed, eager to fight. The sooner they vanquished the last of the Texians, as their army had at Béxar and La Bahía, the sooner they could go back to their homes and families.

Jesús waited with the others. He gripped his rifle and squinted toward the trees from which the Texians would emerge. No one talked. They simply waited. They waited through the morning in the blazing heat of noonday, in the muggy, mosquito-heavy air of afternoon — and on into the damp cool of the evening. They waited until midnight, and into the haunted hours of the early-morning darkness.

And as the sun rose over the field, bright and yellow in the sky, the exhausted soldados continued to wait. And still nothing happened.

Jesús, not for the first time, fought to keep himself from falling asleep. He had found a way to prop himself against the breastwork so that even if he drifted off, he would remain standing up. In this way, he had been able to steal a few winks through the night. But now the sudden blare of bugles jerked him awake. Fear coursed up his spine — it was the Texians! They were attacking!

With immense relief, Jesús saw that it was not the enemy approaching, but the very welcome troops of General Cós. Jesús and the men around him cheered the arrival of the reinforcements. Others might rejoice in the fact that the added numbers would make victory certain. The only thing that mattered to Jesús, though, was that now he might be able to get some sleep. But Cós's men were even more exhausted than the army that was already in place. No sooner did they march into camp than the weary men began to flop down without even removing their packs. Most of them fell asleep immediately.

Almonte surveyed the reinforcements and smiled. "We are safe now."

Castrillón wished he could be so sure. He looked at Almonte, then at the sleeping soldiers, hoping the general was right.

Almonte shouted an order: "Rest, men," he called out. "Rest for battle!"

Houston heard the bugles, too. He was standing with Seguin, watching as Cós's army reached camp.

"How many are there?" he said.

"It looks like six hundred troops, maybe more," Seguin said. "Altogether, that makes thirteen or fourteen hundred. Twice what we have, almost."

Houston considered the odds. Seguin watched and waited, hoping against hope that Houston was not going to once again order a retreat. This, Seguin thought, was the moment of truth.

Houston said, "There is a bridge behind the Mexican army."

"Vince's Bridge," Seguin said eagerly.

Houston nodded. "Send Deef Smith and his boys to burn it," he said.

Seguin almost yelped with relief and started to hurry off to carry out the order. Houston stopped him. "Juan?"

Seguin turned.

"Do we have music?" Houston asked.

Seguin pondered for a moment. "A drummer, I believe," he said.

Houston nodded. "See if you can find him a friend or two," he said.

Seguin grinned and nodded back. Then he raced off, oddly exhilarated.

Word quickly spread around the Texian camp. Eagerly, the men began preparing to fight, loading their rifles, sharpening their knives, checking their reserves of powder and shot. When Seguin returned, Houston motioned him to come to him.

"Captain Seguin," Houston said, "you and your men will guard the camp."

Seguin was too astonished to say anything. Houston's face softened. "There could be confusion out there, Juan," he said. "Some men'll shoot any Mexican they see."

"General, sir," Seguin said evenly, "you

ordered me to stay with you; I stayed. My friends — the friends I left behind — are dead. This is our fight, too. Even more than yours."

Houston exhaled a long sigh. "All right," he said. "You will join Sherman on the left flank. But Juan, put some sort of identifying mark on yourself, so nobody accidentally puts a bullet into you."

"I have a deck of cards," Seguin said. "We will each put one in the bands of our hats."

"Sounds good," Houston said.

"And Sam," Seguin said. "Please be sure and spread the word."

Down in Santa Anna's camp, the Mexicans were sleeping. Jesús was so exhausted that he expected that he would drop right off. But he did not. An odd thought had gotten into his head and would not leave him alone. That night, that awful night. The Texians in the Alamo had been sleeping, relaxing. They had let their guard down because they were so very tired. And now, thought Jesús, we are so very tired. . . . The Texians up in Houston's camp were too excited to be tired. They checked and double-checked their weapons and equipment, tapped their feet nervously, counted the minutes until "Old Sam" would give them permission to get revenge. Almost every man among them had lost friends or relatives at the Alamo or at La Bahía. Now they would make the Mexicans pay.

Seguin passed out cards to his men and instructed them to place them in their hat bands. Whenever a Texian came by, one of the Tejanos made sure he was aware of the signal, and told him to spread the word around camp.

Mathew Ingram sectioned off his powder, his hand shaking as he worked. He had wanted to be a part of this thing, had pled with General Houston to take him along on this great adventure. Now, here he was — and he would give a million dollars, if he had it, just to be anywhere else. Anywhere at all . . . A young drummer named Goldman sat under a tree, tapping his sticks together nervously. Beside him sat two boys with fifes. They were cousins named Hank Harrison and Jack Judson. Harrison had carved a fife as a present for Judson and taught him how to play simple tunes. Now, Seguin had told them they were supposed to play a charge — and how in the hell were they supposed to do that?

"What do we play?" the drummer asked.

Harrison and Judson shared a look — that was a good question.

"I dunno," said Judson. "We ain't never

attacked nobody before. How about 'Yankee Doodle'?"

The other fifer laughed. "'Yankee Doodle,'" Harrison said scornfully. "Who are you, my grandpa back at Valley Forge?"

"Well, you choose then," Judson said indignantly.

The first fifer shrugged and said, "I mostly only know bawdy love songs."

Goldman smiled. "I like 'Come to the Bower.' You know that one?"

"I sure do," Harrison said. "Purty tune."

The fifers put their instruments to their lips and started practicing. They realized soon enough that they did not know the entire song, but they were sure they could get by until the shooting started — and by then, no one would be listening to them anyway.

Deaf Smith rode back into the camp, swung down from his horse and ran into Houston's tent. "General," he yelled, "Vince's Bridge is down."

Houston nodded and clapped Smith on the shoulder. Now no reinforcements could get here to help Santa Anna and Cós. On the other hand, the destruction of the bridge meant that the Texians could not retreat, either. It left them with only one alternative — to move forward, into the camp of Santa Anna, to victory.

"Good work, Deef," Houston said. "Now I believe it is time to raise the curtain."

Houston emerged from his tent and looked at the men. They rose, meeting his gaze, ready to fight. He walked along the lines, looking at them, sizing them up.

Houston stopped and the men instinctively gathered around him. "Men," he said, "you will remember this battle, remember each minute of it, each second . . . until the day you die."

An aide stepped up with Saracen. Houston had had the beautiful white horse groomed to perfection. With a pair of snowy wings, he would have resembled a creature out of Greek mythology. Houston mounted him as the men watched.

"But that is for tomorrow, gentlemen," he said. "For today . . . remember Goliad. Remember the Alamo." He looked across the open field and said, as much to himself as to his men, "The hour is at hand."

With a cluck to Saracen, Houston rode forward. The men started to line up and move through the brush toward the battlefield. Houston exited the brush and was joined by several cavalrymen. He turned to the handsome, eager cavalryman to his right. After a moment, he recognized him. "Lamar, correct?" Houston said.

"Yes, sir, Mirabeau B. Lamar, sir."

Houston said, "What does the B stand for?"

"Bonaparte, sir."

Houston almost laughed. "You, sir, will ride to my right."

Lamar frowned a little and said, "With all due respect, sir, we prefer to be at the front."

"And you shall be," Houston said, riding forward.

He was front and center as the Texians infantry emerged from the woods — two deep and wide across. Mathew was in the middle, barely able to breathe. The two cannon were aimed at the Mexican breastworks. Houston looked to Goldman the drummer and nodded. He counted off for the two fifers and they began a ragged but spirited version of that slightly risqué love song "Come to the Bower." Houston listened for a moment and smiled; he would not have exchanged the silly melody for a standard bugle charge for anything in the world. The general raised one hand, held it in the air for a few seconds, then lowered it. The cannon — the men had already affectionately dubbed them the "twin sisters" — blasted two shells toward the Mexican line. They hit with a double crash. As wood and debris went flying, the sleeping Mexicans awoke with a start. They started to scurry about, grabbing muskets, fixing bayonets. Without clear orders, confusion reigned.

Houston waved his arm toward the enemy lines. "Forward!"

The Texians started walking forward. The Mexicans were starting to return fire. The musket shots, from a distance, sounded like faint pops, and the musket balls whizzed through the air and riffled through the grass around the Texians. But they continued to walk, at a moderate, easy pace, closer . . . closer . . . Houston shouted, "Volley formation!"

The front row of men stopped, knelt and aimed. The men behind them aimed over their heads. When they were in place, Houston called out, "Fire!"

A volley ripped into the few Mexican defenders who peeked over the barricade to fire. A dozen men dropped dead with bullet wounds in their heads and chests.

Houston called out, "Resume advance!" Saracen trotted forward, almost prancing. The sound of battle disturbed him not at all, Houston thought proudly. In fact, he seemed downright chipper. Saracen was a horse born for war.

Mathew got up from his knee, nervously reloading as he walked. His first shot had gone wild; he knew it. But at the moment, he was less concerned with killing Mexicans than with keeping from getting killed himself.

Houston looked down the line of troops. One or two of them had fallen from enemy musket fire, but otherwise the line held steady. He raised his hand again and the twin sisters sent fiery death toward the Mexican ranks, blowing up another section of the barricade.

Santa Anna emerged from his tent, furious. Like his men, he had been enjoying a peaceful nap, and now he had to face the enemy without even being fully dressed. He looked around him wildly and saw chaos everywhere. Only Castrillón had the calm presence of mind to organize his men into an effective defensive position, right in the middle of the breastworks. While the other generals' troops faltered, panicked and ran, Castrillón's lined up, carefully aimed at the distant Texians and fired.

Santa Anna saw a riderless horse near his tent. He ran to it, mounted and rode away. Castrillón watched in disgust as his president fled from the battlefield.

On the left flank, Seguin, Sidney Sherman and two dozen men on horseback moved stealthily behind and through a stand of trees. To their right, Houston was barking orders to the Texian line. "Volley formation!" Houston's voice boomed out louder than the gunfire. The front row of Texians knelt, waiting for his command. "Fire!" he called. When they unleashed withering fire into the Mexican ranks, Houston shouted, "Resume advance!"

The men were anxiously waiting for the order to attack. Held back from fighting for weeks, the anger and lust for vengeance filling their hearts day by day, they were at last getting the chance to bleed the enemy the way their friends, their brothers, had been bled at the Alamo and at La Bahía. At first they moved forward at a steady pace, but when two more Texians dropped from Mexican musket fire, their step quickened to a trot — and then a full run.

Mosley Baker shouted, "Remember the Alamo!"

Others in the line took up the call. Still others bellowed, "Remember Goliad!" or "Remember La Bahía!" Overcome now with righteous fury, their ranks broke and the Texians raced for the Mexican lines, running as fast as they could. They did not bother to stop and reload their rifles. When the time came they would use their muskets as clubs, or spill the enemy's blood with knives or, if need be, bare hands. All they wanted at the moment was to get at them.

Houston saw the order of his army dissolving before him. His carefully staged battle was turning into a brawl. Red-faced with anger, he shouted, "Form ranks! Form ranks!"

But the men weren't listening. Houston realized that not only were the men ignoring him, but that he was in danger of being left behind, out of the fighting. He pulled his pistol from his belt and spurred his mighty Saracen forward into battle.

At the opposite end of the field, Castrillón also saw the order of his men collapsing into chaos. "Hold ranks, hold ranks!" he ordered. But his men could no longer follow his orders. Most turned and fled in terror from the advancing Texians.

Before him, Castrillón saw Seguin and his men racing in from the flank, firing, breaking any chance the Mexicans had of holding the line. The last of Castrillón's men retreated into the distance.

Batres had been looking around wildly for Santa Anna. Unable to find him, the president's aide began to suspect that his master was either dead or had left the field. Either way, Batres was terrified. When he saw Seguin and his men bearing down on the

Mexican line, he screamed to Castrillón, "General, we must pull back!"

Castrillón looked at Batres with something like pity. "Forty battles," he said, "and I have never shown my back. I am too old to do it now." Castrillón turned back to the attack just as the Texians made it to the breastworks and began brutal and desperate hand-to-hand fighting with the remaining brave Mexicans who continued to stand their ground. Castrillón calmly fired one pistol, then pulled another. He fired it — click! — it was empty. He dropped the firearm to the ground and folded his arms over his chest, watching his own death rush toward him over the barricades. T. J. Rusk saw how gallantly Castrillón fixed his enemy, and shouted desperately to the Texians, "Do not shoot him! Do not shoot him!" But the men were too thirsty for vengeance and blood to listen to him. Castrillón was brought down by a volley of musket balls. Several Texians rushed over to him and, seeing that he was an important officer, paused long enough to jab his body with bayonets. They wcre followed by scores of other Texians, who came hopping over the breastworks, screaming like banshees.

One Texian captain named Covner yelled, "Boys, you know how to take prisoners!

Take them with the butt of your guns!"

"That is right, fellers," shouted a ragged private named Buteau. "Club gun right and left and knock their brains out! Remember the Alamo!"

A little Mexican drummer boy, who looked to be about ten years old, cowered before the oncoming Texians. Both of his legs were broken and he screamed in terror and agony. Two Texians, Huthmacher and Laing, ran over to him, rifles leveled. The pitiful child grasped Huthmacher around the ankles and pled in Spanish, "Hail Mary, most pure! For God's sake, save my life!" Laing shook his head in disgust and said, "Let him go. We got bigger fish to fry." Huthmacher had other ideas. He grinned savagely and pulled a pistol from his belt. He held it to the boy's temple and said, "Remember the Alamo." The boy continued praying for his life, but the Texian pulled the trigger, splattering brains all over Laing's boots.

Houston wheeled Saracen toward the barricade. A bullet struck them both, going through Houston's ankle and into Saracen's side. Both horse and rider tumbled to the ground. Houston had no time to mourn the loss of his treasured steed — he quickly got up and limped to another horse, motioning for the cavalryman riding him to dismount.

Seguin's men spread out in the marsh. A musket ball took out a chunk of the calf of a Mexican officer named Lara. He fell to the ground, grimacing in pain. When he looked up, Menchaca was standing over him. A look of relief washed over the officer's face. They had been neighbors in Béxar. "Menchaca, my friend, help me," he said.

Menchaca shook his head sadly. "I cannot help you."

"Please," Lara begged, "we are brother Mexicans. Spare me!"

The sad expression on Menchaca's face slowly changed to one of cold hatred. He raised his rifle. "No, damn you," he said. "I am no Mexican. I am an American." He fired a single shot into the officer's forehead and the man pitched backward, staring in astonishment into eternity.

A group of *soldaderas* huddled in fear near the rear of the camp. Some were wives of the soldados and officers. Others were prostitutes who traveled with the army, offering comfort for a price. But now, all were terrified women, praying for their lives. Chemerka, a recent immigrant from New Jersey, grinned wickedly when he saw them and raised his rifle. Captain Harrigan stepped in front of the musket.

"What the hell are you doing?" demanded Chemerka.

Harrigan pulled out his saber and glared at the man menacingly. "Leave those women alone," he said.

Chemerka sneered. "You cannot knock off a bullet with a sword," he said.

Harrigan pulled out his pistol and aimed it directly at Chemerka's face. "If you harm any woman there, I will kill you," he said.

Now Chemerka was just bewildered. "Are you serious?" he said. "You would kill me to save that trash?"

Harrigan nodded grimly. "I promise you that I would."

The puzzled man shook his head and walked away. Harrigan glanced at the shivering women, none of whom was quite sure what had just happened. He tipped his hat and ran back into the thick of the battle.

The Mexicans ran for their lives into the woods, toward the marshy water of Peggy's Lake, as the Texians gave chase — firing, stabbing and shouting, again and again, "Remember the Alamo!" Some of the Mexicans understood the phrase and held their hands high, insisting, *"Me no Alamo! Me no Alamo!"* The Texians coldly shot down the unarmed men. Some of them hacked and mutilated the bodies of the slain. A few took scalps.

Mathew's fear had become a kind of manic energy, his body pumping with adrenaline. He still had not killed an enemy soldier — and did not intend to — but, caught up in the moment, he found himself shrieking with the rest, running hellbent after the fleeing soldados.

Rushing through some tall river cane, Mathew realized that he had become separated from the rest. He stopped suddenly, eyes dazed, shocked to find that he was all by himself. Jesús, hiding in a bush, praying for the Texians to run past so he could somehow make his way to safety, sensed the enemy soldier standing inches away. Afraid that he had been found and that the Texian was about to casually execute him on the spot, Jesús gripped his rifle and sprang from the bush.

Mathew had not suspected that Jesús was there, and cried out in terror at the unexpected movement. Instinctively, and without thinking, Mathew stabbed at Jesús with his bayonet, hitting the boy in the leg. The pain caused Jesús to flinch and reflexively fire his musket, hitting Mathew in the shoulder. They both fell backward into the muck and lay there stunned, unable to do anything but stare at each other. Jesús had no more ammunition. Mathew was too far away to stab at him again with his bayonet, even if he had been inclined to — which he was not. All the two boys could do was to lie there and bleed.

The retreating Mexicans found themselves on the banks of Peggy's Lake. They realized that they were trapped, threw down their muskets and started jumping into the water, wading or swimming away. The Texians followed them right in, stabbing, firing, slashing, murdering without regard to whether the Mexicans were armed or their backs were turned. Houston appeared on horseback, disgusted by his men's wanton bloodlust.

"Pull back! Pull back!" Houston shouted to the men, who were ignoring him. "Damn your manners, men!"

The Mexicans continued trying to swim across Peggy's Lake for safety. To the Texians on the banks, their attempted flight became something like a down-home shooting match. One grinning Polish immigrant named Malanowski shouted, "This here is better than shooting fish in a barrel!"

Colonel John Austin Wharton stormed along the bank, shouting at the top of his lungs, "Cease fire! You cannot shoot unarmed men in the back! Cease fire!"

"Colonel Wharton," said a rifleman named Musso, "if Jesus Christ himself were to come down from heaven and order me to stop shootin' these yellowbellies, I would not do it, sir!"

Wharton whirled around and saw a redneck farmer named Curtis holding a huge bowie knife to the throat of a Mexican officer.

"Let that man go, Curtis," Wharton shouted.

Curtis ignored him, and continued to threaten the officer. "You killed Wash Cottle," he said. "Now, I'm going to kill you and make a razor strop from your hide!"

Washington Cottle had been Curtis's son-in-law. Actually, Curtis had always hated him and thought he was desperately unworthy of Curtis's daughter. But when Cottle died in the Alamo, Curtis's opinion of him changed, and now all he could think about was vengeance.

Wharton rode in and pointed a pistol at Curtis's face. "I said, let that man go!"

Curtis backed away a little and Wharton pulled the officer up onto his horse behind him. "This man is my prisoner!" he said and started to ride away.

Curtis carefully aimed his musket and

fired, taking off the back of the Mexican officer's head. When Wharton turned around, furious, Curtis chortled, "Remember Wash Cottle!" he shouted. Then he coolly removed a flask from his coat pocket, took a long swig of whiskey, turned his back on Wharton and strolled away.

Batres had left the side of the dying Castrillón and made it to Peggy's Lake as well. But he never made it far enough to do any swimming. He became bogged down in the mud. As he frantically tried to pull himself out, Dr. Labadie, a Texian of French-Canadian origin, saw Batres struggling in the water and waded toward him. Several other Texians raised their rifles and aimed at Batres. Dr. Labadie screamed, "Do not shoot! He is my prisoner!" The gambit worked no better for Dr. Labadie than it had worked for Colonel Wharton. Most of the men only laughed sardonically at the statement. An imposing Texian named Hardin smilingly raised his rifle and fired a musket ball into Batres's head. "Well sir," Hardin said, "then I will leave you with your prisoner."

Batres collapsed into the water, a horrified look on his face. Air bubbled from his lungs. Blood poured from his mouth and from the gaping wound in his head.

The swampy water of Peggy's Lake, never crystal clear to begin with, had become smoky from yesterday's rain and muddy from today's battle; the next day it would be a dull, brackish red/brown, the color of spent lives.

The horror — and the glory — of battle had lasted just a little more than eighteen minutes.

As dusk approached, an eerie calm settled over the battlefield. The ground was littered with the dead and dying, soaked with blood, blackened by soot. To the soldados who had been present at both fights, it was disturbingly reminiscent of the aftermath of the battle of the Alamo. But this time it was the Texians who wandered among the dead, looking for souvenirs, money, clothing or anything else of value possessed by the Mexican corpses. Some of the Texians continued to crave grislier souvenirs, and carved more ragged scalps from the Mexicans' heads.

Nearly seven hundred Mexicans had been killed in the slaughter. About seven hundred escaped, but three hundred of them had been rounded up and brought back to the camp before nightfall.

Houston sat under an oak tree, his

wounded ankle being treated by Dr. Labadie. He pulled out his snuff box and took a pinch to ease his discomfort. The wound was painful, but the escape of Santa Anna was worse. "All is lost," Houston said, near tears. "My God, all is lost!" Seguin squatted by his side. "You have clearly won the day, General," he said.

"But don't you see, Juan?" Houston said. "Without Santa Anna, it means nothing." He pointed toward the ridge. "Do you think these are all the Mexicans in Texas? There are more headed this way right now. If they attack us now, who will be victorious? Our men are exhausted."

Seguin said, "We lost almost no one. Five or six dead, a few wounded. We can still fight."

Houston stared at the woods with a look of terror on his face. "My God, here they come!"

Several hundred Mexicans were emerging from the trees. Seguin stood up quickly and instinctively placed his hand on the hilt of his saber. Suddenly, he relaxed. It was a large group of prisoners being guided back to the camp by T. J. Rusk, Colonel Wharton and two dozen Texians. Seguin recognized Almonte among them but he looked in vain for Santa Anna.

Houston was also looking for El Presidente. He strained to sit up higher, but the pain in his leg forced him back down. He looked at Seguin and shook his head. He did not say it again, but the phrase continued to go through his mind: *All is lost.*

Houston fell asleep beneath the tree and was tortured all night long with strange and disquieting dreams. He was awakened at dawn when someone nearby shouted, "Hey, there, Deef! Got some more for us?" Houston looked up to see Deaf Smith and some of his boys leading in another sixty Mexicans. The string of new prisoners was haggard, bloody and defeated. They were tied together by rope, waist to waist.

As the new arrivals were led over to join the previous prisoners, a low murmur began to go through the crowd. Deaf Smith noticed that one of the prisoners, in a private's uniform, hung his head low, as if trying not to be recognized. The sitting prisoners took note. One man's face brightened and he cried out, "He lives! The president lives! *Viva Santa Anna!*" Other men began to recognize the prisoner, and one by one they began to stand at attention. Several more took up the call, *"Viva Santa Anna!"*

Deaf Smith and the Texians with him turned and stared incredulously at the private. Smith walked over to him, grabbed him by the hair and lifted his head. A broad grin broke out on Smith's face. "Well . . . lookee here," he said. "The head man hisself!"

Delighted, Deaf Smith took Santa Anna across the camp to introduce him to General Sam Houston.

Santa Anna sat on a box near Houston, who was still seated on the ground, his ankle heavily bandaged. Almonte stood nearby to translate. All around them, a group of Texians, thirsting for blood, eyed the proceedings. Rusk and Sherman were, in turn, watching the Texians, alert to any outbreak of trouble that the situation might ignite.

Santa Anna whispered to Almonte, who turned to Houston and said, "That man may consider himself born to no uncommon destiny, who has defeated the Napoleon of the West."

Houston smiled politely and said nothing.

Almonte continued, "And now it remains for him to be generous to the vanquished."

Houston looked at Almonte and then locked eyes with Santa Anna. Although he spoke in English, he never broke his gaze with the dictator. "Generous, eh?" Houston said. "You should have remembered that at the Alamo."

Almonte quickly translated — although from the look on Houston's face, he scarcely had to — and he and Santa Anna looked at each warily, realizing the delicacy of the situation.

"His Excellency," Almonte said to Houston, "is willing to discuss terms of surrender."

Mosley Baker shouted, "I say we hang him from this very tree!"

Other men in the area took up the notion as their own. Several stepped away to fetch a rope. Houston stared hard at Santa Anna, who, feeling the tension, whispered something to Almonte.

Almonte said, "The general would also like to humbly remind that he, like you, General, is a Mason."

Houston waited another long moment, then slowly nodded and took another pinch from the snuff box. Santa Anna watched the action and, indicating the snuff, said to Houston, *"Por favor . . . ?"*

Almonte said, "His Excellency wonders if you might share a bit of your opium? For the nerves?"

"To hell with his nerves," Baker shouted. "Let us kill him and be done with it."

The crowd of men loudly agreed.

Houston looked at the men, then shook his head a little sadly. "No, men," he said. "You will settle for blood — and that ain't enough." He looked at Santa Anna and said, "I want Texas."

Houston leaned forward and handed the Napoleon of the West his little box of snuff. Santa Anna had asked for opium, but this would just have to do.

Seguin did not watch the parley between the generals. To him, it mattered little whether Santa Anna lived or died. He only thought about his people, the Tejanos of San Antonio de Béxar. What did this victory mean for them? He walked slowly through the field, numbly gazing at the destruction. He stopped and dropped to his knees, looking at the bodies of Mexican soldiers lying all around him. Questioning everything.

Further in the wood, Mathew and Jesús were still lying where they fell. They were both dying, breathing with difficulty, too hurt to move, even though they had each lost too much blood to feel much pain. They stared at each other with slightly glazed eyes.

Finally, Mathew spoke, softly, in Spanish. "Where you come from, friend?"

Jesús looked around. "From here," he said weakly. "I am a Texian."

Mathew nodded. "Yeah. Me, too."

Epilogue

The ancient goatherd stood on Powder House Hill, waiting patiently for his little flock to stop grazing and continue their lazy walk into Béxar. The city spread out before them in the distance and it struck the goatherd how large it was getting. Already, new buildings had spread beyond the banks of the river and almost to the walls of the old mission.

Not that there were many walls left. When the Mexican army had defeated the Texians so many months ago, a pompous general had been left behind to refortify the place, to make it strong enough once again to defend Béxar against more threats from the Texians. But after the defeat at San Jacinto, the general had received orders to undo everything he had just spent a month doing.

They tore down most of the north and west walls, spiked and buried the cannon and set fire to the old church. Now, Béxarenos considered it a haunted place. Thousands of bats had returned to live in the ruins of the walls. At sunset, just as during Margarita Fernandez's childhood, they spread a black cloud over Béxar as they emerged for their night travels.

In the courtyard in front of the old church, there were still charred bones and ashes from the funeral pyres that had consumed the bodies of the Texian rebels. Coyotes and rats had made off with much of the ghastly debris, but there was still plenty left, a terrible monument to the horror of that day in March.

The goatherd was startled out of his reverie by the sound of a horse's hooves. Turning, he saw a horseman cresting the hill. The goatherd recognized him immediately.

"Don Juan," he said in surprise. "It has been a very long time."

Juan Seguin did not look at the old man. His eyes were locked on the ruins of the Alamo in the distance. It had always looked like a ruin but now it was decimated. There was nothing left but the old church, part of the long barracks and the main gate. The

Alamo no longer resembled a fort — just a few crumbling, useless buildings.

When Travis had sent him out for help almost a year earlier, Seguin had sworn to return, to stand by his brothers in arms, no matter what the cost. That had not turned out to be possible. Instead, Seguin found himself avenging the deaths of those brothers at San Jacinto. Fate had decreed that he would not die in the Alamo but that he would be present when Santa Anna's life was spared and Texas's independence was won.

But he had promised to return, and today that promise was to be fulfilled. He intended to gather the remains of the heroes of the Alamo and bury them with proper ceremony. There was a lovely spot out near the Alameda, where a long, graceful line of trees lined the roadway. That would be the perfect place for the grave, where grateful Texians could pass by every day and cross themselves at the monument that he would build there.

"Don Juan?" the goatherd said. "Why have you returned?"

"I said I would," Seguin said, his eyes filling with tears. "A man should always keep his word."

Seguin gently spurred his horse. They

began moving slowly down the hill toward the Alamo.

Santa Anna was spared that day at San Jacinto and Texas was won. For the next decade, Texas stood alone as an independent republic. Sam Houston served as the republic's first popularly elected president.

Nevertheless, Houston was plagued until his death by those who blamed him for not going to the aid of the men in the Alamo.

On February 25, 1837, Juan Seguin gathered and buried the few remaining bones of the heroes of the Alamo, both Texian and Tejano. At that occasion he said:

These remains, which we have had the honor to carry on our shoulders, are the remains of those valiant heroes who died at the Alamo. Yes, my friends, they preferred to die a thousand times than to live under the yoke of a tyrant.

What a brilliant example! One worthy of inclusion in the pages of history. From her throne above, the spirit of liberty appears to look upon us, and with tearful countenance points, saying, "Behold your brothers, Travis, Bowie, Crockett as well as the others. Their valor has earned them a place with all my heroes."

I invite all of you to join me in holding the venerable remains of our worthy companions before the eyes of the entire world to show it that Texas shall be free and independent. Or to a man, we will die gloriously in combat, toward that effort.

Within a few years, the marker Seguin placed at the grave deteriorated. Today, no one is sure where the remains of the Alamo dead lie.

About the Author

Frank Thompson is an author and film historian with more than thirty books to his credit. He has written and lectured frequently about the Alamo and has produced five books on the subject. He lives in North Hollywood, California, with his wife, Claire.